D0757944

Beyond
Solidarity

Also by Giles Gunn

F. O. Matthiessen: The Critical Achievement

The Interpretation of Otherness: Literature, Religion, and the American Imagination

The Culture of Criticism and the Criticism of Culture

Thinking Across the American Grain: Ideology, Intellect, and the New Pragmatism

Books Edited by Giles Gunn

Literature and Religion

Henry James, Senior: A Selection of His Writings

New World Metaphysics: Readings on the Religious Meaning of the American Experience

The Bible and American Arts and Letters

Church, State, and American Culture

Redrawing the Boundaries: The Transformation of English and American Literary Studies (with Stephen J. Greenblatt)

Early American Writing

Pragmatism and Other Writings by William James

GILES GUNN

Beyond
Solidarity

**Pragmatism and Difference
in a Globalized World**

The University of Chicago Press
Chicago and London

Giles Gunn is professor of English and of Global and International Studies at the University of California, Santa Barbara.

The University of Chicago Press, Chicago 60637
The University of Chicago Press, Ltd., London
© 2001 by The University of Chicago
All rights reserved. Published 2001
Printed in the United States of America
10 09 08 07 06 05 04 03 02 01   1 2 3 4 5
ISBN: 0-226-31063-9 (cloth)
ISBN: 0-226-31064-7 paper)

Library of Congress Cataloging-in-Publication Data

Gunn, Giles B.
    Beyond solidarity : pragmatism and difference in a globalized world / Giles Gunn.
    p. cm.
    Includes bibliographical references (p.) and index.
    ISBN 0-226-31063-9 (cloth : alk. paper)—ISBN 0-226-31064-7 (pbk. : alk. paper)
    1. Ethics. 2. Pragmatism. 3. Globalization—Moral and ethical aspects.   I. Title.
BJ1031 .G85   2001
144'.3—dc21   00-051219

⊛ The paper used in this publication meets the minimum requirements of the American National Standard for Information Sciences—Permanence of Paper for Printed Library Materials, ANSI Z39.48-1992.

For Deborah, especially, but also for Abby and Adam, without whom

Contents

Introduction

This book was conceived during a period when the U.S. university system, along with segments of the wider world around it, was beset by culture wars. In the larger scheme of things, these wars fought in behalf of identity and difference may not have succeeded in changing as much as their supporters hoped; they were largely skirmishes in the ongoing battle for a more inclusive society rather than turning points in the history of humanity. Nonetheless, to those who found themselves and their own values at risk, under siege, or embattled, those wars were, and remain, far from trivial affairs. What was at stake was not only people's senses of who they are, and want to be, but their convictions about how such senses are best expressed and enacted. Hence, the rapid shifting of terrain in those wars, from issues of identity formation, cultural definition, and national selfhood to larger issues of freedom, equality, liberation, human rights, community, and social hope.

Now that the dust from those wars, as opposed to the enmity they aroused, has begun to settle, it has become increasingly evident that intellectually they stirred up a good deal more than they actually resolved. The wars were initially sparked by a debate about the nature of the literary and cultural canon, but that debate quickly, and not surprisingly, widened into a dispute about the nature and prospects of American multiculturalism as it pertains both to the character of the university and to the restructuring of society as a whole. Partisans on the right claimed to be fighting for cultural standards, those on the left for social and political rights. How much diversity, the right wanted to know, was compatible with real artistic, intellectual, and moral excellence? How much excellence, the left wanted to know, was a mask for social and cultural, as well as racial, ethnic, and gender privilege?

The trouble with both questions is that they left almost everyone on all sides of all divides framing their arguments in terms that were exclusivist. Multiculturalism was not only attacked but also defended in the name of ideals that were too often essentialist as well as restrictive. Thus the debate tended to highlight not only the bankruptcy of much of the language in which it was being conducted but also the problematic nature of some of the motives for which it was being waged. Professing difference became a means both of favoring, and sometimes even of fetishizing, dissimilarity, inimitability, and of remaining politically correct, of riding with the angels, of getting ahead. On too many occasions one was reminded of the spectacle evoked in Albert Camus's *The Fall,* where people raise themselves up on the bodies of those fallen around them so that they can be seen from a greater distance.

Despite some of its less attractive, more self-interested aspects, the debate was not, however, without its achievements. Among its various accomplishments, it forced many of us, both inside and outside the academy, both here in the United States and elsewhere, to rethink the meaning of social, cultural, and ethnic difference, to reflect more deeply on how the category of difference is constructed, empowered, evaluated, appropriated, and deployed in particular contexts. It also raised fresh questions about what binds people together, whether they share anything in common, how they are to be differentiated from each other. Pressing for the importance of diversity has inevitably thrown into new relief the issue as to whether there is anything that can be rightly claimed to be universally human.

This book is an attempt to span the divide represented by these two alternatives without recourse to totalizing solutions. The basic question that underlies all of its maneuvers is whether we have to reject everything associated with the quest for more fundamental values and beliefs to get rid of that quest's absolutist corollaries. This question determines my book's point of departure from the philosopher Richard Rorty's oft-repeated claim, first made in his 1989 book, *Contingency, Irony, Solidarity,* that it is impossible to bridge the gap between the languages we use to express what we wish for ourselves and those we employ to express what we wish for others. Our private dreams of self-fulfillment, he maintained, cannot be squared with our public belief in the need to reduce cruelty, to minimize suffering, to support justice, to increase freedom of speech—in other words, to display solidarity with others. Rorty left his readers with no illusions about his own deep commitments to both projects, both to self-reformation and to social responsibility, but he was insistent that there is no means of reconciling them philosophically. Since the language of personal regeneration is incommensurable with the language of public obligation, all one can do, he insisted, is live uneasily with the tension between them. This amounts to agreeing with the negative critiques of two of the major camps within contemporary liberalism. With the line that runs from John Stuart Mill and John Dewey to Jürgen Habermas, Rorty was prepared to believe that the necessity for personal expression and redefinition must be subordinated to the political goal of reducing social and economic misery worldwide. With the line that runs from Friedrich Nietzsche to Michel Foucault, Jacques Derrida, and Jean-François Lyotard, on the other hand, Rorty was also willing to accept that much of the world's social and economic misery stems from the practice of turning provisional vocabularies that are personal into final vocabularies that are public.

Rorty was in part responding to the philosophical project of Habermas, who has attempted to hold on to Enlightenment liberalism without abandoning Enlightenment rationalism. As Rorty conceives it, this leads to Benthamite panopticons and still more totalitarian regimes of control, and so he has expended much of his political energy since 1989 trying to figure out how to make the claims of freedom, equality, and fraternity work without a general concept of reason. The difficulty of accomplishing this can partly be gauged by remembering that, though Max Horkheimer and Theodor Adorno, two of the Enlightenment's most stringent modern critics, both assumed that reason contains the seeds of its own corruption, they were also "wholly convinced," as they stated in *Dialectic of Enlightenment*, "that social freedom is inseparable from enlightened thought."[1] In fact, Habermas's belief that "a humane collective life depends on the vulnerable forms of innovation-bearing, reciprocal and unforcedly egalitarian everyday communication"[2] echoes a number of pragmatists, such as Charles Sanders Peirce (who was committed to a scientific community of self-correcting inquirers), John Dewey (who viewed democracy as "primarily a mode of associated living, of conjoint communicated experience"[3]), George Herbert Mead (who believed in the inherently social character of language and communication), as well as Hilary Putnam (who advocated, to quote one of his titles, "realism with a human face"). Habermas's view is also not inconsistent with the political agenda of an anti-Enlightenment figure such as Derrida himself. As Richard J. Bernstein asserts, not without warrant,[4] Habermas's commitment to the unfinished social project of the Enlightenment bears an affinity

with Derrida's description of deconstruction as, "in itself, a positive response to an alterity which necessarily calls, summons or motivates it . . . a
vocation—a response to a call,"[5] and his hopes for "a democracy to come."[6]
This observation would be less relevant, perhaps, if Rorty had not made so
much of Derrida's importance in undermining confidence in the traditional
operations of rationality through his attentiveness to the logic of difference,
to the way "otherness ruptures, disrupts, threatens and eludes our logocen-
tric conceptual grids." But the lengths to which Derrida pursues this logic
oddly enough carries us back inescapably in the direction of Habermas by
compelling us to attend ethically and politically, and not just epistemologically, to "the differences that 'make' a difference."[7]

For Bernstein, Derrida nonetheless remains closer in temperament to
Adorno and, particularly, to Walter Benjamin than to Habermas because of
his opposition to what Adorno called "identity logic" and his fascination
with fragments, incidentals, discontinuities, and discards. However, as
Habermas's "other" in the new intellectual constellation they compose together (Bernstein calls it an "allegory of modernity/postmodernity"), Derrida still reveals a desire to encompass, without necessarily integrating
within a single vocabulary, what Rorty imagines to be inherently incompatible. Assuming that reason provides no reliable bridge by which to span the
differences that separate individual minds, much less to delineate the basis
for some common ground of value between them, Rorty is obliged to turn
solidarity into the attempt to expand our sense of "we" to include as many
"others" as possible. But this "liberal" gesture shrinks solidarity into little
more than a form of goodwill and goes a long way toward explaining why so
many of the supposed beneficiaries of fraternal outreach have so often
found its expressions so insufferable. Rorty's reinterpretation of solidarity
bears an uncomfortably close resemblance to an all-too-familiar American
tradition whereby, after a good deal of tacking back and forth, the ever
problematic relationship between "self" and "world" is ultimately resolved
simply by letting the first absorb the second.

As it happens, Rorty's argument that the languages of public accountabil-
ity and personal renewal are irreconcilable also runs counter to another
tradition within American pragmatism itself. This is the tradition of African
American pragmatist reflection first opened up by Cornel West and now
given further examination by Ann Douglas, Ross Posnock, and Nancy
Fraser. This tradition has struggled more vigorously than any other in
America to wrestle private languages of self-creation into alliance with public languages of collective resistance and rebirth.[8] With antecedents in the

writings of Frederick Douglass and Charles Chesnutt, this African American pragmatist tradition, which stretches from Alain Locke and W. E. B. Du Bois through Zora Neale Hurston, Ralph Ellison, and James Baldwin to Adrienne Kennedy and Samuel Delany, has frequently found the terms of that alliance not in the relations between self and world but in those between individual and community, between art and democracy. Yet it is one of the sadder ironies of American intellectual history that many of the most productive formulations of this relationship in African American reflection —and of their larger connection to the sphere of public culture itself—have gone largely unnoticed or underappreciated because its cogitations have been conducted for the most part in the world of letters rather than the realm of professional philosophy or Grand Theory.

With this oversight now in the process of being corrected—along with the equally unfortunate dismissal of the role played by women in the pragmatist tradition[9]—the history of American pragmatism as a more general and diffused intellectual tradition is slowly, if still unevenly, being rewritten as a movement which has continually found itself pushed outward from private, disciplinary concerns to more collective, political ones. Indeed, pragmatism's ability at the present time to offer itself for methodological use in a world without consensual ideological foundations has everything to do with its determination, in America as elsewhere, to span the divide between the personal and the public, the private and the collective.

Beyond Solidarity thus attempts to argue that pragmatism constitutes not so much an alternative to late modernist or postmodernist thinking as a useful intervention within it. Without pretending to claim that there is a simple way to reconcile private aspirations with public answerability, I contend that critical thinkers working within the pragmatist tradition have in a variety of different fields been laboring on and off for many years, and with predictably diverse results, to think through at least one version of what might be called the problem of otherness. In this version, the problem of the "other" amounts to trying to figure out the difference that different kinds of difference make in actual or potential experience, whether those differences refer to distinctions of identity, variations in belief and behavior, or subtle discrepancies in statement. As Charles Sanders Peirce said, there is "no distinction so fine as to consist in anything but a possible difference in practice."[10] A proposition as irresistible to Derrida or Foucault as it was to James and Dewey, it explains why the issue of otherness not only determines the form of most pragmatist arguments but also shapes the purpose of most pragmatist inquiries.

This is one reason, though not the only reason, why the problem of otherness, of alterity, of difference is also large with consequence for the study and understanding of world culture. In confronting this problem in its particularity, if you will, as opposed to its universality, we come up against what some years ago Clifford Geertz referred to as "irremovable strangenesses" that in this new globalized world we "can't keep clear of."[11] And coercing these forms of strangeness into rhetorical terms that we can understand often involves the risk of committing an act of violence against them that is sometimes as destructive, because disguised, as either opposing them outright or disregarding them. But here Derrida may retain, if not the last word, then at any rate the most relevant word. Even if violence can never be expunged from our language or practice, he notes, we must nevertheless

> try to recognize and analyze [violence] as best we can in its various forms: obvious or disguised, institutional or individual, literal or metaphoric, candid or hypocritical, in good or guilty conscience. And if, as I believe violence remains in fact (almost) ineradicable, its analysis and the most refined, ingenious account of its conditions will be the least violent gestures, perhaps even non-violent, and in any case those which contribute most to transforming the legal-ethical-political rules.[12]

In an essay entitled "The World and the Home," Homi Bhabha seems to lend this admonition his support when he entertains the intriguing possibility that "the study of world literature might be [conceived as] the study of the way in which cultures recognize themselves through their projections of 'otherness.'"[13] Bhabha's immediate reference is to those "freak displacement[s]" (as Nadine Gordimer terms them) in postcolonial writing by which hierarchies are inverted, roles reversed, and identities fractured as the experience of alterity reshapes selves.[14] Such displacements, Bhabha maintains, were first identified not only as a possible condition of, but also as a condition of the possibility for, world literature as early as 1830 by Goethe. Goethe associated the development of such displacements with the trauma brought on by national conflicts. He then proposed that they helped create conditions for the possibility of a world literature by exposing people "to many foreign ideas and ways, which they had unconsciously adopted" and by revealing "previously unrecognized spiritual and intellectual needs."[15]

Coupling this line of thinking with Goethe's belief that the interior or cultural life of a nation is, like that of an individual, lived for the most part unconsciously, Bhabha concludes that the problem of otherness, as reflected in the traumas of historical displacement, holds an important key to understanding global literature and culture. If nothing else, it furnishes an explanation for how Walter Benjamin's image of the homeless modern novelist could also be construed as the representative author of a world literature so much of which is, in Bhabha's apt coinage, "unhomely."[16] Beyond this, the problem of otherness defines a trope in modern life which, as I shall be arguing in much of the rest of this book, has proven as adept at producing disconcerting shocks of recognition as at creating violent waves of revulsion.

It is nonetheless pertinent to ask whether pragmatism has ever displayed any interest in what might be called the alterity of the "other." Certainly, the subject is touched on by George Herbert Mead's social psychology and John Dewey's social philosophy, along with some of the more recent work by Nancy Fraser, David Hollinger, Cornel West, and Ross Posnock. Still, critics might well ask whether pragmatism has ever evinced any particular interest in what makes others "other," much less in why cultures, like individuals, are so often predisposed to hypostatize and often deprecate such "otherness," or in what the "otherness" of "others" does either to or for those who perceive them as such. But this is to forget that one of William James's most famous essays mounted a serious critique of what he called, in its title, "a certain blindness in human beings." In actuality, pragmatism's concern with the dialectics of identity and otherness has recurrently appeared in, for example, W. E. B. Du Bois's lifelong study of "the strange experience" of "being a problem,"[17] Jane Addams's efforts to socialize democracy at Hull-House, Gertrude Stein's experiments with William James's psychology in imagining her way into minds so different from her own in early works like "Melanctha" and "The Gentle Lena," and John McDermott's explorations of the significance of pragmatist thought for global culture. This concern is equally evident in West's interventions in behalf of what Frantz Fanon described as "the wretched of the earth"; in Charlene Haddock Seigfried's association of feminism with the emancipatory potential of everyday experience; in Richard J. Bernstein's mapping of the relations between otherness and incommensurability; in Richard Poirier's exploration of the analogies between poetic troping and other life-enhancing activities such as sports, gardening, and sex; and in Henry Louis Gates, Jr.'s explorations of the social criticism and self-fashioning inscribed within the African American practice of "signifying" or playing "the dozens." In fact, this concern is also inscribed in Rorty's own preoccupations with forms of social marginalization and personal humiliation.

This is a tradition within American pragmatism that, to be sure, is rather different from the neopragmatism now associated in the United States with Stanley Fish, Walter Benn Michaels, and the emphatically antifoundationalist and constructivist side of Rorty himself. Theirs is a neopragmatism that repudiates the possibility of any access to the so-called "other" on the grounds that all criticism is tied to the specific practices of some particular institutional or professional community and merely works to reinforce and extend that community's own values. But if criticism offers no basis beyond its own prejudices for deciding between rival claims—"the world offers no criteria for comparing alternative metaphors"[18]—then all interpretive acts reduce to the attempt to state, and sometimes to get, what we want, and pragmatism pits itself "against theory."[19]

This antitheoretical neopragmatism stands in marked contrast to a less exceptionalist or theoretically averse form of pragmatism that is exhibited on Europe's side of the Atlantic by thinkers as different as Pierre Bourdieu, Michel de Certeau, Hans Joas, at times Foucault, and Habermas himself, and on America's by a host of figures not only in philosophy but also in anthropology, education, history, literary criticism, cultural studies, and law.[20] Following out some implications of the other side of Rorty's work, this more transnational form of pragmatism asks what it is like to live without the security of metaphysical reassurance or religious certainty. The task that this alternative form of pragmatism has taken on for itself is, thus, determining how to assess the benefits and liabilities of those devices, disciplines, and discourses that human beings have designed to compensate for the loss of some spiritual and moral safe haven.

Ranging across a number of academic disciplines, this more cosmopolitan version of pragmatism devotes much of its attention to developing critical concepts and methods that cut across many of the categories of modern disciplinary specialization and that afford us some possibility of critically scrutinizing and potentially revising our methods for making sense of the senses we make. Committed to what Salman Rushdie has called "hybridity, impurity, intermingling . . . and mongrelization,"[21] this is a pragmatism less interested in "doing what comes naturally," as Fish put it in the title of a recent book, than in doing, if you will, what doesn't. Doing what doesn't come naturally amounts to being less interested in reducing all theories to a set of themes and then applying them in a variety of different textual contexts (all psychoanalysis is collapsed into the Lacanian postulate that the unconscious is structured like a language and then critics set about looking for linguistic structures in every unconscious trace; all of Foucault is condensed into a theory of power and then critics set about proving that there are no symbolic or epistemic structures that do not attempt to subordinate one form of consciousness to another) than in placing them rhetorically in more dialectical, if not more dialogical, engagement with one another. The moral challenge for this more transnational pragmatism is, therefore, to put it simply, to figure out how the self may be made corrigible to the "other" without turning the "other" merely into a surrogate for the "self." Or, to revert to the language that Rorty sometimes prefers, is it possible to reconcile "private narcissism and public pragmatism" without becoming either solipsistic or ethnocentric?[22] Is there any way of showing how private and public values, both philosophically and in practice, are, if not wholly commensurable, then at least mutually constitutive? Despite widespread skepticism about the existence of universal values and truths and widespread acceptance of the fact that difference has now been established as one of the basic principles of personal as well as social ethics, is it nonetheless still plausible to think in a nontotalizing way about the possible basis of a morality that could be widely shared?

My own belief is that such a reconciliation between public and private is possible, but this requires coming to terms with the disappearance in much later modernist and postmodernist thinking of two necessary components of an argument for solidarity. The first of these components refers to the existence of some truths that are not completely relative, the second to the operation of certain values that are not merely local. In reference to the first, I will seek to show, particularly with the help of William James, how pragmatism developed a notion of truth that was not only personal but also, within certain limits, general. It is a notion of truth, to be sure, of parts arrived at inductively rather than of wholes revealed deductively, but it is a notion of truth nonetheless and not merely a theory of the relative perception of advantage. In relation to the second, I will argue that, while pragmatism acknowledges the contingency of all values, it nonetheless affords the possibility of discovering grounds for values that are potentially sharable. This basis would lie in the experience of those whose sense of solidarity has been achieved, most improbably, not with the relative, friend, lover, neighbor, or countryman, but with the stranger, foreigner, outsider, alien, and even enemy.

This, of course, requires going beyond Rorty's own notion of solidarity. His notion of solidarity is limited not only by the nature of his liberalism, which by my lights is too ironic and culture specific, but also by his take on pragmatism, which is too nativist and exceptionalist. Even if anything can be made to look good or bad by being redescribed, some redescriptions are

more accurate and helpful than others. And even if it was not entirely accidental that pragmatism developed in the shadow of American traditions
that were liberal and democratic, there is no reason to think that America
will always provide the most receptive site for democratic pragmatism. This
is not to gainsay the fact that, if America's "perennial philosophy," as the editor of a recent book on "the revival of pragmatism" put it, "has become
contemporary again in today's post-ideological climate,"[23] credit for that
fact belongs in large part to Rorty himself. His is quite simply the most intellectually interesting, elegantly elaborated, and philosophically challeng-
ing version of pragmatism presently available, and thus, even where I have
disagreed with him, his positions are most often the ones from which I have
pushed off in my own directions.

That said, the alternative to agreeing with Rorty is not to be found in sid-
ing with those who, like the historian John Diggins, denounce pragmatism
for its connivance with postmodern antifoundationalism and blame it for
precipitating the secular crisis of knowledge and authority that we sometimes associate with modernism itself. If Diggins speaks for a good many
others who believe that pragmatism has somehow failed to furnish us with
reliable objects of knowledge, or knowledge of truth, or accuracy of representation, or moral imperatives, or regulative principles, or compelling
truths, or adequate criteria for judgment, all rendering it now "an unwork-
able tool of historical analysis,"[24] his critique is important chiefly because it
suffers from a number of biases that typify other attacks nostalgic for foundationalism. Chief among these biases is that pragmatism lacks humility
and imaginative vision, that it places all its faith in experience as the source
of all value and has substituted sociology for poetry.

As for the charge that pragmatism is too proud and unimaginative, what
else can one rely on in a world without foundations if not ethical experi-
mentalism? Kenneth Burke, whom Diggins wants to use against James and,
particularly, Dewey, only stated the obvious when he pointed out that even
if critical intelligence cannot provide an absolute ground for all values in a
world without stable foundations, it does enable us, in a world already laden
with values like our own, to play them off against one another and thus to
discriminate better from worse. Moreover, it is precisely in the realm of
moral choice, Burke reasoned (anticipating the ideas of contemporaries like
Ross Posnock, Henry Samuel Levinson, and Nancy Fraser), that the pragmatist is at his or her strongest: when as an ethicist he or she is forced, precisely because of the lack of foundations, to operate more like an artist than
a metaphysician. As to the second, who among all modern philosophers
more than Dewey, with the possible exception of Heidegger, has argued

more vigorously that philosophy must reorganize its thinking on all subjects in relation to models furnished not by the sciences but by the arts?

Diggins's dismissal of or indifference to such questions would be less significant if his erasure of an entire vein of reflection within the pragmatist tradition were not so typical of attacks from the right. Pragmatism's profound engagement with the aesthetic, not so much as a category *within* reflection but as a categorical model *of* reflection, is conveniently discounted on the assumption that pragmatism is little more than an extension of one side of that split in America between what, in *America's Coming-of-Age*, Van Wyck Brooks called "highbrow" and "lowbrow," "transcendent theory" and "catchpenny realities."[25] Diggins's own preference is for transcendent theory without the transcendent, but the fact that James actually managed to produce what Brooks was looking for—some "genial middle ground" on which to found a culture capable of possibly reconciling "university ethics and business ethics," "American culture and American humour," "Good Government and Tammany," "academic pedantry and pavement slang"[26]— is apparently lost on him. The choice between the pragmatists and their opponents is for the most part compressed into a choice between the tender-minded and the tough-minded, where James, Dewey, Mead, and others come out as irresponsible optimists and trimmers, their critics as principled pessimists and skeptics.

Yet rhetorical simplifications hardly constitute the most serious difficulty with critiques of this kind. The deeper problem with *The Promise of Pragmatism* is that even if Diggins has asked the right question, his own fondness for a world he knows we have lost has compelled him to ask it in the wrong terms—terms that are not, except in the crudest sense, pragmatist at all. To have asked his question in pragmatist terms would not have been to ask whether pragmatism "worked" historically but to have considered whether pragmatism met its own historical test for intellectual success. If that test has been variously expressed by different pragmatist thinkers, no one came closer to a statement on which all of them might agree than Dewey himself when, in *Reconstruction in Philosophy*, he associated the value of philosophy's hypotheses not with their correspondence with received fact but rather with whether or not "they render men's [and women's] minds more sensitive to the life around them."[27] He then went on to add, in *Experience and Nature*, that those hypotheses must also end in conclusions "which, when they are referred back to ordinary life-experiences and their predicaments, render them more significant, . . . [and] more luminous to us, and make our dealings with them more fruitful."[28]

Judged according to this more appropriate standard, contemporary pragmatism can provide a rich array of intellectual resources for addressing at least some of the issues that now confront us in "today's post-ideological climate," and none of those issues is more vexing or persistent than the pragmatics of otherness. What is one to make of the "other?" With what means or instruments does one undertake such assessments? What role does the "other" play in the construction of the "self" and of "culture"? What roles do the "self" and "culture" play in the construction of the "other"? What does "otherness" teach, illumine, imply? What does "otherness" deform, disguise, or deny?

Beyond Solidarity seeks to probe such questions without pretending that they can be asked as if we already knew their answers. By the same token, Dostoyevsky was surely on the right track when he reminded us that we already know too many answers and that it is the questions we must try to discover.

Part 1 of this book is intended to delineate the field of its questions. In chapter 1, I situate the discussion in relation to the recent debate about multiculturalism and the possibility of developing a transnational cultural criticism of the Americas. These two issues are part of a larger interest reflected throughout this book in the question of what cultures have to learn from and teach one another and how they go about it, particularly in narrative and poetic forms. Thinking about this larger issue in relation to some of the more important colonial legacies in the Americas, I argue that such heuristic possibilities may well depend on grafting what for pragmatism amounts to a critique of essentialism onto what the cultural psychologist Peter Homans calls "the ability to mourn." In chapter 2, I then show what happens to the larger notion of human solidarity itself when mourning simply gives way to the rage in grief, that is, to the anger evoked by a sense of loss, and then cultures, like selves, give in to the need to defend in-group solidarity by disparaging, even demonizing, out-group difference. While the widespread increase of such behavior throughout the world may well reflect alterations associated with the entire global landscape and the changing possibilities of affiliation and opposition it has generated, I contend that they may also require us to reground human identity "beyond solidarity," as it were, in a space where "self" and "other" are no longer conceived either as opposites of one another or as complements, counterparts, or corollaries, but rather as components integral to each other's constitution.

Before taking up this proposal in depth, however, and exploring its realization in several literary and cultural sites in the book's final chapter, I double back in the next two parts to assess the intellectual resources that pragmatism brings to rethinking the issue of human solidarity. In part 2 I show how, as a method of inquiry, pragmatism has been, almost from its earliest formation, always already in some sense global, both because of the circumstances in which it began to evolve and also because of the issues it was initially designed to resolve. In part 3 I take up the way pragmatism has more recently been reshaped into a method suitable for global analysis as it has become more available for reinterpreting the meanings of religion, history, and aesthetics in a global context.

Chapter 3 thus in effect establishes a new point of departure for the book by setting the development of William James's quest for an acceptable vocation against the background of an educational process that was in so many respects transnational. This quest, which James and other members of his theologically deracinated generation inherited from Ralph Waldo Emerson (the latter having been dutifully brought by James's father, Henry James, Sr., to pay him a visit shortly after his birth), could be fulfilled only when James settled on a career given over to determining how a religiously inquisitive and morally sensitive mind like his own is to comport itself in a world without clear metaphysical foundations and ethical boundaries, a world always pressing outward toward peripheries that are more pluralistic, diverse, hybrid, diasporic, and deterritorialized. Chapter 4 then takes up the text in which William's brother Henry most fully appropriated pragmatism to his own cosmopolitan critical purposes. In what still remains, nearly a century later, quite possibly, for all its lapses, the single most comprehensive, searching, introspective investigation of American culture written since Alexis de Tocqueville's *Democracy in America*, *The American Scene* represents as well the most careful working out to date of a pragmatist theory of reading which shows what pragmatism looks like as a form of immanent critique.

Part 3 comprises several, as I call them, re-readings. Chapter 5 circles back to Rorty again and his most recent attempt to redefine pragmatism as a form of Romantic polytheism. In addition to describing how pragmatism functions as a philosophy of religion in a world without foundations, this redefinition permits me to reconsider whether it is still possible to talk about truth without making an essentialist argument. Chapter 6 asks how truth and value are accountable to history, whether they can, so to speak, move with history. Focusing on an interesting marriage that has recently been arranged between rhetorical theory, classical hermeneutics, and pragmatist criticism with the help of Stanley Fish, Walter Benn Michaels, Rorty himself, and Steven Mailloux, it also enables me to examine at greater depth such key terms as *history, interpretation, reading, truth*, and *rhetoric*. Chapter 7 then returns to the notion of the aesthetic and the claim made by some global theorists that, having recently broken free of its traditional moorings in high culture, it now circulates more widely as the primary solvent of culture as a whole. Consideration of this new status of the aesthetic eventually leads me back to the pragmatist insight that the aesthetic has always been sedimented, as Emerson said and Dewey demonstrated so brilliantly in *Art as Experience*, in the logics of the ordinary and opens up a discussion of some of the modern forms in which this insight has been explored—socially and politically in the writings of Hannah Arendt, epistemologically and ethically in the philosophy of Martha Nussbaum and Mark Johnson, literarily and culturally in the criticism of Richard Poirier.

Retheorizing the aesthetic in a pragmatist direction prepares the way in Section IV to retrieve the question at the center of the whole undertaking. How is human solidarity to be reconceived in a world where the pressures of globalization fracture as much as, or more than, they unify and the movements in both directions serve only to broaden rather than narrow the gulf between particular communities? Assuming that this question has often been asked more searchingly in aesthetic rather than discursive forms, I look at several cultural instances where human identity has been compelled, under the most extreme conditions, to reconceive itself not in relation to notions of sameness but in relation to notions of radical difference—postcolonial writing, where the Empire writes back; Holocaust literature or, more exactly, writing in response to the experience of the Shoah, where the world that presents itself as adversary or rival seeks not merely to subjugate the self but to exterminate it; and the cultural and religious experience of African Americans both in slavery and after, where survival has depended less on converting oneself to the gods of others than on converting the gods of others to oneself. Since the intention of this eighth and final chapter is to determine as precisely as possible how symbolic mediations performed in such different cultural settings can simultaneously (as I argue at the end of chapter 1) both edify as well as enhance the humanity of those capable of grasping their significance, chapter 8 can be described without inaccuracy as a study in the pragmatics of modern heroism.

PART ONE

Rethinking Solidarity

Chapter 1

Multiculturalism, Mourning, and the Colonial Legacy of the Americas: Towards a New Pragmatics of Cross- and Intercultural Criticism

One of the many questions posed by the passage nearly a decade ago of the Columbus quincentenary had to do with the relationships among the various cultures that Columbus's voyage, or rather our reconstruction of its consequences, has bequeathed to us. For Columbus's voyage, while producing a holocaust for native peoples, also resulted in an explosion of new cultures in the Americas that has now left us with an elaborate assemblage of societies and nations whose relations with one another, however carefully documented in other terms, are still comparatively unexplored in cultural terms. In other words, despite the fact that these new nations and societies arose out of a common experience of European settlement and colonization involving not only the conquest, displacement, and near extermination of almost the entire indigenous population but also the domestication, often with the assistance of enslaved Africans, of immense tracts of undeveloped wilderness; and despite the fact that the basis of virtually all of the imaginative, and many of the discursive, arts in all of the countries of the Americas would subsequently be furnished by the way these hybrid American societies would eventually undergo a revolutionary break with the colonizing power and then reconstitute themselves as something self-consciously different from their European parents—despite these shared experiences and interpretations of experience, no one would describe the comparative study of American cultures as a thriving academic industry.

This is, of course, not to suggest that the cultural relations among and between the many societies and political formations of the Americas both

North and South, together with the Caribbean world, have gone unexamined. From the period of earliest contact between native and nonnative peoples, these relations have been a source of profound interest in texts ranging from the Mayan "Books of Chilam Balam," Bernal Díaz's *The Conquest of a New Spain*, and *The Narrative of Alvar Nuñez Cabeza de Vaca* to Alejo Carpentier's *Explosion in a Cathedral*, Manuel Puig's *Betrayed by Rita Hayworth*, and Jamaica Kincaid's *Lucy*. These works of primary reflection have been supplemented in recent decades by various distinguished studies of secondary reflection that include everything from Pablo Neruda's meditations on Walt Whitman, Octavio Paz's *The Labyrinth of Solitude*, and Jorge Luis Borges's *Introduction to American Literature* to Howard Mumford Jones's *O Strange New World*, Tzvetan Todorov's *The Conquest of America*, Carlos Fuentes's *The Buried Mirror*, and Doris Sommers's *Foundational Fictions*.

Yet for all its intelligence and insight, such writing—and the enormous body of literary testimony that surrounds it—has not managed, at least in the United States, to diminish, for all but specialists, the general state of ignorance on these matters. Few U.S. students of American history, politics, or literature, for example, think that much light can be shed on their own subjects by a study of racial practices in the Caribbean, or of the appeal of dictatorships in South America, or of environmental policies in the Canadian provinces, or of modernist aesthetic experimentation in Central America. Moreover, the development, during the postwar era, of an interdisciplinary field spanning the humanities and the social sciences called "American Studies," and devoted to the examination of the history of American culture "past and present and as a whole," to quote a famous formulation, has yet to de-provincialize the word *American* in that title so that it may encompass all of the New World societies that find some kind of interpretive shelter beneath its umbrella.

One could, I suppose, try to account for these lapses by resorting to a reductionist argument that lays the responsibility for this ignorance at the door, say, of U.S. imperialism, or Western capitalism, or institutional Eurocentrism, or even of Spanish-American chauvinism, and no small amount of the scholarship that accompanied the quincentenary and has followed it, at least on the left, has been tempted to take such a line. But even if one acknowledges the genocidal horrors that the anniversary of Columbus's voyage brought home to us in the United States and elsewhere—horrors whose replication throughout the centuries and across so many of the emergent cultures of the Americas lead one to reach for explanations that link the structuration of socioeconomic issues to fixed ideas about race and ethnicity—there are surely other reasons why, when employed as a term of hemispheric or continental designation, the word *American* evokes for so many so minimum a sense of solidarity.

No doubt one of those reasons has to do with the entirely different grammar of motives that fueled the original processes of colonization in British and Spanish America and the different effects that these motives were to have not only on the kinds of societies they produced but also on the ways they dealt with everything from native peoples and African slavery to the desire for independence and the rise of nationalism. A second reason why the term *American* is so difficult to bring into focus in a hemispheric or intercontinental context is that even where the cultures of the Americas border one another, they display considerable variations among themselves and, like any cultures, are anything but homogeneous or tightly integrated. Mosaics of diverse, conflicting, and constantly changing traditions whose own inner principles of coherence are frequently provisional, inconsistent, and self-contradictory, the cultures of the Americas represent fairly unstable fields in which distinct and often divisive, or at least contested, social, economic, psychological, political, ceremonial, and aesthetic processes all intersect (when they intersect at all) at odd angles. A third—and, for my purposes here, more interesting—reason for the referential incoherence of the word *American* as a term of hemispheric designation (a reason with special significance for students of literature and ideas) has to do with the extent to which all American cultures were initially, and continue to remain, the products of a complicated process of rhetorical invention and reinvention.

This is as much as to say, following Edmundo O'Gorman, that America was not discovered so much as fabricated or created, and created by Europeans less interested in determining, in all their empirical distinctiveness, the reality of New World conditions than in reimagining those conditions as forms of alterity against which they as Europeans might redefine themselves.[1] To say that they defined themselves against the forms of alterity or otherness by which they imagined American conditions is not to claim that there was nothing to be found on Friday, October 12, 1492, at around 2:00 a.m., when Christopher Columbus first made landfall in the West Indies, on the island of what is now called San Salvador. It is only to assert that Columbus's mistake about what he had come upon that morning was then compounded in characteristic ways when he resisted the subsequent corrections of experience for the sake subsuming his encounters with New World otherness within the image of himself and his mission that he brought with him from the Old World.[2] Looking for a sea passage to India, Columbus supposed that he had actually managed to reach the Orient, but then steadfastly refused to relinquish this conviction despite three later voyages that never carried him further west than, at most, the Paria peninsula of Venezuela.

Columbus was certain that he had found a passage to India because he viewed everything before his eyes with a mental picture he had already constructed. This mental picture derived chiefly from his reading of the Bible, together with his familiarity with the accounts of Marco Polo's overland journey to China and his knowledge of Ptolemaic geography. Ptolemy had postulated that the earth was considerably smaller than we now know it to be and that the Asian landmass extended much farther into the ocean than it does. As it happens, this theory turned out to be admirably suited to Columbus's purposes, since it tended to confirm Marco Polo's speculations about the proximity of Japan's position relative to Portugal and was reinforced by certain prophetic claims found in the Bible. One of the apocryphal Books of Esdras, for example, held that the world was six parts land and only one part water. The Book of Ezekiel, in turn, maintained that Jerusalem was at the center of the world. Such assertions not only persuaded Columbus that the sea voyage from Portugal to Asia was comparatively short (2,700 miles, as opposed to the actual 12,000), they also assured him that in undertaking this expedition he was merely fulfilling the injunctions of the Old Testament. But however much Columbus thought he was fulfilling the words of Isaiah, he was also driven by a complex of other emotions besides religious piety: dreams of glory, the desire for wealth, scientific curiosity, an extraordinary egotism, remarkable courage, and much more.

Amerigo Vespucci, on the other hand, was prepared to take credit for discovering a New World even if he had to fabricate his own account of it. According to his own account in *Mundus Novus*, or *The New World*, ten years later, Vespucci did not actually land on the coast of what is now Brazil until 1501, recording that they had come upon "a new land which . . . we observed to be a continent." But the validity of this achievement was immediately placed in jeopardy by the speculation that Columbus might have touched on the coast of Venezuela during his third voyage in 1498. Thus in his next book, Vespucci changed his story to claim that he, in fact, had reached the South American mainland on a voyage made a year earlier than the one recorded in *Mundus Novus* in 1497.

Nonetheless, Vespucci's fabrication that he was the first navigator to reach the New World might still have come to nothing if his claim had not caught the attention of a little-known German geographer named Martin Waldseemüller who was then preparing a new edition of Ptolemy. Though

Waldseemüller was later to express second thoughts about his decision, and other interested parties, such as the Spanish and Portuguese, were to object to it for centuries, he determined that the new continent ought to bear the name of its first discoverer, and once attached to the newly delineated territory of Waldseemüller's 1507 world map, the name became fixed. At no little cost of symbolic misrepresentation, the New World was from henceforth to be known as "America" (or, to the Spanish, "New Spain").

Both tales tell us something of what it means to say that America was invented as much as discovered. In addition to emphasizing that "America" was hereafter to be a world shaped as much by the energies of the imagination as by the substance of the actual, as much by the ambiguities of desire as by the structures of the empirical, it also makes clear that misinterpretation was subsequently to become a motive force in America's continuous self-making and remaking. Indeed, nothing demonstrates this more dramatically or, perhaps, tragically than the effects this process of misinterpretation was to have on America's original inhabitants.

Whether Columbus reached the shores of the new continent before Vespucci or Vespucci before Columbus is finally of little moment; the point is that neither of them, as even they could see for themselves, were America's first discoverers. That title belongs instead to the ancestors of, as Columbus and Vespucci themselves both reported, those singular and remarkable human specimens who confronted them on the beaches of the Americas. People who, as the Italian cleric Peter Martyr described them, "go naked, . . . know neither weights nor measures, nor that source of all misfortunes, money; living in a golden age, without laws, without lying judges, without books, satisfied with their life, and in no wise solicitous for the future,"[3] these natives and their ancestors had already occupied for many millennia these lands that Columbus and Vespucci claimed to have discovered for the first time. Descendants of nomadic peoples from Asia who, it is still generally believed, first made their way across a land bridge linking the Bering Strait nearly 22,000 years before, these peoples had over thousands of years worked their way down and settled almost the whole of the Northern and Southern Hemispheres, creating in the process some of the great civilizations of the ancient world: the Mayan in southern Mexico and Guatemala, the Incan in Peru, and the Aztec in Mexico. So numerous, in fact, had these descendants of America's nomadic first discoverers become that, by the time Columbus and Vespucci arrived at the end of the fifteenth century, there were then living in the Americas, according to various estimates, somewhere between 60 and 100 million people, speaking as many as 2,200 different languages. All the more ironic, then, that despite the heterogeneity and sophistication of the societies and cultures these people created in the so-called New World (while some Native Americans remained hunters and gatherers, others created written languages, became expert at engineering and astronomy, mastered the art of mathematical calculation, and built such magnificent cities as Palenque, Tikal, Tula, Monte Albán, Uxmal, Tenochtitlán, and Chichén Itzá), they were to be lumped together by the name they received from Columbus when he mistook their homeland for Asia and called them "Indians."

All of this merely helps underline the fact that, if America was from the beginning a product of rhetorical inventions frequently based on misinterpretations, those inventions and the misinterpretations they carried along with them were to compound themselves with each successive wave of reinvention. The first of them began with the appearance of chronicles of discovery, conquest, and settlement—Christopher Columbus's *Letter to Lord Raphael Sanchez, Treasurer to Ferdinand and Isabella, King and Queen of Spain* (1493), Amerigo Vespucci's *Mundus Novus* (1503), Thomas Hariot's *Brief and True Report of the New-found Land of Virginia* (1588), Richard Hakluyt's *Principal Navigations, Voyages, Traffiques, and Discoveries of the English Nation* (1589), Sir Walter Raleigh's *The Discovery of Guiana* (1595)—which erased pretty much the whole inventory of what we might call, within these indigenous societies, "local knowledge" for the sake of celebrating their own triumph over it. But this process of narrative triumphalism then left the descendants of such chronicles with the task of reinventing themselves all over again if they were to develop any form of New World identity independent of those initial colonial stories. Hence, the Empire first began to write back in such early texts as *The Araucaniad* (1569, 1578, 1589) by the Chilean epic poet Alonso de Ercilla y Zúñiga, *The Royal Commentaries of Peru* (1609, 1617) by the Spanish-Incan writer Garcilaso de la Vega, the intellectual autobiography entitled *Reply to Sir Filotea de la Cruz* by the Mexican poet, playwright, and essayist Sor Juana Inés de la Cruz, and *The Uruguay* (1769) by the Brazilian writer José Basílio da Gama, and in such later ones as, say, *The Interesting Narrative of the Life of Olaudah Equiano* (1789) by the African American Gustavus Vassa, *Son of the Forest* (1829) by the Native American William Apess, *Facundo: Civilization and Barbarism* (1845) by the Argentinian Domingo Faustino Sarmiento, *The Posthumous Memoirs of Brás Cubas* (1880) by the Brazilian Machado de Assis, and *Les Anciens Canadiens* (1890) by the French-Canadian Philippe-Joseph Aubert de Gaspé. This process of postcolonial rhetorical invention and reinvention was made more complex still when several of the Americas created out of the inspiration drawn from such early postcolonial texts began to exhibit new colonial ambitions of their own, thus prompting a wave of revisioning, essentially a third fold in the palimpsest of colonial rewritings of America, in such more recent texts as V. S. Naipaul's *The Mimic Men* or Gabriel García Márquez's *The General in His Labyrinth.*

Now, however, this history of rhetorical reinvention and inscription is being extended even further in the Americas, as scholars and interpreters attempt to bring the counter-colonial texts produced in response to it into some form of critical contact and comparison with one another. Such efforts inevitably raise a question as to whether this latest scholarly stage of cultural production can do something other than merely add yet another layer of fabrication to the process. In other words, can it initiate, through the use of comparative and other dialogical techniques, something like a "mutual interrogation" that, in addition to revealing the diverse strategies of representation differentiating this succession of colonial, postcolonial, and neocolonial texts, can also possibly throw into critical relief some of the inner assumptions of the divergent constitutive principles that are buried within these texts?[4] What we need to learn is not simply how people sharing similar rituals of self-creation could have come to inhabit such utterly different social worlds but how, despite the divergences among their narratives, they still share a similar history and are even implicated in each other's fate.

At present the possibility of pursuing this kind of inquiry is still hindered by two kinds of intellectual suspicion. The first has to do with whether comparing and contrasting cultures is anything other than an attempt by one culture to subordinate another. The second has to do with whether cultures, even when, as in the case of the Americas, they are produced by the same processes of invention and redaction, can be compared at all. Implicit in the first suspicion is the assumption that all intellectual work is potentially political and that the politics of the intellect may ultimately be assimilated to the politics of identity. Implicit in the second suspicion is the presupposition that cultures may be inherently incomparable, in which case any attempt to bring them into discursive relations with one another risks violating the integrity of each. If expression of the first suspicion has taken the form of what has typically been called "political correctness," expression of the second has taken the form of what is usually meant by "multiculturalism." Notwithstanding the general erosion of support for the first, which was never entirely acceptable even among some of its strongest advocates, and waning confidence in the second, which is not without its contradictions, both have played an inordinately important role in shaping the critical study of the Americas.

The issue of political correctness originated initially, as is common knowledge, over the need to impose standards for appropriate public behavior and practice in American higher education. But this issue quickly metamorphosed from an interest in regulating campus discourse and conduct, enforcing affirmative action policies, and encouraging the inclusion of more academic subjects in the curriculum into a surveillance operation designed, at least according to its critics, not only to determine what subjects are suitable for academic study but also to challenge the disciplinary boundaries and broader institutional hierarchies that currently define such matters. Carried to extremes, then, the project of political correctness extended well beyond the critique and, if possible, alteration of the self-interested character of all disciplinary and pedagogical arrangements within the academy to encompass a challenge to the cartographic practices of the wider society that legitimates them.[5]

Such arguments were—and still are—often made in behalf of protecting the notion of "difference," and the notion of "difference" is then turned into an unquestioned, even unchallengeable, source of social and political legitimacy. At the geopolitical level, this sometimes leads to the absurd proposition that any people who can differentiate themselves by whatever hereditary or historical arguments from any others deserve, by that very fact, to become a nation. At the social level, it leads to the view that anything that can define itself as "other" to the dominant ideology or group is thus rendered beyond criticism except by its own representatives. Either way, the preoccupation, and in some quarters the obsession, with political correctness has by its very nature actively discouraged intellectual travel across cultural borders in the Americas and elsewhere. As with international travel generally, intellectual exploration beyond one's own country has too often become an affair of valid passports and legitimate visas. Unless one is furnished with an approved ideology of interpretation, a certified subject of inquiry, and the requisite credentials of group membership, the best rule of thumb has been to stay close to home. Educationally this has too often meant in America that, except in selected circumstances, women study, teach, and write about women, blacks study, teach, and write about blacks, Chicanos study, teach, and write about Chicanos, and so on down the line.

Yet, by the same token, this depiction of the climate of restricted movement in the academy, and particularly within the humanities, can be, and at times by the right has been, overdrawn. Fractured as the world of the university may be for other reasons, it is neither as divided as conservatives have made it out to appear, nor divided along the lines that so many of its critics—most of whom are not members of university faculties and are thus ill-equipped to understand the subtlety of academic politics—have caricatured it as being.[6] The great preponderance of those divisions are not sexual, ethnic, or racial, but generational, disciplinary, and methodological, and very few of these divisions set those who want to save the humanities against those who want to destroy them. The real divide within the humanities, though rarely acknowledged as such, is between two strategies for combating their increasing marginalization within the academy. This is the divide between those who believe that the real purpose of humanistic study is to determine the values by which the world should be organized and governed, and those who insist instead that its purpose should be to determine which values should define our experience of the world.

There is substantial irony in the fact that, for all their heat, neither group has shed much light on the far graver issue of how American education as a whole is being transformed. For the new managerial and professional classes currently served by, and increasingly in control of, higher education, public institutions have become too slow to respond to corporate needs and the humanities have lost much of their former glamour and rationale. As private companies generate more proposals for turning much elementary and secondary education into skills training, as businesses set up their own colleges or ask institutions like the for-profit University of Phoenix to train their employees, and as giant corporations like Microsoft and Motorola redescribe their world headquarters as, respectively, campuses and universities, the time is fast approaching when the humanities may be, except in elite institutions, relegated to a supporting role in the world of multinational capital, representing the communication arts and teaching business writing.

But the recent obsession within the humanities (and some social science) disciplines with what constitutes political rectitude is only one factor that has limited interpretive transit between cultural territories in the Americas. A second factor that has inhibited cross-cultural and intercultural interpretation in the Americas has been the debate about the now recherché term *multiculturalism*. Regarded by some, because of its association with a kind of racial, ethnic, sexual, or nationalistic essentialism, as one of the most dangerous and divisive orthodoxies of our time, multiculturalism has been touted by others as one of the only real orthodoxies ever seriously supported in the United States. While the former claim is preposterous and the latter scarcely accurate, the term derives its appeal from the belief that the nation's distinctiveness as a culture and society, if not its very integrity, has always depended not on the uniformity of its citizens but on their heterogeneity. In the minds of its proponents, then, multiculturalism turns on the word *diversity* rather than *difference* and translates *diversity* into a call for a new reign of openness and inclusiveness.

Nonetheless, serious difficulties arise for multiculturalism when "diversity" is transformed politically into the sole, or at least the principal, source of cultural authenticity and then all forms of cultural authenticity are held to be equally inviolate and pristine. At this point, multiculturalism gives up its air of tolerance and flexibility and begins to provide the rationale for a world always on the verge of splintering along lines of prejudice, resentment, and enmity, always ready to fragment into hostile camps. Or when this unhappy fate can be avoided, then the world begins to give way to a more banal environment where wearing one's "differences" simply becomes the only way to belong.[7] Whichever the case, multiculturalism is then quickly transformed into to just another form of monoculturalism, and monoculturalism has a tendency all too often to move in the direction of one of two political extremes: either, where difference is essentialized, in the direction of pogroms and ethnic cleansing or, where difference is normalized, in the direction of conformity and regimentation. In the first scenario, difference becomes sacralized in behalf of a politics of what Kenneth Burke once termed "Holier Than Thou."[8] In the second, difference is "mainstreamed" to satisfy the self-consuming appetites of global popular culture.[9]

No doubt one of the more obvious reasons why multiculturalism is vulnerable to these distortions—distortions that prevent it from fulfilling its otherwise admirable aim to stimulate the exploration and appreciation of cultural distinctiveness wherever it is found—is because the symbolic sedimentation of cultural differentiations goes so deep. However integral and often indispensable such differentiations are to the organization of human life as we know it historically, they derive much of their power from their status as fictions. Cultural differentiations deserve to be called fictions in at least a limited sense both because they often tend, when absolutized as some element of the cultural template, to presuppose a homogeneity or uniformity of experience that their historical development actually belies, and also because they derive their authority from assumptions that are, among other things, decidedly aesthetic. This is not to argue that such significations are any less real or legitimate—or are experienced as being any less real or legitimate—because they are imaginative as well as political, tropological as well as social or economic. It is merely to assert that whatever the experiential terrain on which such artifacts, and the deep attachments they afford, are expressed, these same artifacts, and the emotional appeals with which they are identified, are cultural before they are anything else. They are forms by which people make sense of the sense their experience makes to them, and make more valuable sense the more that sense can be expressed in figurative terms, the more it can be rendered semiotic. Little wonder, then, at the volatility and power of such forms. On the one side, cultural symbols serve as instruments in and through which groups may express an understandable desire to honor and enact their own legacies of identity. On the other, by "naturalizing" those boundaries between peoples, they tend to render them experientially problematic, even impassable.

But this only raises all over again the question about whether it is feasible, or even possible, to look for, or try to define, some common essence or substance that all the cultures of the Americas may be said to share and in terms of which they might be critically compared and assessed. Do the terms for a common American culture lie within history itself, say, in some mythic framework from which all the culturally specific stories of the Americas somehow narratively derive? Or might they be found instead, if not in some genetic link between general myths of origin and specific narratives of destiny, then in the connection between generic interpretive possibilities and diverse interpretive practices in cultural traditions that still remain differentiable? Or yet again, could the premises and procedures of a common culture of the Americas be found in the crosslights that are produced when differing ideational, emotional, and ritual elements from distinctive, discriminable historical traditions are brought into apposite but meaningful relations with one another? Or rather might the preconceptions and customs of an inter-American culture lie embedded, perhaps, within some text, such as Jorge Amado's *Tent of Miracles*, or Isabel Allende's *The House of Spirits*, or embodied in some figure, like José de San Martín, or the woman the Spanish called Doña Marina and the Indians La Malinche, or represented by some territory, such as the Caribbean which, as Antonio Benítez-Rojo has noted, may serve to bridge the differences between the Northern and Southern Hemispheres?[10]

As it turns out, each of these possibilities has been explored with some care during the last several decades. Just as many of the individual cultures of the Americas share a common myth of genesis that is clearly indebted to the Biblical depiction of Eden and the counter-image of humanity's expulsion to an outer wilderness of uncertainty and strangeness, so one can describe systematic relationships between, let us say, the Hispanic and the North American understanding of the family, or between the labyrinth of solitude in the Latin American literary soul and its echo in the soul of North American writers like Edgar Allan Poe, Nathaniel Hawthorne, Herman Melville, and Emily Dickinson. Or, again, just as one can see affinities between the career of a Simón Bolívar and an Abraham Lincoln, or discern telltale similarities and differences between the response to the history of miscegenation in Brazil and the American South, so one can find literary figures like Octavio Paz, Pablo Neruda, Anne Hébert, Clarice Lispector, or Luisa Valenzuela who seem to absorb and express many of the contradictions that make up at least some of the Americas at any given moment. Or, one can discover in a concept such as the *mestizo* something that, on the authority of individuals as various as the African American intellectual Albert Murray, the Nicaraguan poet Rubén Darió, or the Mexican graphic artist José Guadalupe Posada, characterizes the cultures, like the peoples, of both hemispheres.

The question is whether such inquiries finally get us very far, or at least as far as we now need to go, in conceptualizing the kinds of relationship that the cultures of the Americas may potentially have with one another critically. While it is true that common essences can be detected beneath cultural differences, that sets of traits have been shared across cultural boundaries, that cultural homologies can be discovered in the origin and development, as opposed to the appearance and function, of otherwise disparate social practices, and that representative figures may be found who unify, or at least bridge, contiguous cultural traditions, these discoveries merely disclose materials of experience that, for the most part, have yet to be made visible to one another. The real issue is not so much how to bring these things into view as how to make them interpretively accessible and accountable to one another; not how to conceptualize their similarities and differences but how to permit them to have a reciprocal, if not a corrective, influence on one another.

For this to be accomplished, we need an interpretive method that is not only adept, as Clifford Geertz once put it, at translating the performances and practices of one culture into the idioms of another, but that is also capable, as Renato Rosaldo has insisted, of submitting the cultural positioning of its own idioms and perspectives to the critique of the performances and practices it would translate into them.[11] In anthropology this amounts, among other things, to acknowledging that the social analyst is not a *tabula rasa* but a positioned subject who must accept "that the objects of social analysis are also analyzing subjects whose perceptions must be taken nearly as seriously as 'we' take our own."[12] This is far from easy, not only because the cultural field is a site of contestation, of struggles over power, but also because its boundaries are now seen to be infinitely more fluid and permeable than they once were. Hardly more than a space where various trajectories of race, gender, ethnicity, age, class, religious belief, or sexual orientation intersect and diverge, culture is characterized at one and the same time by patterns of movement and by zones of difference, the latter often located, to utilize Gloria Anzaldúa's fruitful term, in the "borderlands" between as well as within cultures.[13]

In a world where "change rather than structure becomes society's enduring state, and time rather than space becomes its most encompassing medium," how, Rosaldo wants to know, is one to bring the other's subject position into view, much less to take it seriously enough to influence one's own?[14] This becomes still more difficult because of the paradox of all ethnographic description: as the "other" becomes more visible "as other" to the ethnographer, the ethnographer becomes less visible "as other" to him- or herself. Thus, what the "other" acquires by virtue of being brought into ethnographic focus, namely cultural distinctiveness or "difference," the ethnographer loses by becoming "culturally invisible."[15] According to James Clifford, what the ethnographer cannot see are the "multiple subjectivities and political constraints beyond the control of the writer" that make up his or her "specific strategy of authority."[16] These subjectivities and constraints include such things as the professional protocols of the discipline of anthropology itself, its institutional positioning within a world that links universities and museums to foundations and governments, and the historical relations between the development of anthropology as a "human science" and the expansion and refinement of European colonization as a political practice. Ethnographers thus find themselves in an epistemological box. The more clearly they see their subject, the less clearly they see, or can correctively discount for, the apparatus of seeing itself.

John Dewey was one of the first philosophers to suggest a way out of this epistemological box when he observed, in his book by this title, that the "knowing and the known" are not wholly independent, much less opposed, entities. Far from being separate, autonomous, and, as it were, self-governing, they are actually reciprocally dependent, really interdependent, in at least two important senses: not only is the "known" in part a construct of the "knower"; the construction and positionality of the "knower" is inevitably affected by the constructedness of the "known." While this is not the same thing as saying that we can see, as the traditional locution has it, "from the native's point of view," it is to say that there is nothing that prevents us from learning how to see ourselves as in some sense "a local example of the forms human life has locally taken, a case among cases, a world among worlds."[17] Seeing ourselves as natives among natives is not, to be sure, the same thing as taking our subject's point of view as seriously as we take our own, but it carries us some way toward recognizing at least some of the things that currently limit our view.

In addition, Clifford proposes that we try to make ethnographic writing more dialogic and polyphonic. The first would exploit the difference between the context in which research is conducted and the interlocutory situation that research wants to explore; the second would open up the field of inquiry to the plurality of voices that currently inhabit it. The problem with both strategies is that, no matter how many voices are added to the mix, nor how successful its various participants are in discursively deepening the relationship between them, any text created out of such discourses will still be the creation of a single author.[18] Short of imagining an ethnographic utopia where responsibility for producing texts would be shared equally, or at least proportionately, by members of all the cultures to be represented in it, we seem to be left with a textual situation where one writer, however adept at ventriloquy, is obliged to speak for others.

José David Saldívar believes that we can circumvent some of the problems associated with this situation if we adopt a self-consciously comparativist perspective that is as seriously prepared to question such oppositions as to acknowledge them. This would entail a rethinking and rewriting of the history of, to recall José Martí's famous essay, "Our America" in terms of "the other America, which is not ours."[19] From this perspective, the challenge is not to rehistoricize cross-cultural comparisons as such but rather to rehistoricize such comparisons, in Carolyn Porter's reformulations, "*as* intercultural relations."[20] What needs to be played off against one another are not the historicized differences between "us" and "them" but the way those differences as historically constituted have created forms of life in which both of us share and by which both of us have variously been shaped.

Such sharings and reshapings bring us back to Dewey, who defined his version of pragmatism as a critique of prejudices that involves a kind of "intellectual disrobing." Without pretending that the garments of cultural sense-making can ever be shed entire, Dewey held that there is "a discipline of severe thought" that enables us to determine not only what cultural garments do to the wearer but also what the wearing of them does to the garments. If this form of immanent critique still fails to let us know what cultural forms mean to the "other," it does enable us to gain a deeper comprehension than Rosaldo and, perhaps, Clifford allow of what cultural forms and their instrumentalities do for those who try to use them dialogically to understand and, if possible, engage the "other."

Problems arise for pragmatism, as they do for most other theories of cultural hermeneutics, chiefly when particular cultural perspectives prove impervious or inimical to one another or, almost worse, incommensurable with each other. Liberals have typically responded to these challenges by attempting to create the kind of pluralistic system recommended by the late Sir Isaiah Berlin, where one tries insofar as possible to prevent situations from arising in which human beings are necessarily compelled to act in ways contrary to their own deepest convictions. But this liberal tactic has proved notably ineffective in curbing the use of those more insidious symbolic practices where the opposition or at least difference between various cultural mindsets is turned into an instrument for idealizing, if not reifying, one of them at the expense of deprecating another. Often linked to the construction of identity, this psycho-moral reflex works to shore up and defend senses of self, whether collective or individual, that are threatened or at least unstable. The triggering device is usually some experience of loss, or the threat of such an experience, which can then be assuaged only by laying blame for the distress on someone or something else who or which can then be stigmatized, even demonized. The question to be asked is whether there are any intellectual remedies for such practices and for the social and political pathologies they trail in their wake. Though the word "remedy" may convey the wrong impression, implying that these problems merely await the application of the right medicine to undo the psycho-cultural knots they tie us in, pragmatism seeks to combat the effects of this practice by, in effect, ministering to its cause.

The source of such practices most often lies in a sense of identity that has been weakened or endangered, presumably through exposure to and encounters with senses or expressions of self that are different, or, more precisely, through threats to those idealizations of the past that permit identity to be constructed around a self-reinforcing dialectic of sameness and difference, of "I" and "other." Pragmatism, on the other hand, is to be associated with those interpretive strategies that, like psychoanalysis, cultivate what the cultural psychologist Peter Homans has described as "the ability to mourn."[21] The ability to mourn presupposes, with psychoanalysis generally, that the experience of loss, as I am calling it, need not be restricted to the loss of other selves but can also pertain to the loss of any loved object, from a cherished possession to a valued ideal. The experience of mourning is thus not to be restricted to the traditional model of personal grief, because it can be aroused by the loss of anything that plays a symbolic role in the formation and maintenance of the self. For this reason, mourning is as often associated with the loss of meanings as it is with the death of persons; it occurs whenever selves lose whatever situates, fixes, intensifies, and buttresses their own sense of identity, whether it be other selves, institutions, customs, practices, ceremonies, ideologies, narratives, or what-have-you.

As is well known, Freud's work on mourning was initially provoked by his reflections on the related subject of melancholia, a malady which from the beginning he understood as demonstrating that loss is essential to the formation of the ego. As is less well known, however, Freud did not figure out until much later that the mechanism he had identified with melancholia, a mechanism that enables the ego to construct within itself a replacement for the lost object, is in fact essential to the development of all selves and not just those who are pathologically ill. Having perceived from the start that melancholia involves substituting a new object for the one from which the self has been separated, he did not immediately appreciate just how common this substitution procedure is or how large a role it plays in forming all selves and maintaining their ego-strength. It is not simply that the self is constituted by loss but rather that the experience of loss itself initiates a procedure by which, as Judith Butler has recently remarked, the self can reproduce a potentially acceptable substitute for the missing object.[22]

In this sense, mourning for Freud involves not only a special kind of grieving but also, as Paul Ricoeur was the first to realize, a special kind of remembering.[23] In other words, mourning does not entail a rejection of the past or, even less fateful or dramatic, a willed alienation from it. Instead it enables one to come to terms with the past by, in effect, recreating one's image of it and redefining one's relation to it. More exactly, mourning involves a relinquishment of all attempts to compensate for the continual dissolution of the past's previous forms of unity, coherence, and significance by "monumentalizing" or absolutizing some version of them as an appropriate model for the construction of selfhood.

Thus, the relation between mourning and the formation of identity, whether personal or cultural, might be thought of still differently as a crisis of representation and its resolution. This crisis is precipitated, one might say, by the initial movement of mourning itself, a movement that records, in addition to the abjection of a self that has suffered the loss of some object determinative of its own sense of presence and empowerment, the consequent negation of that self's ability to compensate for such loss except through the creation and then valorization of a representation of its own experience of it. This crisis can be resolved only if the self can relinquish its fixation on a symbolic representation that memorializes merely its experience of its own loss and in its place can reconstruct a representation that memorializes instead the object that occasioned its loss, and in a form that can eventually be contemplated and enjoyed rather than simply lamented and endured.

The process here described is not unlike the movement delineated by Henry James in his famous essay on immortality. Taking up the question, "Is There a Life After Death?" James answered by referring to the change he himself underwent in mourning the death of his beloved cousin Minny Temple. His initial experience, James notes, was almost a complete collapse of the power to represent that loss to himself, but this collapse was eventually reversed, he goes on, when she whose death he grieved was transformed (mercifully) from the occasion of his experience of bereavement into an object of reverie, or, as he remarked in a letter to his brother William, translated into "the realm of pure thought."[24]

Gathering up hints from Freud, Jacques Lacan, and Melanie Klein, Mitchell Breitwiesser has deftly shifted the description of this arduous process into a more contemporary psychoanalytic register, depicting it as one in which the initial image, or, better, sense, of what has been lost *to* the self, and thus of what has been lost *of* the self, is subsequently challenged by a resurgence of memories that mark the passage of the deceased's life through the mourner's world. This surge of memory threatens what Lacan calls a "second death" and begs to be blocked by the nearest instrumentality at hand, which turns out to be, as previously noted, a defense of that initial image that the mourner has constructed of his or her own sense of felt loss.[25] Promising to immunize both the mourner and the mourned against further encroachments of the experience of death, and also to help reverse the mourner's sense of impotence in the face of the loss of his or her object of attachment, this defensive strategy nonetheless carries with it the additional risk of creating within the self what Nicholas Abraham and Maria Torok have termed a "crypt," or inert area, which then obstructs the return of further memories and permanently blocks the continued work of mourning.[26]

To remove these impediments—and the fantasies of spurious empowerment that accompany them—requires "working through," as conventional

Freudian wisdom has it, the return of those resurgent memories so that the self can eventually reconstruct a different representation of the deceased that is based not on the self's experience of its own loss but on what Lacan calls "the unique value/valor of the dead's being."[27] In other words, without a return of the repressed (in this case, the memories of the deceased), the self cannot construct out of, and for, the imagination a representation of the passage that the deceased has made through the mourner's world, much less a representation that is distinguishable from the mourner's image of his or her own grief. For the work of mourning to succeed, then, the dead must be allowed, as Breitwiesser aptly observes, to die "honorably," adequately assigned to "being something symbolized . . . rather than [remaining as] a crippling defect in a survivor who would otherwise be whole."[28]

"Honoring the dead" would be a good deal easier for individuals as well as groups to accomplish if the experience of grief were not accompanied by so much anger. In addition to evoking a sense of sorrow often too deep for words, feelings of numbness and unreality, uncontrollable weeping, and other emotions, devastating loss can also trigger an anger that is no byproduct of grief but rather an integral aspect of it. This is what Rosaldo confesses to having experienced himself, after the accidental death of his first wife, as "the rage in grief."[29] Whether or not this "rage in grief" is to be explained as a result of those "crypts" within the self that can block the full return of the repressed and thus cut the self or mourner off from symbolic resources that might otherwise assuage it, this is the kind of rage that leads Ilongot men in the Philippines to want to cut off human heads and leads other mourners to take up paramilitarism, espionage, and terrorism. The link between loss and rage, as Freud also discerned, has to do with the inability to represent loss as anything other than an impoverishment of the ego, which turns the ego vengeful. Left to themselves, these feelings threaten to tear apart groups no less than individuals. The only way they can be curbed, or rather managed, is through the intervention of symbolic forms that can draw off some of the anger in grief while at the same time providing a structure for redescribing it.

Chief among those forms that enable us to honor the dead without murdering the witnesses is what, in psychoanalytic terms, is known as the technique of transference. But the technique of transference, as post-Lacanian psychoanalysis has emphasized, is none other than a transactional, or what might be described as a pragmatist, theory of interpretation. What defines this theory of interpretation is the way it creates what Freud viewed as a region situated somewhere between illness and real life, a region where the patient's blockage, now manifested in a symbolic reification centered on the patient's grief rather than on the meaning of his or her loss, can become accessible to the interpretive interventions and reinterpretations of the analyst. In other words, transference turns the therapeutic relationship into the form of an exchange that is less monological than dialogical, where the story to be reconstructed is a product of the transactions between analyst and analysand as each contributes—because of, and in anticipation of, the interventions (whether merely envisaged or literally enacted) of the other—to the production of a narrative. This is a narrative whose veracity, as in William James's theory of truth, has less and less to do with its correspondence to buried fact, that is, to a reality that is reflected or copied, and more and more to do with its plausibility as the model for an alternative future. The meaning produced by this narrative of interpretation results, as in literature, neither from the author's intentions alone, nor from the reader's responses, but instead from their collaborative interaction. The aim of the therapeutic exercise is to create an interpretive environment where, in clinical terms, both patient and therapist, and in aesthetic terms, both artist and critic, may work on a "text" that simultaneously "works" on them. They work together in the belief that the fullest measure of so-called truth will be found, to utilize Peter Brook's helpful formulation, through the deepest possible penetration of the semiotic, the imaginative, and the hermeneutic into the domain of the psychological.[30]

But if transference can be applied to the psychodynamic process of individual therapy, where it exhibits its analogies with the work of reading, can it not also be applied, as I have intimated all along, to the psychosocial process of what might be termed cultural therapy, where it exhibits albeit looser analogies with the work of inter- and transcultural criticism? Here, as it happens, transference finds its most obvious parallel in the historical development of psychoanalysis and pragmatism themselves, both of which could be said to have been devised, as I have noted elsewhere,[31] as strategies for responding to the loss of a felt sense of religious and cultural unity at the end of the nineteenth century. Both theories responded to that loss by converting the experience of lamenting the loss—and consequently of reorganizing self-identity around an image of the passing of that sense of unity—into an opportunity to remake the self, and the self's relations with the world around it. The remade self was built out of the interpretive activities, at once critical and self-reflexive, that had to be brought into play in order for some other form of psycho-cultural organization to take the place of the unity that had been lost.

More specifically, the development of pragmatism and of psychoanalysis was made possible by, and replicated in, a personal experience of "working through" in the lives of their founders (I am thinking in particular of Freud and James) that was almost identical to the intellectual "passage" conceptualized as the principal therapeutic paradigm of their respective theories. This involved for each man a passage from the encounter with the death of meaning (or at least an encounter with the fear of that death), through a countermovement designed to dispel that fear (by redefining the self in terms of an image of its loss), to an eventual recovery not only of meaning itself but, more crucially, of the ability to produce and take pleasure in new meanings.

The point to be noted is that recovery of the self's ability to create and enjoy new meanings, which is synonymous with the work of mourning itself, is made possible only by a liberation of the self's capacities for imaginative as well as interpretive and critical reflection. The work of mourning thus eventuates in the development of a new emotional and intellectual space between, as it were, the self and the social order and its historical surround. An intermediate space that enables the self to fashion its relations through symbols with structures of meaning that it creates and at the same time inherits, this is the cultural space that, as Homans observes, Freud himself could never quite conceive but that pragmatism necessarily presupposes and seeks critically to colonize.[32] An at least partially fictive space created in no small measure by fantasy, conjecture, inference, hypothesis, surmise, and prediction, this domain of the cultural imaginary, I am arguing, is not only where, as James and Dewey contend, our most fateful (and fanciful) reasoning occurs, but also where societies, like selves, must continuously learn to remake themselves.

And just like selves, societies learn to remake themselves by learning how to trust themselves, so to speak, to the imaginative, interpretive, and critical energies that are released and enabled when they resist the temptation to compensate for the loss of meaning that inevitably accompanies historical change by pretending that the past can still remain effectively present—and thus available to the self—if the past, or at least certain qualities associated with it, are "monumentalized" in some unchangeable form. The ability to mourn the loss of these qualities is decisive if the imagination is to be freed to perform its work of developing images of the culture's relations with the world around it which are not merely solipsistic.

This is as much as to say that if, as Jamesian and, more specifically, as Meadean and Deweyan pragmatism have always assumed, selves develop only in relation to other selves, or, more exactly, in relation to the symbolic materials by which those other selves represent themselves to themselves, the same holds true for entire cultures. Cultures constitute themselves, as Christopher Miller has pointed out, "*by reference to each other.*"[33] But this intercultural referentiality can, and does, cut in more than one direction. If cultures can find out how they might become other than they are only by imaginatively relocating themselves in the narratives and fables of other cultures, so it is also true, as Carlos Fuentes has observed, that only by discovering ourselves already in some sense situated in the stories and tales of others, often as their despised antagonist or nemesis, can we fully understand all that we presently are. The stories, narratives, interpretations, and representations of the other Americas not only allow us to begin rereading and re-imagining ourselves but also enable us to recognize aspects, dimensions, and elements of ourselves that we did not even know existed.[34] Such discoveries, entailing as they do a sense of loss as well as a sense of recognition, inevitably run the risk of awakening the rage in grief no less than the pleasure in self-fashioning. Intercultural and cross-cultural concourse may always be a mixed blessing, but if we were unable to participate in it, we would remain as much in ignorance of ourselves as of others.

We thus return in this chapter to where we began, but now found in translation rather than lost in it.[35] To find oneself in the processes of cross- and inter-American cultural translation is to realize that our relations with others, and particularly with socially and culturally significant others, are rarely direct, simple, or one-way. They occur most often in that intermediary space between selves and the social and historical surround known as culture where contacts and exchanges are as much symbolic and imaginative as they are material or empirical. More precisely, they occur through the mediation of images, fictions, and ceremonies that, however different and distinctive their particular references, have become consequential for ourselves and for others in oddly similar ways: not because they possess the same symbolic significance in our respective cultural-historical contexts, but because they have served—and can be comprehended as having served—the same, or at any rate similar, functions in our respective epigenetic development.

What we identify with through these mediations are the psycho-cultural processes by which other people, often so different from us in so many other respects, have become more interesting, and sometimes more admirable, but in any case more instructive, for us through their ability to redraw the coordinates of their own autonomy and dependence, their own originality and belatedness, by reinterpreting the way they can be represented symbolically. They rework the temptation to lament the loss of previous forms of cultural identity into an opportunity to create new alternatives for self-definition out of the imaginative and interpretive energies brought into play by the decomposition and recomposition of former ones. On the other hand, what we sometimes rather miraculously achieve through such symbolic interventions is that fuller enlargement of ourselves that comes from recognizing, in terms and forms often so alien and even unsettling to us, traces of that common and unending imaginative struggle for meaning that not only still marks us all as human but also still marks our humanity as necessarily a corporate rather than an individual accomplishment.

If the possibility of creating a mutually interrogative and genuinely critical cultural criticism of the Americas depends on recognizing this double truth, it is worth asking how pragmatism developed into a theory of inquiry that might inform it. To answer this question fully, it will be necessary to turn to the James brothers, William and Henry, who between them turned pragmatism into a critical method that was both dialogical and transnational. But before we do so, we need to ask what a sense of solidarity in the Americas or elsewhere can mean in a world being rapidly globalized.

Chapter 2

Rethinking Human Solidarity
in an Age of Globalism

In the present multicultural environment in the United States, conventional understanding of the terms *self* and *other* may carry us only so far, I want to propose, in enabling us to reconceive the pragmatics of a new interor transnational criticism, whether restricted to the Americas or not. There are no doubt many reasons for this, but the one I wish to focus on here has to do with liberalism's seeming inability, beyond a certain point, to rethink the issue of alterity in a multicultural world. As instances of this difficulty, I want to select from a fairly broad spectrum of thinkers that might include, on liberalism's right flank, Arthur Schlesinger, Jr., Robert Bellah, and Michael Sandel, or on liberalism's left, Michael Walzer, Cornel West, Todd Gitlin, and David Hollinger. The work of Gitlin and Hollinger, who have written two of the best books on the subject, seems to reflect the fact that a position within American liberalism seems to be slowly formulating itself around the issue of multiculturalism and democracy, a position that, as no one would be surprised to learn, is at once agonized and critical. What further troubles me is that this position may well underestimate the problems of conceptualizing the relations, at best somewhat discordant and vexed, between multiculturalism, otherness, and solidarity.

Of the two books, Gitlin's is more distressed and angry than Hollinger's, partly because his own "leftist universalism," as Michael Walzer describes it, has been so savagely attacked and undercut by the militant identity politics sometimes spawned by multiculturalism itself. But Gitlin's *The Twilight of Common Dreams* also provides a denser history of the run-up to America's recent culture wars and a more broad-gauged psychosocial explanation of why America has been so wracked by them. Hollinger's *Postethnic America*, on the other hand, furnishes a sharper analysis of the logic of multiculturalism and a more extended proposal for how to get beyond it. Both writers agree, however, that multiculturalism has failed, and both are equally convinced that a chief reason for this failure has to do with multiculturalism's inability to balance the centrifugal pressures for cultural diversity against the centripetal pressures for some kind of shared, or sharable, sense of cultural identity.

Much of their critique circles around the way the notion of solidarity has been turned against itself. On the one hand, the new appreciation of cultural differences has rendered the whole notion of human solidarity suspect. On the other, the often volatile, but at the same time often beleaguered, politics of identity have simultaneously recuperated the idea of human solidarity as a defense of ethnocentrism. Thus, Hollinger's rehearsal of the inherent conflicts within multiculturalism itself constitutes what sounds like a catalogue of failure:

> Mixed-race Americans demand recognition from the United States census, while many black politicians defend a "one-drop rule" for identifying African Americans that was designed to serve slaveholders and white supremacists. Women's rights activists try to help victims of clitoridectomy, while cultural relativists warn that westerners have no standing to instruct Saudis and Sudanese on culturally specific rights and duties. Educational reformers add new cultures to school curricula, while guardians of civility demand the banning from campuses of speech that might offend certain groups. Illegal immigrants from Mexico complicate the public services of California, while prophets of postnationality explain that the boundary between the United States and Mexico is an imperialist fiction.[1]

Hollinger's diagnosis, not unlike Gitlin's, is that these problems stem from a conflict within multiculturalism itself that sets pluralist against cosmopolitan. This conflict, whose origins go back to tensions latent within William James's pluralist vision of experience and its later reappropriation in John Dewey's theory of democracy, was first played out in the contrary positions taken up in the 1920s by Horace Kallen and Randolph Bourne. Because cultural pluralism was used, then as now, to defend a kind of ethnic provincialism, Gitlin and Hollinger each argue that cultural pluralism must presently give way to a new kind of critical cosmopolitanism. This critical

cosmopolitanism would be sensitive to the contribution that a particular-
ized ethnicity can make to the formation of both human character and political citizenship when each is seen both as rooted in history and as subject
to change. Hollinger goes on to describe this critical cosmopolitanism as
"postethnic" because, while abandoning the reference to any generalized
sense of humankind, it nonetheless holds that we are all affiliated with more
than one historically rooted sense of particular solidarity, or ethnos, and
that we all can—and in some sense continuously do—often affiliate ourselves with numerous others at will. Hollinger thus concludes, not unlike
Richard Rorty, that we have the capacity, and should exercise the power, to
extend our sense of "we," our feeling of solidarity with our own kind, as far
as our capabilities, and the sensibilities of those "others" we wish to include,
will allow us.

Though Hollinger is unable to predict how strong the forces in America
may be that stand opposed to a postethnic orientation—how deep the
racism of whites or the anger, suspicion, and despair of various ethno-racial
minorities—he invokes the Henry James of *The American Scene*, who called
upon members of his own ethnos to surrender at least part of their idea of
the country to the new immigrants arriving from Eastern and Western Europe. The children of these immigrants struck James as "the stuff of which
brothers and sisters are made" since "'they' are no more 'alien,'" he went on
to add, "and no less the 'American' than we.'"[2] By contrast, Gitlin is less
certain than Hollinger is that discovering how all our senses of solidarity are
constructed will, in turn, encourage "us" to go more than half way to meet,
or at least to engage, the solidarity of others, but he nonetheless insists that
our only political hope in the United States is to build as many bridges as
possible between our sense of "us" and their sense of "them." Both writers
are, of course, alive to the fact that building bridges raises decidedly political questions—Who has access to them? How much traffic flows in either
direction? What sort of material is granted passage?—but neither expresses
any serious doubts that democracy, as commonly understood, can show us
the way.

Thus, if each of these powerful apologias for the need to move beyond
multiculturalism—and thus beyond the wrong kind of human solidarity—
reflects what I am calling an emerging liberal consensus on the subject, they
nevertheless strike me as partially unconvincing because of their mutual assumption that the individual is still sufficiently unencumbered by cultural
and other determinants to act in behalf of its own, let alone other peoples',
self-interest. When Hollinger, for example, quotes Joseph Raz, the distin-

guished liberal theorist, on what the latter calls the "right of exit" from communities of identity—be they religious, ethnic, racial, or whatever—he means to defend the possibility that people can, within reason, resist the argument that "grandparents are destiny," that descent, as it were, goes all the way down.[3] While agreeing with the noted communitarian thinker Michael Sandel that we all "move in a history [we] neither summon nor command, which carries consequences nonetheless for [our] choices and conduct,"[4] Hollinger still insists that the real issue "is how much choice there is in relation to given desires."[5]

Like Gitlin, Hollinger is aware of the structures of power in society—who controls them, how far and deep they extend, and with what intensity and effects they are experienced in any given moment or sphere of existence—and of how these power structures constrain the realm of choice. But this way of putting "the real issue" also leaves unanswered a related question as to what controls the grammar of desire. Like most liberals, Hollinger answers that the grammar of desire is ultimately in the hands of the individual, even if this individual is threaded together with numerous other individuals in various overlapping, and sometimes conflicting, communities of identity. And like any good utilitarian pragmatist, Hollinger also assumes, or at any rate hopes, that the individual can, through the voluntary exercise of such choices as are available, not only enact her or his freedom but at the same time encompass within the scope of this desire wider spheres of what I will call, for want of a better term, social and cultural otherness.

As an ideal which, as Hollinger notes, "prefers voluntary to prescribed affiliations, appreciates multiple identities, pushes for communities of wide scope, recognizes the constructed character of ethno-racial groups, and accepts the formation of new groups as part of the normal life of a democratic society,"[6] this is an attractive option; but as an option which hinges for its achievement, as Hollinger and Gitlin both presume, on summoning the will, both individual and collective, to actualize it, an ideal is in truth all that it remains. For if America's most recent experience of multiculturalism has taught us anything, it has reminded us that the will to realize this ideal, here as elsewhere in the world, is deeply troubled, unpredictable, divided against itself, dispersed, sublimated, and often repressed; in short, that good will carry us only so far in comprehending, much less coping with, what has been loosely termed "the problem of the 'other.'"

Among pragmatists, no one deserves more credit for placing this issue center stage than Richard J. Bernstein.[7] Associating the acquisition of all

knowledge with concepts of the "alien" and the "other" (without, as it happens, ever quite addressing the issue as to whether all that we always want to
understand is always alien and "other" to the same radical degree), Bernstein maintains, in a manner foreign neither to James nor to Dewey, that the
basic condition for understanding inevitably remains the self's willingness
to place its own convictions and assumptions at risk for the sake of encoun-
tering that which is inevitably different. The corollary to this conviction is
that "it is only through an engaged encounter with the Other, with the otherness of the Other," Bernstein goes on to observe, "that one comes to a
more informed, textured understanding of the tradition to which 'we' belong."[8]

But now the claim that understanding is founded on otherness is itself
likely to activate a question from another quarter. For example, the Jewish
philosopher and Talmudic scholar Emmanuel Levinas has pondered at
length as to whether such formulations threaten to reduce the alterity of the
"different" or the "other" to what Levinas calls the "Same." If, as Levinas
has long argued, the self is ethically constituted by an encounter with that
which is radically "other," how does the "other" in this transaction, or even
merely the "different," retain its alterity? As Bernstein notes, Jacques Derrida, Levinas's old friend and sometimes critic, may well have answered this
question more cogently than Levinas himself has.[9] While Levinas is prepared to sacrifice any connection between self and "other" for the sake of
preserving the integrity of otherness itself, Derrida asserts that the so-called
"other" can maintain its alterity only if in fact it actually remains part of the
"Same." While "the other," Derrida writes, "is the other only if his alterity
is absolutely irreducible, that is, infinitely irreducible,"[10] its otherness must
be recognized as part of the ego, actually as a kind of alter ego, if that otherness is not to dissolve. Hence Derrida concludes that "the other as alter ego
signifies the other as other, irreducible to my ego, precisely because [as
Edmund Husserl maintained] it is an ego, because it has the form of the
ego. . . . This is why, if you will, he is a face, can speak to me, understand me,
and eventually command me."[11] To put this in slightly different terms, only
if the "other" is represented as something that our "I" must address (because
it possesses the form of an ego) can it remain something to which our "I"
must remain accountable, to which "we" are required to be answerable.

For Bernstein, then, "self" and "other" constitute a relationship of co-
implication, even if that relation also contains within itself dimensions of estrangement, enmity, and violence, even of abjection and horror. Rather like
Mikhail Bakhtin, Bernstein allies himself with Derrida (who is not usually

thought of as agreeing with Bakhtin on this issue) in thinking that "self" and "other" are not absolutely opaque to one other, much less always reflective of mindsets or frames of reference that are utterly incommensurable. Indeed if, as Bakhtin holds, understanding is necessarily transgredient and exotopic,[12] then the so-called "other" cannot be understood at all except from a point of view outside itself, which within the terms of this binary formulation is to say, from the point of view of the so-called "self." Bernstein therefore reasons, in conformity with Derrida but in disagreement with another liberal, Sir Isaiah Berlin, that the "other" cannot be totally incompatible, let alone fundamentally alien, to the "self," so long as the "self" feels some kind of ethical obligation, if not to understand the "other," then at least to understand itself in reference to the "other."

But what if selves no longer feel this sense of ethical obligation? What if, along with the religious and social as well as epistemological transactions it once sponsored, this ethical sense has dissolved into thin air, or, more likely, been reduced to ash by the furnace of hatred that has been set ablaze in this century by ideologies of race, ethnicity, nation, class, religion, and gender? What if, as the political theorist William E. Connolly has asserted, identity, whether personal or cultural, can establish itself only by defining itself paradoxically in relation to a set of differences that it is constantly tempted to view not simply as "other" but also as contrary, inimical, hostile, and malevolent.[13] The temptation to view those differences as "other," rather than simply as divergent or discrepant, arises because identity can best define and reinforce itself in terms of a series of oppositions whose operations are for the most part carried out beneath the levels of conscious reflection. The temptation to view "otherness" as antagonistic, even pernicious, emerges because of the sense of uncertainty already built into the need for identity itself. This uncertainty is exacerbated in our late-modern era by a generalized feeling of resentment against all the globalized structures, disciplines, and practices that threaten to control, constrain, destabilize, or dismantle the self—hence, the risk that identity will be further dogmatized, difference further stigmatized.

Connolly's hope that the "dogmatization of difference" can be restrained rests on the possibility of cultivating a new ethics based on the care for difference. This hope depends on instituting new genealogical modes of reflecting about the relation between identity and difference and will need to draw on a democratic politics sensitive to the abundance of difference that exceeds any given political or personal identity.[14] But in a world where questions of cultural as well as personal identity seem so often locked in destructive embrace with issues of cultural difference, where people not only seem to prefer their own values to the values of others but appear to be able to maintain their own values too often only at the expense of disparaging or demonizing the values of others, is it actually possible to imagine that the forms of life that we traditionally encompass within the structure of "self" and "other" can any longer have a constructive impact on one another?

This is a question that can now no longer be begged, a question that indeed, it seems to me, has now cast a dark shadow, at least in the West, over our whole notion of the human. That notion of the human is linked to a sense of solidarity that has enjoyed a very long career in the history of human thought and that for at least the last century or two has been one of the Western world's, if not one of the rest of the world's, most significant "god-terms." Premised as it was (and, for many, still is) on the concept of a unitary humanity, the notion of human solidarity has historically offered a way of symbolizing the nature of the human bond not only within cultures but potentially across them during a period when, in the West itself, formulations of a more orthodox kind, theological or otherwise—*imago dei*, original sin, divine spark, the sacredness of the human spirit, inalienable human rights—could no longer be employed as easily, or at any rate as widely, as they once were to define our commonality as creatures. It is not only in the master paradigms of some of those prominent nineteenth-century social thinkers who became, in the twentieth, our secular theologians—Alexis de Tocqueville, Karl Marx, Max Weber, Ferdinand Tönnies, and Émile Durkheim—that the appeal to human solidarity has been at least one way, even if not the only way, that we have expressed, enacted, and critiqued our shared attributes as a species. It is also in the master narratives of many of those nineteenth-century writers who took upon themselves the task of supplying us with a new set of what Northrop Frye was rightly to call our "secular scriptures"—Jane Austen, Honoré de Balzac, Leo Tolstoy, George Eliot, Herman Melville, Joseph Conrad, and Virginia Woolf.

If cruelty, as Judith Shklar once stated, is the worst thing we do,[15] solidarity is among the best, not just according to Rorty but also according to the Anti-Slavery Society, Amnesty International, Human Rights Watch, B'nai B'rith, and countless other NGOs (nongovernmental organizations), governmental institutions, and moral and religious traditions. A term that has found significant if partial (and some might say imperfect) historical realizations in the Universal Declaration of Human Rights established by the United Nations in 1948, the Polish Solidarity Movement, and the Czech Charter 77 movement, and which possesses powerful advocates and defenders in Václav Havel, Elie Wiesel, Nadine Gordimer, Amartya Sen, and numerous others throughout the world,[16] *solidarity* is not a term with which we can easily dispense.

Joseph Conrad gave what is perhaps the most affecting testimonial to the nineteenth-century faith in human solidarity in his remarkable preface to *The Nigger of the Narcissus*, defining human solidarity as a feeling "that knits together the loneliness of innumerable hearts . . . in dreams, in joy, in sorrow, in aspirations, in illusions, in hope, in fear, which binds men to each other, which binds together all humanity—the dead to the living and the living to the unborn." Conrad associated this feeling not with anything that philosophy or science can describe but only with what the highest art can express. If philosophy and science both speak to our sense of credulity, Conrad wrote, the first appealing to ideas, the second to facts, art appeals by contrast directly to the emotions and thus "speaks to our capacity for delight and wonder, to the sense of mystery surrounding our lives; to our sense of pity, and beauty, and pain; to the latent feeling of fellowship with all creation."[17]

Nonetheless, such feelings all too easily turned inward for Conrad, as when the phrase "one of us" in *Lord Jim* and *Nostromo*, no less than *The Nigger of the Narcissus*, *Youth*, *Under Western Eyes*, *Victory*, and other tales, begins to contract its putatively universal or global reference and becomes more restricted to something merely European, white, male, and even Christian. As an augury of things to come, Conrad's writing presages the extreme pressures to which the notion of solidarity has been submitted in the century just past. Cambodia, the Sudan, Rwanda, Chechnya, Bosnia, and Kosovo name only a few of the places where the potential for solidarity has all but been engulfed by the penchant for cruelty; nor should one forget that the Universal Declaration of Human Rights was itself created in the hope of putting an end to the genocidal policies that led to the Holocaust.

But even if these barbarous events had not called the idea of solidarity into serious question—in what Eric Hobsbawm calls the cruelest and most bestial century in the history of human records—its usages over the years have caused it to be viewed with considerable suspicion, where it has not been totally discredited. Initially problematized and censured by social and political historians who have linked it closely to the history of Western imperialism and the practices of European colonialism, the notion of human solidarity has now been subjected to renewed attack by the very science that imperialism begat, anthropology. We are now told that human beings, instead of sharing a common nature, as was once assumed, now merely share a certain predisposition to define themselves by means of their practices, or, rather, by the connection, as Clifford Geertz puts it more exactly, between their generic capacities and their specific performances.[18] Either way, human beings are no longer understood to be creatures possessing a universal nature to whose collective ethical center one can appeal but rather are viewed as members of a species given to defining itself relentlessly in terms of the disparagement of human difference.

Ethnic and religious violence of the sort that sets Serbs against Albanians, Palestinians against Israelis, Tutsis against Hutus, Azerbaijanis against Armenians, and Russians against Chechnyans may represent only the most dramatic spectacle of this fact, but it is a fact nonetheless. And it is a fact all the more disturbing simply because the appeal to blood loyalty so easily and sometimes inevitably legitimates the need for blood sacrifice. Nationalism has, of course, always been defined in relation to the conditions that permit a people to resort to force or violence in their own defense, but ethnic and religious nationalism all too readily transform the warrant for violence into a mandate for it. An essential ingredient in this process that connects blood loyalty with blood sacrifice is a psychology that, as Michael Ignatieff has recently reminded us, appeals to peoples' better instincts rather than their worst. In other words, the sanctions for violence derive not from what people hate but from what people cherish, which helps explain why ethnic and religious nationalists are so often, and without contradiction, sentimentalists. They are in the grip of a set of feelings stronger than enmity, stronger even than the desire for self-preservation. Hence, as Ignatieff observes, "there is no killer on either side of any checkpoints that will not pause, between firing at his enemies, to sing some nostalgic song or even to recite a few lines of some ethnic poem."[19]

More disturbing still, this psychology that puts murder in the service of love helps illumine the logic of ethnic cleansing, which permits groups that have lived together on terms of the greatest intimacy and understanding, often for centuries, to become the targets of each other's most murderous rage. While all societies may practice some forms of symbolic sacrifice that permit them to prevent their aggressive instincts from running unchecked and allows those instincts to be rechanneled and concentrated on the society's or group's perceived enemies, ethnic and religious communities in particular respond to perceived threats to their identity with a ritualistic virulence that is without parallel. The more dire the imagined threat to the community's social being, the more important must be the victim sacrificed to preserve that identity. Under such circumstances, former neighbors, and even family members, offer themselves as the perfect vehicles of sacrificial mediation. The community of significant selves can be saved only by exterminating those "others" who were once so valuable to it.

There is, of course much here that is reminiscent of Freud's later theory of aggression in *Civilization and Its Discontents*, where violence is not an aberration or abnormality of social behavior but an inevitable outcome of it. Aggression for Freud is a response to the disappointments, postponements, and sacrifices of civilized life. Whether or not this aggression represents what Freud called the death instinct, the instinct for life to which it is opposed cannot be maintained if the propensity for aggression is not contained. In classical Freudian theory, this containment is accomplished through a process of internalization by means of which aggression is turned back against the ego, or that part of the self which splits off and is known as the superego, and is then used by the superego to keep the ego in line. Thus aggressive impulses that would otherwise be projected outward beyond the self against others are supposedly enfeebled, or at least curbed, by being diverted back to and introjected by the superego, which then manages them by redirecting them back at the ego in the form of punishment.

Freud's somewhat hydraulic explanation of this process may account for how violence against others is partially kept in check and prevented from spreading any further, but it doesn't offer much assistance in helping us understand why the chief mechanism for such work seems to be the displacement onto others of responsibility or blame for this psychologically painful state of affairs. Nor, for all of its reasonableness, does the decidedly less primitive view of the etiology of aggression that has been more recently supplied by Peter Gay in *The Cultivation of Hatred*. Gay rejects Freud's theory of aggression as based on too mythological, albeit "picturesque," a theory of the instincts. Instead he sides with Otto Fenichel who—when Freud's theory of Eros and Thanatos was declared pretty much dead and aggression was being reinterpreted as merely one among a number of other assertive activities by psychoanalysts like David Rapaport and ego psychologists like Heinz Hartmann—proposed that aggressive drives lack any instinctual aim of their own and are merely, in some cases, responses to the frustration of other drives, and in others, violent reactions to whatever is experienced as unpleasurable. In either case, these drives can, and often do, work themselves out in a variety of circumstances.

While this revisionist smoothing out of Freud's theory of aggression may represent an important improvement over Freud's more primitive account (Gay maintains that it suggests "where psychoanalysts now stand"[20]), it still fails to account for the ritual behavior that seems almost universally to underlie and reinforce communal as well as personal violence. Such behavior, as Orlando Patterson has recently pointed out, is intimately linked to rites of sacrifice in which the shedding of blood is associated symbolically with the preservation of a social world threatened with destruction. Such rites may be as old almost as time immemorial, having been employed by people throughout the ages as a traditional way, to follow Henri Hubert and Marcel Mauss, of binding the sacrificers into a community of ritual cleansers and of linking their community to the larger structures of life itself through the mediatorial role played by the sacrificial victim.[21] These rites also need to be understood, however, as Mark Juergensmeyer has suggested, in the context of war.[22] Sacrificial victims are selected because, like enemies in battle, they are discovered to be out of place and therefore represent a form of disorder that endangers the security of the community. Moreover, their identification and destruction helps renarrativize social history as a redemptive story of persecution, resistance, liberation, and salvation. Thus, as social repetitions of organized conflict, forms of blood sacrifice not only reinforce one of the deepest needs of the human spirit but exemplify one of the most ancient religious practices, known as "scapegoating."

Scapegoating is a rite that, according to René Girard, is designed to prevent conflict from destroying the social fabric. Social strife can be avoided if the community can realign itself around its common repudiation of a victim symbolically held responsible for the aggression against it. Community can then be preserved because a mimetic surrogate has been found to divert and absorb its violence.[23] But this in turn does little to account for the religious virulence of scapegoating. Kenneth Burke maintains that this virulence cannot be fully understood without explaining how the scapegoat permits the community, like the self, not just to protect itself from unwanted evil and pollution but to purge itself of them. To Burke, the relation between victimizer and victim is thus much closer than even Girard assumes. What the scapegoat offers the community is nothing short of "vicarious atonement."[24] The victim in scapegoat rituals becomes a "chosen vessel" whose function is to enable others to "ritualistically cleanse themselves by loading the burden of their own iniquities upon it."[25] And once this process of deprecatory displacement has been initiated, the scapegoat's therapeutic properties tend to increase in direct proportion to the violence by which it is attacked. In this ritualistic scenario, then, victimage and the violence that accompanies it are not merely instrumental to personal and social health but are absolutely indispensable to it. Self-formation and cultural renewal are inextricably linked to a sacrificial procedure that enables those who feel threatened, inadequate, or guilty to find expiation and deliverance by projecting their senses of vulnerability, deficiency, or corruption on some "other" who can then be vilified, shunned, humiliated, tortured, or exterminated.

Such rites of sacrifice, which prevent violence from spreading any further and function to keep vengeance in check only by naturalizing it, pose a moral, not to say political, challenge of enormous magnitude. If "blood and cruelty" are not, as Nietzsche feared, "the foundation of 'all good things,'" how is one to break the cycle of the dogmatization and deprecation of difference that now characterizes the behavior of so many destabilized groups as well as individuals throughout the world? One doesn't need to accept Nietzsche's view of religion, Orlando Patterson writes, to appreciate his insights into the ubiquity of human sacrifice:

> When man thinks it necessary to make for himself a memory, he never accomplishes it without blood, tortures and sacrifice; the most dreadful sacrifice and forfeitures (among them sacrifice of the first-born), the most loathsome mutilation (for instance castration), and the most cruel rites of all the religious cultures (for all religions are really at bottom systems of cruelty)—all these things originate from that instinct which found pain its most potent mnemonic.[26]

Global theorists like Giovanni Arrighi, Stanley Jeyaraja Tambiah, and even Arjun Appadurai are inclined to explain the upsurge, really explosion, of ethnic and other forms of violence in other ways. Arrighi attributes the increase in this violence not to atavistic groups or local warlords but to the operations of the world market, which forces society to protect itself in response to the disruption and dismantling of more established ways of living.[27] He also agrees with Tambiah and Appadurai that this violence has grown less containable because of the decline of the modern state and, as Appadurai puts it, the "incapacity of many deterritorialized groups to think their way out of the imaginary of the nation-state."[28] According to Appadurai, this forces "many movements of emancipation and identity, in their struggles against existing nation-states, to embrace the very imaginary they seek to escape."[29]

Much as this observation has to commend it, it nevertheless needs to be qualified by a realization that the problem of ethnic "belonging," as Ignatieff has termed it—which clearly has been exacerbated by the recent destabilization and collapse of so many nation-states in, say, the territorialities that once made up the borders of the former Soviet Union, or that remain as the legacy of colonialism throughout Africa, or that still mark the existence of people like the Kurds and the Palestinians, as well as those millions of deterritorialized guestworkers and diasporans from the Middle East to Australia and from South Africa to Northern Europe—produces a problem that is not primarily one of recognition, as Charles Taylor would have it, but one of security. Now that people have been deprived of the shelter of larger political structures like the nation-state, who is going to look out for them if not representatives of their own kind? Urging them to think their way out of the imaginary that supposedly blocks their route to emancipation and identity, as Appadurai proposes, is a good deal more difficult when they cannot easily survive without either the protection or the support that, in Ignatieff's estimation, such imagined communities once routinely provided.

Burke, on the other hand, may have come up with a way of breaking the cycle of ritual violence that so often attends the demarcation of difference when he urged us to consider reconstructing human identity not only in terms of our sense of solidarity with our own kind but also in terms of what he called, only half-humorously, our "sense of fundamental kinship with the enemy."[30] By "enemy" Burke did not necessarily mean only "adversary," "antagonist," or "assailant," but in fact anyone in opposition to whom—or constructed in opposition to whom—we find it necessary to define ourselves, in other words, the "other." Affording what he thought of as a "perspective by incongruity," this essentially comic recognition depends less on reversing the subject positions of "self" and "other," however much that maneuver might have to recommend it, than on using each as a kind of prismatic mirror to refract back to its opposite undetected aspects of itself.

In recommending such a stratagem, Burke was not intending to preempt the fashionable postmodernist view that we can know others only in ways that are always already forms of ourselves; nor was he implying, to the contrary, that there are no forms of ourselves that are also forms of others. He was merely asserting, with a contemporary critical theorist like Satya P. Mohanty, that even in our differences, whether lived or only imagined, we are still intertwined with these others by virtue of the fact that we share histories that are not entirely separate, and have suffered a fate that, however discrepant, is never entirely discrete.[31] Thus, to turn the subject positions of "self" and "other" into prisms that reflect is not simply to see elements of the "other" within the "self" or elements of the "self" within the "other." Nor it is even, and this is much more difficult, to see elements of the "self" as "other" and elements of the "other" as potentialities of the self." It is, rather, to see how, even in their opposition and, possibly total, antagonism, "self" and "other" remain constructs that are at once implicated in one another's fabrication and necessary to each other's moral constitution. The kinship between "self" and "other" is thus predicated less on any intrinsic qualities they may possibly share than on the pragmatic truth that neither can understand itself except from a position outside of and different from itself. Alterity is thus the lens by which "self" and "other" come into focus, at least as enablers of each other's self-knowledge, possibly as aspects—however obscure, remote, ambiguous, or discomfiting—of each other's identity.

To call that truth "pragmatic," however, is, in the current intellectual environment, to invite the response that pragmatism is not, in fact, political at all, since it possesses no way of appreciating how completely the relations between "self" and "other" are always determined by distributions of power. Some of the responsibility for this view of pragmatism's indifference to politics has to be laid at the door of William James himself. In his well-known definition of the pragmatic method in his chapter on "What Pragmatism Means" from *Pragmatism*, James insisted that pragmatism stands for no particular results. It is, he insisted, a method only, though one more attractive than other empiricisms because more radical and at the same time more congenial. Turning its back on many inveterate philosophical habits and biases, it is both more concrete than other empirical methods and also more free-spirited and adaptable. Pragmatism was to James less a theory than an orientation or attitude, and to the degree that it considered theories at all, it viewed them as instruments for further inquiry rather than as solutions to problems.

Rorty has since fastened on this disclaimer more than once to argue that pragmatism lacks a political consciousness. But this assertion simultaneously disregards the limited point that James was initially trying to make about this new method of philosophical analysis—or, rather, as he phrased it, this "new name for some old ways of thinking"—and to discount what, in any case, it quickly became as a generalized intellectual perspective on experience. If the pragmatic method was originally designed to mediate the otherwise interminable disputes among rival metaphysical claims, it proposed to do so by, in effect, translating questions of meaning and truth into questions of practice, that is, by deflecting attention away from "first principles, closed systems, and pretended absolutes and origins" and redirecting it—as James believed such predecessors as Socrates, Aristotle, Locke, Berkeley, and Hume had also done—"towards concreteness and adequacy, towards facts, towards action, and towards power"[32]

The further claim, or at least imputation, that pragmatism lacks what, for want of a better term, I will call a political inclination or sensibility seems stranger still when applied to a philosophical orientation which accentuates not only the active but also relational and unfinished character of existence; which insists that experience is plural, diverse, unpredictable, ambiguous, and messy; which maintains that all epistemological positions and philosophical standpoints are potentially unstable and thus susceptible to revision and correction; which holds that life presents us not with a hierarchy of answers but rather with a hierarchy of problems; which posits that all values are merely prejudices, or at least preferences, that need to be weighed and assessed against the preferences of others; which claims that culture needs to be democratized by dismantling the distinctions between high and low, between elite and ordinary; which assumes that the understanding of difference—and not just the difference difference constitutes, but the difference difference makes—is the key to understanding itself; and which implies that one of the essential tasks of political life is to render such differences conversable so that the conflicts between them can, insofar as possible, produce human community rather than destroy it. Rorty would not dispute the fact that pragmatism has been so conceived; he merely denies that you can derive grounds for a politics, or, for that matter, grounds for anything else, from a philosophy that, like pragmatism, is antifoundational. If one is a pragmatist, he believes, one's politics are a matter of personal preference, not of philosophical persuasion. We adopt the politics we do, not because we find better reasons for practicing it, but because practicing makes us look and feel better.

The social philosopher Nancy Fraser, on the other hand, disagrees. She believes that pragmatism does offer better reasons than, say, poststructuralism does for a feminist politics because its theory of discourse, like those of a host of modern thinkers from Mikhail Bakhtin, Michel Foucault, and Pierre Bourdieu to Julia Kristeva and even Luce Irigaray, views discourses as contingent and plural and construes signification as a form of action as well as a mode of representation. Thus, it furnishes feminism with a better, and not just a more attractive, model for politics because it treats speaking subjects not as products of immutable structures but rather as socially situated agents in emergent political processes, processes whose conflicts of interpretation need to be politically negotiated constantly if society is to address such issues as power, inequality, and injustice. Fraser thus concludes that "the pragmatic approach has many of the features we need in order to understand the complexity of social identities, the formation of social groups, the securing and contesting of cultural hegemony, and the possibility and actuality of political process."[33]

The contemporary reprisal of pragmatism's political dimensions—which were given their most extensive treatment in the series of books that John Dewey wrote between 1920 and the outbreak of World War II—has more recently been reinforced by the political philosopher Chantal Mouffe in a book entitled *Deconstruction and Pragmatism*. Denoting in its title a relationship that Rorty himself first explored in *Contingencies of Pragmatism*, Mouffe (who is the author of *The Return of the Political* and the coauthor, with Ernesto Laclau, of *Hegemony and Socialist Strategy*) argues that pragmatism is not only saturated with political consequentiality but possesses a special affinity for a politics that is democratic. This is a politics to which pragmatism can, and must, make a significant contribution, she feels, in light of its commitment to pluralism. But if this pluralism is to remain consistent with pragmatism, it must resist the lyrical and unrealizable kind of democratic consensus that Rorty currently recommends in favor of a more Derridian or Cavellian comprehension of the place of conflict, division, and undecidability in all democratic processes. In short, Mouffe maintains that democracy as reconceived and advanced by pragmatism brings us back to the epistemological proposition that originally launched this excursion into pragmatist theory in the first place, by presupposing an unending, but not uninstructive, process of negotiation and renegotiation between "self" and "other" in which the moral constitution of each is determined by the way they both appropriate the tension, ambiguity, and inevitable contradiction between them. The challenge, to return to Burke, is to discover what it could possibly mean to base a politics on what one shares in common not only with one's ally but also with one's opponent, even one's "foe."

Such reflections are not, as it happens, all that unfamiliar to us, having been entertained in, among other strange places, a variety of literary cultures that have recently acquired new importance for reasons that are simultaneously aesthetic, moral, and political. In the literature of the West, the best known of these reflections is the concession that Shakespeare wrings from Prospero in "The Tempest," when Prospero says of Caliban, "this thing of darkness I acknowledge mine" (V. i. 275–76). An admission that echoes some of the most troubling fantasies once entertained about the "wild man" by the European mind, Prospero's declaration in no sense carries with it an assertion that Caliban now belongs to the human family. It merely registers, as Stephen Greenblatt notes, Prospero's unsentimental realization that Caliban is somehow part of him without, like Philoctetes's wound, entirely belonging to the being that Prospero is.[34]

Somewhat closer to us in time is the similar acknowledgement that Conrad's Marlow makes, as his steamer works its way upriver in *Heart of Darkness*, of a sense of "remote kinship with this wild and passionate uproar" that greets him from the dense jungle edging the bank. Similarly sedimented with some of the West's deepest racial fantasies connecting Africa and blackness with the primitive and the savage, Marlow is nonetheless reluctant to brand this outburst of the otherness that greets him from the bush as inhuman, because he dimly senses within it something that not only elicits from him "the faintest trace of a response" but that will eventually permit him to recognize images of what is so conspicuously lacking in virtually all the Europeans he meets, and most notably in Kurtz. Marlow refers to this missing element by various names—"inborn strength," "deliberate belief"—and accounts it wholly responsible for restraining the African boatmen, who practice cannibalism and are now near delirium from hunger, from making a meal of him and his fellow whites. Speculating on the possible sources of such restraint—"superstition, disgust, patience, fear, or some kind of primitive honour"—Marlow rejects all but the last:

No fear can stand up to hunger, no patience can wear it out, disgust simply does not exist where hunger is; and as to superstition, belief, and what you may call principles, they are less than chaff in a breeze. Don't you know the devilry of lingering starvation, its exasperating torment, its black thoughts, its sombre and brooding ferocity? Well, I do. It takes a man all his inborn strength to fight hunger properly. It's really easier to face bereavement, dishonour, and the perdition of one's soul—than this kind of prolonged hunger. Sad, but true. And these chaps too had no earthly reason for any kind of scruple. Restraint! I would just as soon have expected restraint from a hyena prowling amongst the corpses of a battlefield.[35]

This exhibition of restraint remains for Marlow a mystery he cannot penetrate, an enigma that remains, like the jungle, the great river, and Africa itself, simply unfathomable, but the resonance of that "sense of primitive honour" on which it is based deepens as the book progresses and the reader witnesses the extent of its utter collapse in Kurtz. Since Kurtz is assumed by his fellow Europeans to epitomize those ideals that are supposed to redeem the depredations of imperialism, his eventual depravity stands in starkest possible contrast to the restraint of the natives themselves.

Nonetheless, this exhibition of restraint on the part of the natives is itself qualified by, or rather subtly undercut by, the note of condescension that determines the way its abnormality, and, indeed, inexplicability, are expressed narratively. Even as the lawlessness of Kurtz and the other whites is judged and condemned in *Heart of Darkness*, that condemnation is enfolded within a narrative that never succeeds in entirely escaping all of the shadows of white racism that paradoxically make up so much of the darkness in this tale itself. Just as Marlow cannot acknowledge native restraint without turning the natives into objects of weirdness, grotesquerie, and mystification, so Conrad does not manage to transcend all the imperialist structures of domination and subordination even in exposing them.

To see those structures fully challenged and revised, if not supplanted, we must eventually turn to texts where such narratives have been explicitly or implicitly rewritten. But before turning to such texts in chapter 7, where the colonial paradigm, like other structures of dominance, are not so much reversed or inverted as surpassed in narratives of violation and survival, it is important to consider another alternative. Could it be that the terms in which this inquiry has been framed have been rendered problematic, if not obsolete, by recent alterations in the nature and fabric of the human community worldwide? In this most recent era of globalization, it might be asked, is it even possible to think about the nature of human solidarity, much less reconceive it, in such dualistic terms? In a world increasingly shaped around diasporan communities and global flows of information, haven't such binaries as "self–other," "us–them," "native–foreign," "center–margin" become increasingly superfluous, if not downright misleading? It is one thing, we might agree, to resituate ourselves and others in a world of "imagined communities";[36] it is quite another to realize that those communities have themselves been radically destabilized, displaced, and reconstituted in ways that now defy more traditional notions of peoples, regions, homelands, identities, centers, and peripheries.

As global theorists rarely tire of reminding us, we now live in a world where geopolitical as well as cultural boundaries have become so porous and fluid that paradigms once employed to describe the nature of their relations and interactions, such as the "borderlands," may no longer be of any use to us. Communities, like identities, are too multiple and dispersed, imaginations too supple, adaptable, or, by some accounts, easily manipulated to fit the old oppositions by which they were formerly defined. To map the real configuration of human difference, we must come up with new coordinates that attest to how completely and rapidly the new lines of global affiliation and division have been redrawn. Moreover, it would seem that we now need maps that are not two- but three-dimensional to allow for the fact that these lines intersect at different angles in different spheres of experience and practice.

This task of mapping the global is still further complicated by what Benedict Anderson has recently termed the "spectre of comparisons," which is now assumed to "haunt" the cultural construction of all social and political imaginaries. The spectre of comparisons is a process that refers to the way perceptions are so often shadowed by the memory of images that are sufficiently analogous to the very thing they are patently not to create a doubling of vision that is deeply astigmatic. This spectre enables the imagination to become a still more potent source of social and political structuration.

As the creation of but one such system of spectres, Anderson holds up his own area of academic specialty known as "Southeast Asia." Owing variously to the absence of any hegemonic power in its earlier history, the heterogeneity of its religious traditions, and its highly differentiated history of imperialism, this is a region that didn't exist either as an academic specialty or as a geopolitical entity until after World War II, when, as a result of the Cold War, the United States decided to fill the vacuum created by the departure of the Japanese by turning the region into a bulwark for the defense of democracy and the free world. This process of turning Southeast Asia into the "imagined reality" it is taken for today was accomplished not only through political treaties like the SEATO pact but also by, first, creating the field of Southeast Asian Studies as a locus of academic study and research; next, redefining the region's thousands of different peoples as themselves "Southeast Asians"; and, finally, training countless specialists in the histories, cultures, and politics of these myriad peoples who, because of their invented subject, eventually became known as "Southeast Asianists."[37] What was once a polyglot area of the world comprising myriad traditions, societies, and cultures that had not, except accidentally, had very much to do with one another over the course of human history suddenly became, within the space of two generations, a discriminable region of the world framed by distinctive customs with its own cadre of specialist interpreters. So much for the simple plotting of distinctions between "self" and "other" when cartographic practices become captive to global forces.

But the practice by which cultural construction is filtered through ghostly comparisons did not commence with this most recent phase of globalization. The spectre of comparisons has been in operation as a global process at least since the beginnings of the nationalist era. It reveals itself in the way national monuments—which are themselves capable of being recirculated through a variety of different media (posters, tee shirts, postcards, placemats, license plates, stamps)—testify to the "originlessness" of the nation itself, or, rather, to the way the nation is now often constructed imaginatively as a replica that oddly enough lacks an original. Anderson's chief specimen is the Lincoln Memorial in Washington, D.C., an edifice that is itself composed of replicas of something else (in this case a medieval church on the inside and a pagan Greek temple on the outside). More to the point, if we didn't know that the exterior of the Lincoln Memorial was architecturally designed to resemble a temple, we might otherwise suppose that its facade is contemporary since it is "not too stylistically different from those of many banks, fraternity houses, insurance companies, and courts of law."[38] But the real "spectre" Anderson is after is to be found within the temple itself, where what one finds enshrined is not so much a statue of Lincoln (a replica with an original) as a memorial to Lincoln's "memory" (a replica without an original). One might argue that the "memory" is Lincoln's, after all, were it not for the fact that the "memory" of Lincoln didn't come into being until after he died, when its only purpose was to create out of those who came after him a people who could reconstitute themselves around its imaginary existence as "American." Hence, the memorial stands as a replication of what has no copy, a memorial, if you will, to the imaginary.

If this digression into ghostly reminiscences and imaginary hauntings tells us anything, it does not tell us that people lack common experiences that help forge shared notions of consciousness—many diasporan peoples have developed senses of community around experiences of discrimination, loss, marginalization, exploitation, exclusion, and exile or, more positively, around shared experiences of larger historical, cultural, political, or religious forces—but that such senses of community often resist being defined in absolutist terms even when such terms are routinely invoked. Such diasporan worlds, whether in Southeast Asia or northwest Africa—being products of intercultural and cross-cultural contact and association that are endlessly in motion, richly hybridized, constantly redefined, and inevitably shadowy—are far less likely to share a common identity than a common set of identifications. As James Clifford observes, this is no less true of Paul Gilroy's brilliantly evoked "Black Atlantic," composed of peoples produced by the slave trade but defined by all the movements of emancipation, cultural expression, nationalist aspiration, and historical memory that now define them, than it is of S. D. Goitein's "Geniza world" of cosmopolitan Jews in the Middle Ages, composed of urban people living under Muslim rule in Mediterranean societies that stretched from the Atlantic to the Indian oceans. In Goitein's Mediterranean world of Jewish communities, these identifications were composed of shared kinship systems, commercial guilds and practices, travel routes, and cultural as well as religious attachments to particular centers of Jewish faith in Babylon or Palestine, while in Gilroy's Black Atlantic they were created out of common struggles for freedom, political rights, and citizenship. Today such communities are changing even more rapidly, so the argument goes, in a world of increased migration, instant communication, and the free circulation of capital.[39]

Appadurai claims that because the relations between these flows of people and information are constantly shifting, expanding, and overlapping, context becomes almost everything. By "context," he refers to the angle of vision from which such changes in the relations between and among groups, just like the relations across and beyond them, are perceived.[40] Far from being "objectively given," such contextual relations comprise what Appadurai calls "deeply perspectival constructs, inflected by the historical, linguistic, and political situatedness of different sorts of actors, nation-states, multinationals, diasporic communities, as well as subnational groupings and movements (whether religious, political, or economic), and even face-to-face groups, such as villages, neighborhoods, and families."[41] With everything so mobile and deterritorialized, then, oppositional structures based on sharply defined ideological boundaries become far more easily traversable and less normative. The question is *how much* more easily traversable and less normative?

We know, for example, that enmity between and within groups continues to exist because the sources of resentment and fear that generate it continue to persist. In too many instances (some critics think most), globalization does not abolish inequities so much as sometimes mask them from all but those who suffer them. As boundaries become harder to preserve, or to define, or, for that matter, sometimes to imagine, individuals and collectivities alike—and especially those who do not see how they benefit from such actions—grow still more deeply menaced, vulnerable, and angry. Thus, while it is true that some senses of animosity and hatred, just like some philosophical controversies, can be outgrown, some just as surely cannot. Oppression, exploitation, and cruelty continue to exist on a scale many human beings cannot take in or absorb, but so does the will to resist them, or at least, to expose them, whether directly in the form of political action, or more indirectly in the form of artistic expression and other modes of symbolic action. In a world where MTV threatens to homogenize all of culture and the Internet threatens to commodify it, such interventions may be continuously in danger of being co-opted or neutralized, but they are not without effect.

In the sphere of transnational politics and economics, Saskia Sassen has defined three "arenas" where the normative functions of the state, and more particularly the homogenizing effects of globalization, have been challenged and at times thwarted. One such arena is the international movement for human rights, symbolized, perhaps, by the World Conference on Human Rights sponsored by the United Nations in 1993. This conference led to the establishment of transnational or supranational legal institutions that have given new power to marginalized groups, while at the same time compelling nation-states to begin responding to people as human beings first and citizens second. In other words, states are no longer legitimated solely because of their right to self-determination but must also be held accountable, as we have seen most recently in the Balkans, by the respect they show for human rights codes established by international bodies.

A second arena where the notion of state sovereignty has been, to use Sassen's word, "unbundled" is in the global economy itself. For all of its seeming indifference to human rights and its lack of respect for national courts, the global economy is now itself creating the possibility of resolving at least some transnational disputes among corporations through the use of international commercial arbitration. Thus, such institutions as the World Trade Organization have acquired the authority to override national sovereignty and to discipline individual states when they violate the terms of their agreements. Still more important, the notion of the state is itself being transformed, as was made evident in the recent meltdown of southeastern and east Asian economies, because of a growing consensus that individual states must now take responsibility not only for their own economic well-being but also for the development of the global economy as a whole.

Third, and most important, millions of people throughout the world have, from the beginning of the Cold War on, been mobilized around a variety of global issues, from nuclear disarmament and human rights to health, poverty, immigration, children's welfare, and the environment. Central among these selective formations of global relationships that are helping to create an ever widening "transnational civil society," as Susanne Hoeber Rudolph describes it,[42] is the international women's movement. As women find new spheres for cooperation and contestation outside the borders of the nation, Sassen writes, "we are seeing the formation of cross-border solidarities and notions of membership rooted in gender, sexuality, and feminism, as well as in questions of class and country status, i.e., First versus Third World, which cut across all of these membership notions."[43]

It is not my intention to minimize the political and moral significance of any of these developments, or of others like them. All of them are products of globalization itself, and each of them, like NGOs, hold the promise of creating new forms of human association and cooperation that span enormous divides of culture, race, class, ethnicity, nation, gender, religion, region, and sexual preference. It is worth remarking, however, that a lengthy report published on July 13, 1999, by the United Nations Development Program notes that forces of economic and cultural globalization have further widened the gap between rich and poor in the world, and that these forces, so largely reflecting the dominance of the United States, need to be reorganized if this gap is not to become catastrophic. To prevent such developments as Sassen describes from producing increasing polarization—which in the short term will benefit the United States and its rich allies but in the long term will benefit no one—there must be not only a reform of "global governance," as the report calls it, but also more massive and efficient debt relief, the redirection of aid to the poorest countries, the reform of resource allocation and corruption in those countries whose mismanagement discourages foreign investment, and much more.

Important as these initiatives are in advancing the cause of human solidarity, there is a question as to just how far they extend into the neighborhoods of ordinary existence throughout the world. Hasn't recent world history shown us that certain expressions and experiences of difference continue to resist incorporation within some of these newer structures of global aspiration, commitment, and action? If more traditional notions of solidarity have experienced difficulty holding up under the pressures of twentieth-century experience, will these newer forms of global solidarity, however admirable and promising in other respects, be capable of containing, much less defusing, some of the more extreme forms of mistrust, resentment, antipathy, detestation, and malevolence that still divide the human community and continue to provide models for the creation and maintenance of the self? To think our way through the dilemmas that globalization, like its predecessors, have created for human community, we may need to look, as it were, "beyond solidarity." We may need to look to those who have created their sense of humanity not out of the possibility of overcoming their differences with others, or even in the hope of regulating their relations with others, but rather out of their need (frequently amidst harrowing circumstances) to determine what constitutes their sense of fundamental kinship with others, despite their differences. Before undertaking this, however, we need to examine what intellectual resources a cosmopolitan pragmatism brings to this task and how that pragmatism has articulated itself in relation to such issues as the nature of religion, of history, and of aesthetics.

PART TWO

Jamesian Matters

Chapter 3

William James and
the Globalization of Pragmatism

> Those of us who give up the quest for certitude do not thereby give up the quest or hope of truth itself.
>
> William James

William James is a thinker whose charm as well as importance is so often assumed to derive, at least in part, from his ability to appeal to different readers in different eras and for different reasons that it is often forgotten that it also has something to do with the cosmopolitanism, indeed the transnational cast, of his mind. To be sure, his remarkable availability for repossession by such varied readers in so many eras and from so many cultures would be less likely if James were not so protean a philosopher, if in fact to call him a "philosopher" in the traditional sense at all was not to risk doing him a certain kind of injustice. But James's continuing appeal in a period of intensified globalization of thought also has to do with the extraordinarily international circumstances in which his thought first took shape and the global environment in which it continues to resonate intellectually.

James's first book—which some still consider his greatest—was entitled *The Principles of Psychology* and was published in two volumes in 1890. This pioneering study, which immediately received wide acclaim on the Continent and adopted as a text in many British and American universities, was then followed seven years later by a collection of essays in what appeared to be moral and religious thought entitled *The Will to Believe and Other Essays in Popular Philosophy.* The essays collected in this volume (a volume James almost immediately wished he had called instead *The Right to Believe)* turned out in some respects to prepare James for the internationally prestigious Gifford Lectures that he was invited to give in May and June of 1901 and 1902 in Edinburgh, Scotland. These lectures were published in 1902 as *The Varieties of Religious Experience.* It was not until five years later, in 1907, however, that James put the finishing touches on the lectures in "practical philosophy," as he termed it, that would ever after provide his thinking with its signature description throughout the world.

James first delivered these lectures as a set in Boston to a large and receptive audience at the Lowell Institute in November and December 1906, and then later to a much larger and still more enthusiastic audience at Columbia University in January and February 1907. He gathered these essays under the title *Pragmatism* and dedicated the volume to one of the great exponents of liberty, John Stuart Mill. They were almost immediately to define James's reputation in the public mind, even as they produced some consternation in more specialized philosophical circles. *Pragmatism: A New Name for Some Old Ways of Thinking was* preceded by several additional texts in practical, really popular, philosophy, such as his one-volume condensation of *The Principles of Psychology* entitled *Psychology: Briefer Course* (1892) and *Talks to Teachers on Psychology: And to Students on Some of Life's Ideals* (1899), based on a lecture series he frequently gave at Harvard. After *Pragmatism*, James quickly produced a succession of other volumes. These include *The Meaning of Truth: A Sequel to "Pragmatism,"* in which he attempted to clarify some of the misinterpretations that the earlier *Pragmatism* immediately produced (and still does), and the posthumously published and unfinished *Essays in Radical Empiricism*, in which he sought to flesh out the lineaments of his metaphysics. James's additional works include *A Pluralistic Universe* (1909) and *Some Problems in Philosophy* (1911), published the year after James died, along with more than a hundred essays he wrote on similar or related subjects, as well as a plethora of articles on issues of more topical concern. Together, these many volumes describe a thinker who was a master not only of philosophy (as it classically defined itself in his age around questions of epistemology, metaphysics, ethics, and the theory of truth) but also of critical thinking generally. James wrote at a time when critical thinkers were seeking to create a form of public discourse capable of reflecting on such philosophically nontraditional subjects as psychology, religion, educational theory, social thought, politics, cultural experience, and contemporary morals and manners.

Yet what sets all of James's writing apart, rendering it simultaneously so attractive and so accessible, are his immense and varied gifts not only as a thinker but also as a writer. James was brilliantly adept at producing an American middle style that makes up in suppleness, wit, grace, and fluidity for what it sometimes lacks—at least for certain kinds of readers—in coherence, rigor, and internal consistency. James writes always out of the decencies and commonplaces and reasonableness of ordinary experience, which he welcomes into his thinking not only as an old and trusted, if also frequently amusing, friend but also as an ever-renewing and renewable source for reflection. Thought should never rise so far above the plane of common life, James seems to say, that it forgets where it came from and to what it must finally answer.

There is, moreover, a cordiality as well as forthrightness to his prose that functions to draw readers in rather than hold them off. James clearly wanted to communicate and convince, but he also hoped to bring his readers into the processes and play of his own reflections. The mind is not a passive receptor of information that is then simply translated into another medium, James believed; it is a creative, inventive, imaginative instrument that responds to previous descriptions of reality as though they existed not simply for themselves but as stimulants to further thought. "We *add*," James wrote in one of his most famous formulations, "both to the subject and to the predicate part of reality. The world stands really malleable, waiting to receive its final touches at our hands. Like the kingdom of heaven, it suffers human violence willingly."[1]

This is what James wanted his readers to experience in his own prose—not just the creativity of his own reflections but the stimulation of their own minds in response and the accompanying sense that such stimulations actually "enhance the universe's total value."[2] In this he was assisted by a feeling for vernacular language and the rhythms of everyday speech that was as "game-flavored," to quote another of his famous figures of speech, "as a hawk's wing."[3] James's colleague at Harvard and sometime fellow pragmatist, the philosopher George Santayana, got it just about right when he described James the writer as "an impulsive poet: a master in the art of recording or divining the lyric quality of experience as it actually came to him or to me."[4]

Beyond that, however, there was the sheer vitality, brilliance, edginess, unconventionality, and disarming candor of the man. To his students, James was ready for almost anything and hated any system that closed off further possibilities for thought. "We must never set up boundaries that exclude romantic surprises," Santayana again remarked. "He retained the primitive feeling that death *might* open new worlds to us . . . ; also the primitive feeling that invisible spirits *might* be floating about among us, and might suddenly do something to hurt or to help us."[5] How was one to resist such a man who so perfectly fit the description he provided in *A Pluralistic Universe* of the German philosopher Gustav Theodor Fechner?

> The *power* of the man is due altogether to the profuseness of his concrete imagination, to the multitude of the points which he considers successively, to the cumulative effect of his learning, of his thoroughness, and of the ingenuity of his detail, to his admirably homely style, to the sincerity with which his pages glow, and finally to the impression he gives of a man who doesn't live at secondhand, but who *sees*, who in fact speaks as one having authority, and not as if he were one of the common herd of professorial philosophic scribes."[6]

Little wonder, then, that just as James's own contemporaries turned again and again to him for illumination of their own quandaries, so subsequent generations of readers have inevitably brought to him their own very different questions and concerns. James's earliest readers looked to him either as one of the first—and still one of the greatest—psychologists of the inner life, or as a moral thinker who could adumbrate the experiential grounds of reasonable belief, or as an anatomist of religious experience. Later admirers, during the middle part of the twentieth century, valued him instead for developing a simpler calculus for weighing the merits of ideas, or as the proponent of a worldview that was radical in the seriousness with which it took the relational character of existence, or as an advocate of the social theory known as democratic pluralism. Now, at the end of the twentieth century and the beginning of the twenty-first, we find still other things to value in James, whether it be his conviction that most of our certainties (even about matters of fact) are susceptible to correction in the light of future experience, or his emphasis on contingency, chance, and novelty, or his sensitivity to what he calls, in the title of one of his most famous essays, "a certain blindness in human beings." But this only confirms what James would have anticipated himself. If philosophy is, as James's fellow pragmatist John Dewey later contended, merely the history of its own time in thought, then no one should be surprised to discover that different historical eras put very different queries to themselves, or at least find themselves confronted by very different challenges and conundrums.

James was living at a moment when the spirit of the "modern" was beginning to break free of the ethos of the "Victorian." The Victorian era had been marked by a strong belief in the permanence and validity of certain moral values associated with words like *truth*, *duty*, *selflessness*, and *decency*. It also assumed that such values are inscribed nowhere more deeply than in the texts and practices associated with high culture and that as long as such values are permitted to influence the course of the present, then human history would continue to display a record of steady progress.[7] The modern era, on the other hand, and particularly modernism of the sort that James helped stimulate in America, assumed that values are, like life itself, more unstable, provisional, and circumstantial, that the monuments of high culture have lost touch with their roots in the soil of day-to-day experience, and that history refuses to present us with a spectacle of uninterrupted advancement and enlightenment. T. S. Eliot captured this benighted side of James's modernism perfectly when he remarked that it is in the struggle for cultural and spiritual values that we fight to keep something alive, rather than in the belief that anything is certain to prevail. Or, as James put it for himself at the end of his essay "Is Life Worth Living?" what matters is not having won but having tried.

But there was a good deal more than this—and a good deal that was more radical—to James's American modernism, much of which is proleptically present in the great early essay James wrote on the nature of human consciousness entitled "The Stream of Thought." I refer not simply to his view that life confronts us with a series of obstacles to be overcome, of problems to be addressed, but to his belief that consciousness comes before sensation, that thinking can be likened to the behavior of a stream, that thought can therefore be differentiated into moments that are substantive and moments that are transitive, that the relations between such moments are as much a part of experience as the moments they connect, that we can have feelings about those moments as well as about the things conjoined by them, that thought is therefore a kind of algebra that does not need to translate all its operations into images in order to perform its work, and that, as a result, consciousness should be reconceived as a process rather than a substance. I also mean that "The Stream of Thought" gives early expression to James's belief that modern philosophy needs to redirect its efforts toward reinstating the elements of the vague and the indeterminate in our mental life; that it foreshadows his later opinion that philosophical history is to a large extent a conflict of different dispositions rather than merely of differing opinions; and, finally, that it reveals his lifelong penchant for meliorism, for exploring the middle ground between opposites. In all these ways—and one could name others—James already possessed some of the most radical elements of his own modernism, to say nothing of many of his most recurrent themes, by the time he had published his first major work, which, as already noted, was not in philosophy but psychology!

James has now, of course, been rediscovered in a different historical and cultural moment than the one he first helped to energize. This is a moment we have come to call "postmodern," if only because it seems to exist both in continuity with and also in disjunction from the cultural moment just preceding it. Viewed in these terms, the contrast between James's so-called modernist moment and our so-called postmodernist one might be reconceived. In the modernist era belief in life's fundamental unity and coherence had been seriously eroded, or at least fundamentally questioned, but a nostalgic desire to recover such coherence survived. In contrast, the postmodern era, in its bleaker version, acknowledges that life seems to lack any sense of underlying unity or purpose at all beyond, perhaps, the pursuit of pleasure and the creation of a therapeutic culture to sustain it, while in its more sanguine version it views bricolage, parody, irony, playfulness, anarchy, and *jouissance* as auguries of a potentially new age of the sublime.

The American poet Wallace Stevens can help us sharpen one side of this distinction, just as the French philosopher Jean-François Lyotard can assist us in honing the other. Stevens associates modernism with an age of disbelief, in which people who have experienced the disappearance of many of the gods are forced to look elsewhere for the consolations once provided by religious faith. If such consolations formerly included the mediation of a reality not their own, a "something wholly other," as Stevens refers to it in *Opus Posthumous*, "by which the inexpressive loneliness of thinking [and feeling] is broken and enriched,"[8] they must now be sought in secular forms such as literature, painting, dance, and philosophy itself. Here spiritual survival depends on what, in "Of Modern Poetry," Stevens describes as "the finding of a satisfaction, and may/Be of a man skating, a woman dancing, a woman/Combing."[9]

Lyotard, on the other hand, deems such spiritual substitutes ineffective at best, self-deceiving at worst. He has asserted that the great metanarratives of the past—which once taught us, if not exactly what the world is really like, then at least in what direction to think about the world and how to care for it—have collapsed, or at any rate have been outgrown, and there is little to console the self but the endless recirculation, often narcissistic, of outmoded images of such things. This means that all storytelling, all narrativizing, all yarnspinning is plural, provisional, sentimental, and genealogical: an attempt to rewrite the story of the past out of the various, fragmentary plots at hand in light of the outcome we would like it to have. In such a cultural climate, James's pragmatism presents itself less as a simple philosophical and moral alternative to postmodernism than as an intellectual correction and deepening of some of postmodernism's own preoccupations with the fluidity, open-endedness, belatedness, randomness, and undecidability of experience.

Such terms, which have almost come to be regarded as hallmarks of the postmodern itself, should also serve to remind us that pragmatism has never been an exclusively American phenomenon or movement. Long before James had settled on the vocation of philosopher, much less developed any sense of the pragmatist project, he had undergone, while reading the French philosopher Charles Renouvier's writings on the will, a kind of "conversion" that would stay with him throughout much of his life. And once James's range of intellectual interests acquired clearer philosophical focus, he was to find himself in extended conversation with various like-minded philosophers from abroad who put their own spin on pragmatist themes and motifs, including F. C. S. Schiller in England and a small circle of thinkers gathered around Giovanni Papini in Italy.

But the transnational extension of pragmatism never was, nor now is, confined to James's own conversational partners. Almost as soon as James's ideas began to circulate beyond the shores of the Atlantic, following the publication of *The Principles of Psychology* and, particularly, *The Will to Believe*, people were detecting European precedents for his thinking in the work of everyone from Johann Gottlieb Fichte and Friedrich Nietzsche to Friedrich Schelling and Henri Bergson. Moreover, some were claiming that James's work communicates in interesting and important ways with the writings of contemporaries or near contemporaries like Georg Simmel, Edmund Husserl, Hans Vaihinger, and even members of the Vienna Circle such as Ernst Mach and Ludwig Wittgenstein. Before the end of World War I, pragmatism had established itself on the Continent as a philosophy one had to take account of. In 1917, at the time of his death, the great French sociologist, Émile Durkheim, was preparing to deliver a major series of lectures on pragmatism in Paris. In the years between the wars, pragmatism became a frequent object of attack—as an example of technological reasoning at its worst—by a whole generation of German philosophers from Martin Heidegger and Max Scheler to Theodor Adorno and Max Horkheimer. Less then half a century later, it would in turn be recuperated by another generation of German philosophers, led by Jürgen Habermas and Hans-Otto Appel and followed by Hans Joas, who embraced it as a model for communicative and creative action at its best. Nor does the story end with its Continental influence. If pragmatism has provided a resource for contemporary thinkers from Pierre Bourdieu, Michel Foucault, and Julia Kristeva in France to Gianni Vattimo in Italy and Cornelius Castoriadis in Greece, it has also found echos in the work of, among others, Roberto Unger from Brazil and Charles Taylor from Canada.

This rehearsal of some of the global resonances of James's work, along with that of other American pragmatists, would not be worth mentioning if we were not so accustomed to thinking of James as quintessentially American, indeed, in a certain sense, provincial. Yet James was anything but provincial, almost literally from the time of his birth, having been subjected from earliest adolescence to an education that for its time could only be called international. During William's most formative years, James's restless father, Henry, Senior, moved his family of five children, together with their Aunt Kate and his wife, Mary, back and forth across the Atlantic, searching for the perfect educational setting he would never find. The story of this peripatetic education is too well known to bear repeating, but the stimulus that this transcontinental itinerancy provided James's thinking deserves further assessment if we are to appreciate how naturally, if not inevitably, that thinking evolved into a philosophy that, so to speak, travels.

James's first recorded impressions are to be found in the extraordinary series of letters he began to write back to the United States from abroad after his family had settled for the first time in Paris and begun the wanderings between European capitals and watering places and American residences that were to carry James from early adolescence into adulthood. The earliest of these letters, written when James was only fourteen, is typical of many in showing the delight he took in observing the world around him. He reserved his keenest discriminations for the inhabitants of Paris, particularly its shopkeepers, who, because of their crudity, aggressiveness, and greed, presented an interesting contrast for the young teenager with the more servile behavior of their English counterparts. Indeed, the sharpness of scrutiny in these youthful letters, their descriptive wittiness, their tone of self-assurance, their readiness to moralize, all convey the impression of a mind at work, however juvenile, that is strikingly reminiscent of the kind of spectatorial intelligence more often associated with his brother Henry, but

which also bore a resemblance to that of his acutely and often wickedly observant father. One also discerns habits here, already bred by long experience, of one of the James family's chief pastimes in their travels, namely,
trenchant commentary and criticism of local customs and character traits
that was both unsparing and amused.

Though William would soon shed much of the distaste for the English
that he expresses in this early letter—deciding by 1870, in the midst of the
Franco-Prussian War, that England is by far the healthiest nation in Europe
and its people among the most reliable—he would retain, during the next
twenty years, much of his early suspicion and disapproval of the French, always thinking of them as in some sense untrustworthy. It was to the Germans that James was more closely drawn in his early years, and not only
because their language was so marvelous to think in. Though he found German peasant women spectacularly dirty and the German people as a whole
overly sentimental and fastidious, he felt great respect for the German way
of working and was deeply impressed by their sensible, easy way of living. In
a later letter from Berlin to Edmund Tweedy, an old Newport friend of the
James family, William notes that "there seems to be such a good fat homely
atmosphere about the inner family life of the people, as well as about much
of their public life, that a German child's early associations must have an un-
common richness and stoutness, so to speak, even if they have not much
artistic elevation."[10] In a letter to his Geneva friend Charles Ritter, sent after his return to the United States, William expands upon the effects of this
middle-class solidity, so "full of patience, of respect, and of concentration":

> You could not imagine, my dear fellow, you who have been reared in a
> somewhat similar environment, the appeal for us Americans, without
> forebears, without tradition, without customs—I mean without cus-
> toms that have been handed down from father to son and which one
> reveres—floating here and there, far from the paternal home, which,
> if there ever was one, has long since been demolished and replaced by
> a more beautiful and wonderful one—the appeal, I repeat, of that very
> personal part of German life in which the present still seems com-
> pletely imbued with the past, in which people are still satisfied with *be-
> ing* and seem to be entirely unaware of this madness of *achieving* which
> here has us all by the throat—achieving anything, anywhere, as long
> as it takes one out of where he is or what he is today.[11]

One can, of course, hear in this passage a good deal more than William's
idealization of the bourgeois family. There is also an echo of the loneliness

and desolation he must have felt, living frequently at such great distance both from the family circle and also, by extension, from the moral and spiritual roots, however complex his own relationships with them, that he associated with that circle.

But if America left much to be desired—there was so much less to remark about it—William is still prepared, as in the very first letter mentioned, to make the United States and its culture the standard of measure for most of his comparisons with other countries. While much of what he believed worthy of appreciation in his country lay in its potentiality, its rawness, its inchoateness, he was not unmindful of the liabilities this entailed. As he observed at age 26 from Dresden to his Cambridge friend Arthur George Sedgwick, a people committed for most of their brief history to wresting from "the hands of Nature," a vast territory in which a new human society might be laid out, "the details of wh. the Future must fill in," was likely to suffer from an impatience for results, a reckless optimism, a mental coarseness, an insensitivity to the feelings of others, and, not least, a basic intellectual insincerity.[12] His countrymen impressed him, in fact, as an essentially untruthful people not because they were given to deceit or dissimulation but because they were indisposed to take themselves, or, for that matter, anyone else, with full seriousness. The typical American's "only notions of the functions of thought," William continued in the same letter, "apart from its applications to industry, trade & politics, seems to be derived by extension from these, that it is useful to get over some temporary difficulty to stop, justly or not, the mouth of an importunate antagonist, or to wile an hour ingeniously away."[13]

But even where William found much in America that was vulgar, disingenuous, and self-serving, he was generally willing, if not to excuse these deficiencies, at least to explain them as deriving not from want of character but from historical and cultural circumstance. And in the same letter to his Geneva friend Charles Ritter, sent from the United States after his family had resettled in Cambridge, Massachusetts, James described quite precisely the peculiar nature of that historical and cultural circumstance which was to prove one of the chief obstacles to his own process of maturation:

> Here everything is so free and optional, no privilege, no traditional limitation, no hereditary presumption, a much less restrictive competition in every occupation than over there, so that the individual blossoms, so to speak, without experiencing any external resistance, resistance which is, however, necessary for defining him, for giving

him a distinct and stable form, for focusing him. Plaster which sets without a mold remains without form, and we have, we Americans, compared to the Europeans, something *locker* [slack], as the Germans say, in our character and in our ideas. We have too much elbow-room to concern ourselves with the details of life, with the small change of things; only the broad outlines interest us, only the results which, by the same token, we want to be immediate.[14]

As it happens, this defines the same set of cultural conditions that James himself would have to transform from a personal impediment into a professional advantage if he was ever to find himself as an adult. In the absence of traditional limitations, hereditary presumption, or restrictive competition, where was he (or any other bright but spiritually deracinated young American) to find the external resistance necessary "for defining him, for giving him a distinct and stable form"? Where, one might ask, if not precisely in the experience of freedom from such restraints, a freedom that, even more than his brother Henry, he would find so distracting, confusing, and physically incapacitating?

As early as age sixteen, for example, James was confiding to his friend Edgar Beach Van Winkle that "the choice of a profession torments every one who begins life, but there is really no reason why it should; that is, there is no reason why it should, if society was decently ordered."[15] Were society decently ordered, then "everyone . . . should do in society," the youthful James surmised with conviction, "what he would do if left to himself." Subsequent years, however, were to disclose to him how much more difficult this was to accomplish than he first imagined. Society, at least American society, was not ordered in a manner designed to accommodate this problem, and the solution to the problem, at least as William experienced it, was not simply social. Not only were there choices to be made between "material comfort," which seemed "a kind of selling of one's soul," and "mental dignity & independence combined however with physical penury," as he once put it to his mother, but also personal demons to confront, family ghosts to exorcise, social prejudices to surmount, the whole connected world of mind and body to suffer and survive.[16] Over and above these challenges, there stood in addition the cultural issue of what to do, of who to become, in a world where one still felt a sacred obligation to serve but could no longer believe in most of the titular deities of service, institutional or otherwise.

This was the spiritual situation that Ralph Waldo Emerson had first defined in "The American Scholar" and that Emerson, like William's father,

Henry, Senior, had resolved for himself by taking up the vocation of "Man Thinking." In Emerson's case, much of that thinking proceeded without benefit of traditional theological formulations; in the elder James's, by turning them somewhat on their head. But Emerson and the elder James both retained an essentially religious understanding of what they were about. They were seeking to articulate the contours of Being Itself through an articulation of the meaning of their own spiritual experience. Merely one generation removed from the world of these forefathers, William's response to this crisis was, with the help of Peirce's initial definition of pragmatism, to formulate an alternative vocation for thought itself and the thinker. William was to redefine thinking not as the articulation of the being of the thinker, nor as the articulation of the being of Being Itself, but rather as the articulation of the consequences for experience if this or that idea about being, or this or that conception of the intellectual, were held to be true. The Emersonian intellectual thus underwent a kind of metamorphosis, being transformed into the figure of cultural statesman whose vocation becomes the job of assessing the practicable differences entailed in adopting one way of thinking rather than another, in accepting this worldview rather than that.[17]

William's vocational challenge, in other words, was to learn how to exploit his situation by converting the experience of cultural deprivation that comes of being an American from a spiritual liability into a spiritual asset, into a remedy for the question of *how* and not just *what* to be.[18] But this was far easier said than done. This process was perhaps initiated when James was fourteen, as the result of a fateful visit to the Louvre that would encourage him, less than two years later, over his father's strenuous protests, to try painting for a year to see if he had any talent. It may also be reasonable to conclude that James's long quest for a vocation did not end, if it ever ended at all, until almost thirty years later when, in 1884, he laid to rest the ghost of his father's objections not only to an artistic career but to his way of seeking life for himself in the world by editing a selection of his father's posthumously published writings under the title *The Literary Remains of the Late Henry James*. His father's permissive attitude with regard to many other aspects of his children's lives did not, as it happens, extend to pursuits that conflicted with his own theological views. Yet, it would not be an exaggeration to say that the frustration of William's youthful desire for an artistic vocation would determine much of the direction that his own tortured quest for a vocation would take as well as the form that pragmatism would itself eventually acquire when James wrested it, as it were, from Peirce's hands.

The elder James was apparently of the opinion that there is something incompatible between the realms of the aesthetic and of the spiritual, but in this view, as in his general resistance to his son's desire to pursue an artistic career in the first place, there was something potentially disingenuous even if self-consistent. In two different essays composed in the early 1850s, essays of which William was probably unaware at this point in his life but with whose ideas, or at least with the gist of them, he may well have been made familiar during family discussions over meals, Henry, Senior, had idealized the artist as prototype of the divine man and then exalted art as representing the image of the perfect life.[19] At the same time—and true to his own spiritualist assumptions—he had pointed out that he did not mean by artist anyone who pursues a distinctively aesthetic vocation, nor by art some object shaped exclusively for contemplation. Defining artists in contradistinction to those who, like artisans, work for gain or fame, the elder James conceived the aesthetic person as someone who, possessing a specific talent, seeks to fulfill it by following the laws of his or her own inward nature, laws that Henry, Senior, assumed to be universal to the nature of all human beings. According to this view, art was to be radically differentiated from all its particular, expressive manifestations and identified instead with the spontaneous revelation of the true being of its maker.

Whether such opinions were known to William or not, he based the defense of his own choice of an artistic career on the conviction that the spiritual and the aesthetic are not mutually incompatible, and that far from diminishing his spiritual life, his own exposure to art had actually nourished it. But this defense proved ultimately futile. For even if the elder James quickly yielded ground by offering to place William in study under the painter W. M. Hunt in Newport, the initial patriarchal challenge had nonetheless already begun to erode William's self-confidence in his decision. Within a year, he had thrown over these plans for an artistic career altogether and moved the next autumn from Newport to Cambridge, where he enrolled in the Lawrence Scientific School to pursue the kind of career in science that his father had originally planned for him.

This abrupt shift in William's vocational plan understandably carried with it certain psychic costs. The concurrent development of a serious case of eye-strain and of nervous indigestion merely presaged deeper psychological problems that in the months and years ahead would be extended and compounded by crippling back pain, severe headaches, and increased nervousness. By the spring of 1863 these problems caused him to withdraw for a period from his medical studies in Cambridge. Abandoning his dreams of painting also left an aesthetic wound that would in later years take contrary forms by expressing itself in irritability with his brother Henry's elusive and recursive writing style and a deeper dependence on aesthetic models for his own thinking and writing. By the following fall, William was healthy and stable enough to return to Harvard, where he switched his concentration from chemistry to comparative anatomy. This change in his field of concentration was the first in a series of adjustments in his scientific education that would carry him from anatomy to physiology and then, some thirteen years later, to psychology, where he would begin to explore—with an interest now vividly awakened by his own physical and emotional problems—the relationship between the human body in all its parts and the human mind.

The first and almost inevitable step in this set of intellectual moves was William's decision to enroll in the Medical School at Harvard, not because he wanted to practice medicine but because he wanted to continue his scientific study. This plan was soon interrupted, however, when the distinguished Swiss naturalist Louis Agassiz, who had come to America in 1846 and been appointed professor of zoology at Harvard two years later, announced the organization of an expedition to Brazil to collect specimens of unknown species of fish for the Museum of Comparative Zoology he had founded at Harvard. With the help of a generous offer of financial assistance from his Aunt Kate and the promise of the companionship of his friend Thomas Wren Ward, William decided to sign on. An arduous trip, it was also an eye-opening one. In addition to hospitalizing him for nearly three weeks with what the Brazilian doctors diagnosed as smallpox—Agassiz claimed it was only varioloid, a lesser form of smallpox—the Brazilian adventure was to cure William once and for all of an early boyhood ambition to become a naturalist. In the process, his loneliness, self-doubt, and sense of isolation convinced him that he was better suited for a speculative rather than an active life.

Obviously one of the catalysts of these discoveries was Agassiz himself. On first acquaintance, Agassiz struck William as something of a buffoon— "The Professor has just been expatiating over the map of South America and making projects as if he had Sherman's army at his disposal instead of the 10 novices he really has"[20]—but this impression was quickly changed. Despite Agassiz's childlike devotion to science, his rashness, and his grand displays of feeling, William soon was unable to resist his charm, remarking in a letter to his parents, "I could listen to him talk by the hour."[21] By August he was prepared to admit that he was acquiring excellent training from Agassiz, "who pitches into me right & left and wakes me up to a great many of my imperfections. This morning he said I was 'totally uneducated.'"[22]

And from Manaos on the banks of the Rio Negro in September he was able to admit to his father: "No one sees farther into a generalisation than his own knowledge of details extends, and you have a greater feeling of weight & solidity about the movement of Agassiz's mind, owing to the continual presence of this great background of special facts, than about the mind of any other man I know."[23]

The expedition to Brazil taught William about the scientific pursuit of fact, about a very different part of the world, and especially about himself— having complained about his lack of grit at the beginning of the expedition, he returned from a 300-mile canoe trip from Santarém up the Amazon to Manaos feeling elated by his own perseverance, as well as by the startling scenery along the way. Nonetheless, the expedition exacted an alarmingly heavy toll. Upon his return to Boston, William entered what was to become one of the two darkest periods of his life. Precipitated in part, perhaps, by the fact that he had returned from South America too late to enroll for the spring term at the Medical School, thus postponing his graduation until the spring of 1869, this bleak phase of his life was made more difficult by a real- ization that may have grown more insistent during the long days and weeks of comparative solitude in Brazil: the realization that neither medicine nor science could supply him with the kind of faith that he seemed to need— faith that his father so confidently possessed and that painting might have been able to provide him earlier if he had stuck with it—in some power or force larger than himself.

During the course of the expedition, William had apparently sparred vigorously with Agassiz over Charles Darwin's *Origin of Species*, taking a view diametrically opposed to Agassiz's supernaturalism by maintaining that evolution is not a divine process but a natural one; that species survive be- cause they adapt, not because it is decreed; and that struggle rather than ac- quiescence is the law of life. This "tough-minded" stance, as William was subsequently to call it, nevertheless defined a position that was finally to feel unsatisfactory to a man who in later life would always look for the balance with its "tender-minded" opposite and whose father was continuously re- minding him of what William was himself to call, in *The Varieties Religious Experience*, the sense of "the More" that surrounds and supports all created life.

Finding himself thus blocked by the very path he had chosen, William withdrew from school and returned to Europe to find some relief from his ambivalence and confusion. William's trip to Europe, which lasted from April 1867 to November 1868, constituted what he felt was another wasted period in his life. Much of this period was spent reading widely in, among other things, French fiction—George Sand, Théophile Gautier, Erckmann-Chatrian, Denis Diderot—and in November 1867 he placed his third piece of writing, with his brother Henry's assistance, in the *Nation*, a notice of Hermann Grimm's novel *Unüberwindlichhe Mächte* (Invincible Powers).[24] Forced by worsening backaches and personal distraction to withdraw before the term ended, William then wandered fitfully for the next five months between Teplitz, Dresden again, Geneva, and Divonne, constantly in search of physical and emotional relief. Struggling by turns with experiences of lassitude, indecision, and self-accusation, and then giving in to them, William found himself gravitating, as he told Oliver Wendell Holmes, Jr., toward "an empiristic view of life":

> I don't know how far it will carry me or what rocks insoluble by it will block my future path. Already I see an ontological cloud of absolute Idealism waiting for me far off on the horizon, but I have no passion for the fray. I shall continue to apply empirical principles to my experience as I go on and see how much they fit. One thing makes me uneasy. If the end of all is to be that we must take our sensations as simply given or as preserved by natural selection for us, and interpret this rich and delicate overgrowth of ideas, moral, artistic, religious & social, as a mere mask, a tissue spun in happy hours by creative individuals and adopted by other men in the interests of their sensations—how long is it going to be well for us not to "let on" all we know to the public? How long are we to indulge the "people" in their theological and other vagaries so long as such vagaries seem to us more beneficial on the whole than otherwise? . . . If God is dead or at least irrelevant, ditto everything pertaining to the "Beyond," if happiness is our Good, ought we not to try to foment a passionate and bold will to attain that happiness among the multitudes? Can we not conduct off upon our purposes from the old moralities and theologies a beam which will invest us with some of the proud absoluteness which made them so venerable by preaching the doctrine that Man is his own Providence, and every individual a real god to his race, greater or less in proportion to his gifts & the way he uses them?[25]

The answers to questions inspired by his continuing internal conversations with the work of Darwin, when they came, would take a very different form from what is here anticipated. Rather than learn how to be contented with a "sensationalism" that seemed to leave him a prisoner of his physical and psychological infirmities, William was to discover from Renouvier that the human will gives one the freedom to believe what one wishes and that one of the things one might wish to believe in is the freedom of the will itself. But the comfort these writings were eventually to bring—laying the foundation for the assertion in "The Will to Believe" that one has the right to believe in whatever presents itself as a live, forced, and momentous option—would have to await the more or less complete disintegration of William's sense of self that followed upon his return to America.

Within seven months, in fact, he had suffered a complete mental collapse, but a collapse of which there is almost no record in the letters—though there are intermittent references, going back as far as his trip to Brazil, to a "slough of despond" and admissions of deepening depression, even thoughts of suicide. In a letter to his father from Berlin in 1867, for example, after an unusually bad bout with his back and "chronic gastritis of frightful virulence and obstinacy," he confesses that "thoughts of the pistol the dagger and the bowl began to usurp an unduly large part of my attention";[26] earlier that same year, he had reminded his parents of his continual difficulty preserving the "golden mean between an inane optimism & a stupid pessimism wh. has always distinguished me."[27] Ten months later, he was asking Oliver Wendell Holmes, Jr., "the question which all men who pretend to know themselves ought to be able to answer, but wh. few probably could off hand,—'what reason can you give for continuing to live? what ground allege why the thread of your days shd. not be snapped *now*?'"[28] But it was not until six years later, in a letter to his brother Bob nearly four years after his darkest moment, that William refers at any length to the collapse that occurred in early January 1870. Alluding to this moment in his diary in the entry dated February 1, William wrote: "Today I about touched bottom, and perceive plainly that I must face the choice with open eyes: shall I *frankly* throw the moral business overboard, as one unsuited to my innate aptitudes, or shall I follow it, and it alone, making everything else merely stuff for it?"[29]

The "moral business" to which he alludes in this candid admission involves the whole question of the will and thus of one's responsibility, in the last analysis, for one's actions. It was the question that William had been wrestling with for most of his conscious life: Is salvation to be found in submission to a power or force outside of and greater than the self, as his father steadfastly maintained, or is it to be discovered, if at all, as his sister Alice was later to confess in her own *Diary*, through "the resistance we bring to life and not the strain life brings to us"?[30] As he put it in a letter to Henry later that spring:

> It seems to me that all a man has to depend on in this world, is in the last resort, mere brute power of resistance. I can't bring myself as so many men seem able to, to blink the evil out of sight, and gloss it over. It's as real as the good, and if it is denied, good must be denied too. It must be accepted and hated and resisted while there's breath in our bodies.[31]

This is the "moral business" that his father had effectively rejected during his own experience of spiritual vastation, or emptying out, and complete psychological abjection back in May 1844. Henry, Senior, found his own salvation in the surrender of his will to that which he imagined to be sovereign over it, and then insisted, in book after book, that those who took the other path, the one less traveled in the nineteenth century, were guilty of the sin of pride, of inordinate self-love.[32]

But if William could not bring himself to describe to anyone his own experience of vastation when it occurred in the winter and spring of 1870, he did reinscribe it twenty-two years later as the suffering of another in the pages of *The Varieties of Religious Experience:*

> Whilst in this state of philosophic pessimism and general depression of spirits about my prospects, I went one evening into a dressing-room in the twilight to procure some article that was there; when suddenly there fell upon me without warning, just as if it came out of the darkness, a horrible fear of my own existence. Simultaneously there arose in my mind the image of an epileptic patient whom I had seen in the asylum, a black-haired youth with greenish skin, entirely idiotic, who used to sit all day on one of the benches, or rather shelves against the wall, with his knees drawn up against his chin, and the coarse gray undershirt, which was his only garment, drawn over them inclosing his entire figure. He sat there like a sort of sculptured Egyptian cat or Peruvian mummy, moving nothing but his black eyes and looking absolutely non-human. This image and my fear entered into a species of combination with each other. *That shape am I*, I felt, potentially. Nothing that I possess can defend me against that fate, if the hour for it should strike for me as it struck for him. There was such a horror of him, and such a perception of my own merely momentary discrepancy

from him, that it was as if something hitherto solid within my breast gave way entirely, and I became a mass of quivering fear. After this the universe was changed for me altogether. I awoke morning after morning with a horrible dread at the pit of my stomach, and with a sense of the insecurity of life that I never knew before, and that I have never felt since. It was like a revelation; and although the immediate feelings passed away, the experience has made me sympathetic with the morbid feelings of others ever since. It gradually faded, but for months I was unable to go out into the dark alone.

In general I dreaded to be left alone. I remember wondering how other people could live, how I myself had ever lived, so unconscious of that pit of insecurity beneath the surface of life. My mother in particular, a very cheerful person, seemed to me a perfect paradox in her unconsciousness of danger, which you may well believe I was very careful not to disturb by revelations of my own state of mind. I have always thought that this experience of melancholia of mine had a religious bearing.[33]

William's rescue from the brink of despair was completed later that spring. He had been reading the British psychologist Alexander Bain's *Senses and the Intellect*, but it was returning to Renouvier that saved him from disaster by convincing him that it was no illusion to believe that the power to sustain a thought when one might have other thoughts was evidence of free will. As William noted in his diary marking this crucial discovery on April 29, Renouvier had provided him grounds for concluding that life consists of "doing and suffering and creating," that meaning is to be found "in the self-governing *resistance* of the ego to the world."[34] With this reassurance, or at least possible reassurance, William was in a position to begin the process of healing himself, a process that was probably hastened somewhat by the timely offer that same spring of a one-year instructorship in Comparative Anatomy and Physiology at Harvard. Finally, at age thirty, with the acquisition of his first professional appointment, William was no longer financially dependent for complete support on his family. For the next two years his great success in teaching, together with his further reading in Renouvier and Wordsworth, would effect an at least partial, if precarious, recovery.

Among all the more interesting letters about James's state of mind during this very long process of self-discovery and emotional rehabilitation, none tell us more about his evolving feelings and ideas, and their global scope, than those he addressed to his father. If James's relationship with his father was one that he could not completely understand or reconcile himself to until 1884, when he edited and introduced the collection of his father's writings, it nevertheless influenced everything he thought about himself and the life he wanted to live. A relationship that had already experienced severe strains as a result of his father's resistance to an artistic career, it was obviously marked by differences of perspective and belief that went far beyond the aesthetic. By age twenty-five, for example, William was already expressing strong skepticism about his father's incarnational view of creation—"I cannot understand what you mean by the descent of the Creator into nature you don't explain it, and it seems to be the kernel of the whole."[35] Moved only weeks later by the spectacle of his father's "mental isolation," which made even his children seem "strangers to what you consider the best part of yourself," William is eager to take back some of his previous hostility to his father's position and sounds a more conciliatory note: "I want you to feel how thorough is my personal sympathy with you, and how great is my delight in much that I do understand of what you think, and my admiration of it."[36]

Nonetheless, William's reactions to "Father's ideas," as they were referred to by the James family household, could be pointed and unsparing. Responding to an article his father had sent him in Teplitz during the beginning of one of his own most difficult spiritual periods, William made no effort to protect his father's feelings: "I must confess that the darkness wh. to me has allways hung over what you have written on these subjects is hardly at all cleared up. Every sentence seems written from a point of view wh. I nowhere get within range of, and on the other hand ig[n]ores all sorts of questions wh. are visible from my point of view."[37]

William's deeper source of disagreement with his father stemmed inevitably from the discrepancy of their theological views, or, rather, at this moment in his life, from William's lack of any. Even if he could embrace, in many of its particulars, the world his father's theory of creation described, he could not accept his father's view of how that world came to be as it is. What Henry, Senior, credited to divine initiation and governance, his son was just as prepared to attribute to magic, accident, or contingency. Yet much as they might differ over these and many other points of philosophical and theological doctrines, William still found himself sharing his father's nonoptimistic view of nature and his belief in the reality of evil.

In a particularly full letter written in early January 1868 to cheer up a despondent Tom Ward, his former crewmate from the Agassiz expedition to Brazil, William reveals exactly how much he was his father's son intellectually and how much his own person. He gets at the issue that divides and at the same time links them when he confesses that "the thought that with me outlasts all others, and on to wh. like a rock, I find myself washed up when the waves of doubt are weltering over all the rest of the World . . . is the thought of my having a will, and of my belonging to a brotherhood of men possessed of a capacity for pleasure & pain of different kinds."[38] Henry, Senior, had no doubts about the brotherhood of men to which we all belong but believed that the individual will is the very instrument that must be sacrificed if this relationship is to be achieved. William, on the other hand, could conceive no expression of what his father called—in the title of his most successful book—*Society the Redeemed Form of Man* that was based on anything other than the will of individuals desiring to create such a society.

Nonetheless, William's disagreement with his father's ideas, here and elsewhere, still testifies to the depth of his spiritual engagement with them. It was an engagement that not only helps suggest why William was eventually driven toward philosophy itself but also goes a long way toward explaining the kind of philosopher he was to become. As he said as early as May 1868 in a letter to Oliver Wendell Holmes, Jr., "The only thing I can now think of is a professorship of 'moral philosophy' in some western Academy, but I have no idea how such things are attainable, nor if they are attainable at all to men of a non-spiritualistic mould."[39] The challenge posed by his father's arguments was how to counter them without simply dismissing them. The solution William in the end devised was to try to reinterpret for himself what his father's beliefs empirically amounted to, and then explain why on that basis he could not completely accept them. At that moment, if not before, the future pragmatist was really born. Thus, in the famous letter he wrote to his father as the latter was dying—the letter that failed to reach his father in time and that his brother Henry read over the elder James's grave—William could confess without dissimulation or exaggeration that for better or worse he owed virtually the whole of his intellectual life to his father. The relations with his father had compelled him to develop a method for understanding and more fairly assessing the ideas of others, ideas that, on their face, one neither shares nor fully comprehends. Pragmatism was thus produced as a hermeneutic of otherness.

As is well known, James first employed the term *pragmatism* in a lecture entitled "Philosophical Conceptions and Practical Results," delivered before the Philosophical Union at the University of California at Berkeley in August 1898. He was borrowing the term from his friend and sometime colleague Charles Sanders Peirce, who had first developed it in an essay that appeared in *Popular Science Monthly* in 1878 entitled "How to Make Our Ideas Clear." Peirce had in turn reported discovering the term in Kant's *Metaphysics of Morals* where, interestingly enough, it is contrasted with the term "practical"—Kant associates the "practical" with a priori moral laws, the "pragmatic" with rules of art and technique derived from experience—but for both Peirce and James pragmatism was essentially a new name for some older ways of thinking that could be found in everyone from Socrates and Aristotle to Spinoza, Locke, Berkeley, Hume, Kant himself, and Mill.[40] Peirce's interests centered more narrowly than James's on the problem of meaning: the pragmatic method, which he was at one point tempted to call "practicalism" and at another "pragmaticism" (the latter being an ugly enough term to prevent it from being stolen by James and his followers), addressed this problem by proposing that all distinctions of thought can be ultimately reduced to differences in practice. Assuming further that our conceptions of things are no more than our idea of their sensible effects, Peirce devised the following pragmatic rule: "Consider what effects, that might conceivably have practical bearings, we conceive the object of our conception to have. Then, our conception of these effects is our whole conception of the object."[41]

Peirce wanted a procedure for determining the rational meaning of a word or concept, which for him lay "exclusively in its conceivable bearing upon the conduct of experience." Hence the "rational meaning of every proposition," said Peirce, "lies in the future," its meaning being "that form in which the proposition becomes applicable to human conduct, not in these or those special circumstances, nor when one entertains this or that special design, but in that form which is most directly applicable to self-control under every situation, and to every purpose."[42] This was Peirce speaking like a scientist intent on establishing a rule for intellectual clarity that was sufficiently rigorous to stand up to laboratory conditions of exactitude, consistency, and logical coherence. Ideally, Peirce felt that scientific investigation should operate like a force of destiny, carrying the most radically antagonistic minds toward the same inevitable conclusion: "No modification of the point of view taken, no selection of other facts for study, no natural bent of mind even, can enable a man to escape the predestinate opinion." Truth is no more than "the opinion which is fated to be ultimately agreed to by all who investigate," Peirce maintained, "and the object represented in this opinion is the real."[43] That, and that alone, is what we should mean by reality.

By contrast, the artist in James was convinced that reality constantly overflows our intellectual formulas and findings, and may be, as James observed only much later in *A Pluralistic Universe*, "if not irrational then at least non-rational in its constitution."[44] James therefore wanted a less scientifically scrupulous or psychologically sanitized method for clarifying the meaning of principles, ideas, and language which would concede the fact that reality may encompass more than the conclusions on which reasonable people can logically agree. More to the point, most of James's potential readers were not scientists, and the issues and concerns with which they were confronted did not, for the most part, lend themselves to scientific analysis. What they wanted were answers to larger and more unwieldy questions, such as why to go on living, what constitutes the moral life, how to reconcile the many with the one, why truth matters, and what makes one view of the world better or truer than another. Consequently, philosophy needed to stop concentrating all of its attention on its own problems and begin asking itself, as James put it in the chapter on "What Pragmatism Means" in *Pragmatism*, "what definite difference it will make to you and me, at definite instants of our life, if this world-formula or that world-formula be the true one."[45]

Thus, when James decided, in his Berkeley lecture to the Philosophical Union, to borrow the pragmatic method from Peirce (he had actually heard Peirce invoke it in the early 1870s and had himself employed less developed versions of it in his earlier writing), he sought to give it much more general application. While remaining in complete agreement with Peirce that beliefs are guides for action and that truth must be measured by the consequences to which it leads, James nonetheless felt that the pragmatic principle should be opened up. If the ultimate test of any truth is the conduct that it produces, James reasoned, then one must grant that it produces or inspires this conduct only because it initially "foretells some particular turn to our experience which shall call for just that conduct from us." James was thus prepared to revise Peirce's principle to say that "the effective meaning of any philosophic proposition can always be brought down to some particular consequence, in our future practical experience, whether active or passive; the point lying rather in the fact that the experience must be particular, than in the fact that it must be active."[46]

The upshot of this expansion of Peirce's original definition is, first, that it permitted James to apply the method to a vastly larger terrain of experience than Peirce had considered. He was not interested in a method that works only under the controlled conditions afforded by laboratory apparatus or the classroom. He wanted a method that could be employed across the board, in all concrete cases. Second, it enabled James to turn pragmatic reasoning into an exercise that was less severely rational or deductive and more loosely interpretive and conjectural, one involving a good deal of mental guesswork as well as more stringent intellectual calibrations. To attain intellectual clarity, then, as James paraphrased Peirce both in his University of California address and, as here, in his chapter from *Pragmatism* entitled "What Pragmatism Means," "we need only consider what conceivable effects of a practical kind the object may involve—what sensations we are to expect from it, and what reactions we must prepare. Our conception of these effects, whether immediate or remote, is then for us the whole of our conception of the object, so far as that conception has positive significance at all."[47] In *Some Problems of Philosophy*, James simplified the method still further:

> The pragmatic rule is that the meaning of a concept may always be found, if not in some sensible particular which it directly designates, then in some particular difference in the course of human experience which its being true will make. Test every concept by the question 'What sensible difference to anybody will its truth make?' and you are in the best possible position for understanding what it means and for discussing its importance.[48]

James's definition of the pragmatic method, however phrased, clearly opened up Peirce's formulation to more comprehensive use while at the same time rendering it, much to Peirce's displeasure, a good deal less precise. The new imprecision of James's description of the method derived partly from some of the phrases it left open for further elucidation—"conceivable effects," "practical kind," "may involve," "sensations . . . to expect," "reactions . . . may prepare," or, in the phrasing from *Some Problems of Philosophy*, "sensible difference" and "course of human experience"—but it also stemmed from the way James put imagination back into the operations of rationality. To determine "some particular difference in the course of human experience which [a concept's] being true will make," as in the latter definition, or, to calculate, as in the former, "what sensations we are to expect from [the object], and what reactions we must prepare," was to put much greater reliance on the inferential and the projective capacities of the mind than Peirce had done. "Pragmatism unstiffens all our theories," James proclaimed in "What Pragmatism Means," "limbers them up and sets each one at work,"[49] and the work our theories do is suppositional, hypothetical, and presumptive as well as analytic. Assessing notions in terms of their practical consequences often entailed reflection on matters that had not taken place yet, that could only be surmised rather than substantiated, only imagined rather than corroborated. Where theories and beliefs had been for Peirce merely precepts, templates for action, for James they became instruments for imaginative speculation as well as catalysts for change.

Pragmatism could thus be said to coincide with, and reinforce, many philosophical orientations. "It agrees with nominalism, for instance, in always appealing to particulars; with utilitarianism in emphasizing practical aspects; with positivism in its disdain for verbal solutions, useless questions, and metaphysical abstractions."[50] It could also be seen as continuous with the practice of everyone from Socrates to Hume. But all of these forerunners had practiced it piecemeal. James was recommending that pragmatism be applied more universally and in a form that was intellectually more supple, accessible, and predictive. Even if it seemed to lack any presuppositions of its own and stood for no particular results, the pragmatic method could nonetheless serve as the solvent of all other philosophical theories, as the medium in which they conducted their investigations. Giovanni Papini, the Italian pragmatist, had caught exactly this dimension of the pragmatic method when, in a particularly apt metaphor, he likened its operations among all theories to the way a corridor functions in a hotel. While innumerable philosophical chambers open off of and onto this corridor, each housing a particular way of thinking, and all having rights to it, the corridor itself is philosophically neutral. It merely serves as the conduit that all schools of thought must use if they are to exit their rooms, much less circulate among one another.

If this was to say that the pragmatic method lacks an intellectual agenda, it did not mean that it was bereft of any philosophical presuppositions or, more to the point, that its adoption was without consequences. In fact, James was convinced that its broad-scale employment would spell the end of many of the practices to which philosophers had become habituated over the centuries. More specifically, it meant, as James emphasized in "What Pragmatism Means," *"looking away from first things, principles, categories, supposed necessities,"* and *"towards last things, fruits, consequences, facts."*[51] More generally, it suggested "the open air and possibilities of nature, as against dogma, artificiality, and the pretence of finality in truth."[52] If pragmatism was a method only, then it was a method, as we would now say, with an "attitude." James considered the implementation of the pragmatic method nothing short of revolutionary and even imagined for a time that he might be launching a new Protestant reformation.

With ambitions such as these, it should come as little surprise that James shared with the British writer G. K. Chesterton the belief that the most important and practical thing one can know about individuals is their philosophy or worldview. By "philosophy or worldview" he did not refer to anything derived chiefly from books but rather, as he stated in "The Present Dilemma in Philosophy," to one's "more or less dumb sense of what life honestly and deeply means."[53] Something acquired from the whole course of one's experience, one's philosophy is in this sense simply "our individual way of just seeing and feeling the total push and pressure of the cosmos."[54] James was prepared to concede that most of us have no very clear idea of such matters; indeed, he was persuaded that on large issues the great majority of us rarely know our own minds at all. But he was also of the opinion that no individuals, professional philosophers included, are indifferent to their, as he called it in "Is Life Worth Living?," "*Binnenleben*," that mute "region of the heart in which we dwell alone with our willingnesses and unwillingnesses, our faiths and fears."[55] "The history of philosophy," he therefore boldly proclaimed, "is to a great extent that of a certain clash of human temperaments."[56]

That philosophical divisions can to a large degree be reduced to no more than differences of temperament is a claim that philosophers were no more prepared to hear then than they are now. Violating all their preconceptions of, and pretensions about, their work as reasonable, objective, and disinterested, it provoked, not surprisingly, a torrent of criticism. But if philosophers for the most part insisted on defending themselves against such a charge, James was no less tenacious in pressing it. Temperament might well be the last thing that philosophers wanted to admit into their practices, much less admit about them, but it was the first thing they trusted, James was certain, when it came to reaching their conclusions. Temperament "loads the evidence . . . just as this fact or that principle would," he went on in "The Present Dilemma in Philosophy."[57] The philosopher wants a universe that matches his or her temperament and rejects any universe that doesn't. James argued that the philosopher "feels men of opposite temper to be out of key with the world's character, and in his heart considers them incompetent and 'not in it,' in the philosophic business, even though they may far excel him in dialectical ability."[58] In *A Pluralistic Universe*, James went even further:

> If we take the whole history of philosophy, the systems reduce themselves to a few main types which, under all the technical verbiage in which the ingenious intellect of man envelops them, are just so many

visions, modes of feeling the whole push, and seeing the whole drift of life, forced on one by one's total character and experience, and on the whole *preferred*—there is no other truthful word—as one's best working attitude.[59]

The conflict of temperament that marked his own period, James believed, set rationalists, as he called them, against empiricists. Rationalists were committed to abstract or timeless principles and tended to be intellectualistic, idealistic, optimistic, religious, monistic, and dogmatic. Empiricists, on the other hand, were committed to facts and thus tended to be materialistic, sensationalistic, positivist, pessimistic, fatalistic, pluralistic, and skeptical. While neither type was pure—traces of these differences can be found in some mixture in most of us—the clash between them could be discerned throughout literature, government, art, religion, social thought, and contemporary manners, as well as philosophy, and seemed to be reducible to a basic distinction between two types of personality. On the one side are the "tender-minded," who cling to the belief that facts should be related to values and values should be seen as predominant; on the other are the "tough-minded," who want facts to be dissociated from values and left to themselves. Just as the "tough-minded" find such things as idealism and intellectualism laid too heavily over the path of life, so the "tender-minded" complain that the path of life is choked with the weeds of positivism, relativism, utilitarianism, and naturalistic determinism. The "tender-minded" find the "tough-minded" callous and unfeeling, the "tough-minded" charge the "tender-minded" with sentimentality and fuzzy thinking. This clash has produced what James described as "the dilemma in philosophy," a dilemma that has left thoughtful people who seek a philosophy for the whole person suspended between two seemingly irreconcilable and equally unattractive alternatives: either an empirical philosophy that leaves too little room for values and principles, or a rationalistic or intellectualistic philosophy that has lost touch with the concrete facts of human experience.

James offered pragmatism as a solution to this dilemma. Pragmatism could reconcile the ideal with the material, the rational with the concrete, because in addition to being a theory of meaning, pragmatism was also a theory of truth. As a theory of truth, James argued, pragmatism holds that ideas are not only abstractions from experience and generalizations about it but also aspects or components of it. Ideas, that is, do not simply comment on experience but actually constitute important elements of it. For example, ideas are the forms that life takes for us when we are living under the sway of ideologies or experience a feeling of solidarity with others who belong to those "imagined communities" called nationalities, religions, ethnicities, and so forth. More than that, ideas are what experience consists of for us when, even temporarily, our sensibilities undergo the reshapings of art and serious thought. Were this better understood, James assumed (and Dewey never tired of remarking) the importance of education, and the directions it should take, would be much more apparent to most people than they currently are.

But if ideas are in fact aspects of experience and not simply interpretations of it, then ideas become true, James reasoned, or, at any rate, become true instrumentally, just insofar as they help place us in more constructive, more effectual, more valuable relations with other parts of our experience—just to the extent that they exhibit what James termed, borrowing a metaphor from business, "cash-value." James's use of such commercial metaphors was not intended to imply, as Oliver Wendell Holmes employed them himself to mean, that the truth of ideas or concepts is determined solely by, or is reducible essentially to, what they are good for in the intellectual, cultural, or any other marketplace. He was merely restating and reaffirming what he believed Dewey and other members of the Chicago School had established, and what other disciplines as various as geology, biology, and philology now routinely accepted: truth is not an inherent property of ideas as such but rather a property of their working connection with other things that already belong to the assemblage of what is taken to be true.

James was here drawing from a familiar theory of how individuals typically acquire new opinions and establish their veracity. Truth normally lives on what James referred to in "Pragmatism's Conception of Truth" as a "credit system": "Our thoughts and beliefs 'pass' so long as nothing challenges them, just as bank-notes pass so long as nobody refuses them."[60] When some new experience emerges that unsettles the stock of already accepted opinions and thereby creates discomfort, the mind seeks to escape from this discomfort by attempting initially to modify the mass of already accepted opinion as much as possible. If this doesn't relieve the sense of inward unease, then one must await the discovery of some new idea that can be grafted onto the stock of older opinions with a minimum of difficulty. In "What Pragmatism Means" James contended that new truth functions as a kind of "go-between, a smoother-over of transitions. It marries old opinion to new fact so as ever to show a minimum of jolt, a maximum of continuity."[61]

One of James's chief interests in this subject derived from the part played by older truths in the acquisition of new truths. Even as knowledge grows, it grows only in spots and leaves most of what is already known completely intact. The greatest enemy of a new truth is thus likely to be the rest of our other truths. And even when a new truth can get itself grafted onto the stock of the old, as James noted in "Pragmatism and Common Sense," it almost always comes "cooked" rather than "raw": "New truths . . . are resultants of new experiences and of old truths combined and mutually modifying one another."[62] In this connection, James's most startling assertion is that the body of truth that strikes most of us as no more than ordinary common sense may actually represent the distilled wisdom of some ancient genius whose discoveries have survived the long night of historical obscurity to subsequently form a kind of "stage of equilibrium in the human mind's development," a level that later stages of knowledge supplement without ever completely replacing."[63] Thus, even if common sense does not represent the most complex or advanced stage of human understanding—James reserved this for science and critical philosophy—it shows us how knowledge increases and why truth is always relational. Truth is relational because it is never encountered alone or in isolation; it always emerges in association with its antecedents and allies, its previous models and affiliated figurations.

James deduced from this that truth is not so much found as rather made, and made in part out of former truths constantly remade because they prove useful both as material for such remaking and as beliefs that do something for us.

> We plunge forward into the field of fresh experience with the beliefs our ancestors and we have made already; these determine what we notice; what we notice determines that we do; what we do again determines what we experience; so from one thing to another, altho the stubborn fact remains that there *is* a sensible flux, what is *true of it* seems from first to last to be largely a matter of our own creation."[64]

Truth, therefore, ceases to be a category distinct unto itself and becomes for James a species of the good. "*The true is the name of whatever proves itself to be good in the way of belief, and good, too, for definite, assignable reasons.*"[65] In purely functional terms, despite whatever else it may be, truth is what we say about it: James notes in "What Pragmatism Means" that "the reason why we call things true is the reason why they *are* true, for 'to be true' *means* only to perform this marriage-function."[66] We accept things as true, then, not because of what, in and of themselves, they say about the real but rather because of what saying this about the real does to and for our relations with it.

Such views were, of course, bound to arouse a storm wind of criticism, since they put James on a collision course with all those philosophers and lay people who maintained instead that truth represents a correspondence with reality. In this more conventional notion of truth—which, as it happens, is the same notion that common sense holds, even if common sense portrays truth as something else—truth is a reflection of what is already there in experience prior to our perception of it. And what is already there in experience prior to our perception of it is simply the realm of the real that our ideas are supposed to copy. Empiricists in James's time, no less than in our own, supposed that the realm of the real is composed essentially of material facts. The rationalists and idealists who opposed them insisted instead that the real also includes our perception of purely mental notions like goodness and beauty and the relations between them. From James's perspective, however, both groups overlooked the fact that, as James had shown in his discussions of common sense, our sense of reality is also composed of the whole funded tradition of experience that has already been accepted as true.

Although this latter claim, even if not original with him, was one of the distinctive contributions of James's theory of truth, it immediately created problems for anyone who wanted to champion the view that truth is simply a matter of correspondence. How could one square the idea of truth as correspondence or agreement with this threefold conception of the real as relating to facts, to ideas, and to history. James's answer in "Pragmatism's Conception of Truth" was simple. Inasmuch as the idea of copying never worked in the first place for many of the things we already take for reality—James's examples include such things as "power," "spontaneity," and "time past"—he concluded that truth as "agreement" between an idea of something and the thing itself could only in the widest sense mean *"to be guided either straight up to it or into its surroundings, or to be put into such working touch with it as to handle either it or something connected with it better than if we disagreed."*[67]

James's phrasing here is very important. Without disputing the fact that some ideas do indeed copy the reality they name, and thus coincide with reality more or less perfectly, he wanted to indicate that "agreement" in this literal sense is far from essential to what is most salient in our working notion of truth. For many purposes of truth—and particularly those we can never corroborate, so to speak, face-to-face—it is sufficient, James believed, for ideas to lead us in the direction of reality and to aid us in our dealings with it. He speaks of this process of worthwhile *leading* as one by which an idea's truth is verified. Truth is not, in other words, an ingredient in ideas from the outset but is instead acquired by them. Truth is what "happens" to an idea when it is put into the relations that confirm it. More than a description of the agreement that obtains between an idea and its referent, then, truth is an action, an event, a process, by which an idea's "agreement" or "correspondence," in only this widest sense James is talking about, is verified, validated. Yet an idea's verity is not to be confused with the process of its, as James called it in the same chapter, "veri-*fication.*"[68] Truths are verified only retrospectively, and are always subject to further revision by later experience.

James was willing to admit that others might find this way of talking about "agreement" confusing, if not disturbing, but it was necessary if "agreement" was to apply to "any process of conduction" by which a present idea moves constructively, or, to use James's term, "profitably," to a future conclusion. In any case, what all truths have in common, James was convinced, is that "they *pay.* They pay by guiding us into or towards some part of a system that dips at numerous points into sense-percepts, which we may copy mentally or not, but with which at any rate we are now in the kind of commerce vaguely designated as verification. Truth for us is simply a collective name for verification-processes."[69]

Describing truth as but another name for verification processes was scarcely likely to silence James's critics because verification processes so often occur only at second or third hand. Their belated nature derives from the fact that thinking, as James put it, anticipating the insights of philosophers from our own time such as Jacques Derrida and Michel Foucault, is so wholly discursified. By "discursified," James meant that thinking is always mediated through intertextual systems of communication and exchange. Thus, as truth "gets verbally built out, stored up, and made available for every one," and verifications are lent and borrowed through textualized social intercourse, fewer and fewer of these ideas receive direct verification but are instead confirmed or disconfirmed by their relations with other discourses and discursive regimes.[70]

James's notion of truth thus contains several elements that must be kept in view if we are not to be misled by its somewhat informal and digressive articulation. Assuming that truth involves agreement with reality only in the most general sense, James was careful to resist any imputation that "agreement" involves "one and the same relation in all cases," or that "agreement" is ultimately achievable only in some infinite mind that transcends the limitations of all human points of view.[71] Moreover, while truth involved for him something that works, that has practical effects, that is conducive to change, James's theory also owes something to Peirce's association of truth with reasoned consensus. James may have come closest to clearly sorting out these various elements in an interview he gave to the *New York Times* the same year that *Pragmatism* was published. Countering charges that pragmatism denies any possibility of a theoretical knowledge of reality or truth, and that it functions for too many people as a practical substitute for philosophy itself, he insisted, a bit defensively, that pragmatism has "proved so over-subtle that even academic critics have failed to catch its question, to say nothing of their misunderstanding of its answer":

> Whatever propositions or beliefs may, in point of fact, prove true, it says, the truth of them consists in certain definable *relations between them and the reality* of which they make report. . . . Philosophers have generally been satisfied with the word 'agreement' here, but pragmatists have seen that this word covers many different concrete possibilities. . . . Thus the vague notion of 'agreement' with reality becomes specified into that of innumerable ways in which our thoughts may *fit* reality, ways in which the mind's activities cooperate on equal terms with the reality producing the fit resultant truth.[72]

Statements such as this—or his more famous claim in "Pragmatism's Conception of Truth" that "*'the true' . . . is only the expedient in the way of our thinking, just as 'the right' is only the expedient in the way of our behaving*"[73]—have always furnished James's opponents with an excuse to brand him as irresponsible subjectivist, and nothing he said later in *The Meaning of Truth*, where he attempted to address the strongest arguments of his best critics, has fully silenced his detractors. Indeed, when James tried to explain some of the implications of his theory by describing truth as "a relation, not of our ideas to non-human realities, but of conceptual parts of our experience to sensational parts" in the chapter entitled "Humanism and Truth" in *The Meaning of Truth*, he only aroused his critics the more by maintaining that the "truth-relation," as he termed it, describes something that works, whether physically or intellectually, actually or merely possibly, in establishing relations within concrete experience.[74]

Critics have taken this as further evidence that James denied the existence of real objects outside of or independent of the mind, but James considered this malicious nonsense. Neither he nor any other pragmatist (he pointed to Schiller and Dewey) had ever denied that the object in a truth relation, if it can be experienced at all, is transcendent to the subject. How, otherwise, he asked in the preface to *The Meaning of Truth*, explain Dewey's insistence (with which he himself concurred emphatically) that the whole purpose of thinking is to intervene in and attempt to change the world outside the mind?: Dewey's "account of knowledge is not only absurd, but meaningless, unless independent existences be there of which our ideas take account, and for the transformation of which they work. But because he and Schiller refuse to discuss objects and relations 'transcendent' in the sense of being *altogether trans-experiential*, their critics pounce on sentences in their writings to that effect to show that they deny the existence *within the realm of experience* of objects external to the ideas that declare their presence there."[75]

While it seemed incredible to James that his most intelligent critics could have gotten him so far wrong, some of their misunderstanding was at least partially intelligible. Part of the problem, as I have indicated earlier, was that James was not writing primarily for professional philosophers but for members of an educated public that was more in need of intellectual encouragement and moral support than of precise definitions and logical arguments. In addition to being a source of irritation for some, this was also a source of bewilderment to others. A second factor was James's talent for vivid expression and pointed argument. If this produced a continuously ambulatory prose style that was rich in figurative maneuvers and surprises, it frequently yielded metaphorical analogies that left much room for alternative and sometimes discrepant interpretations. Still a third reason for his problems with critics had to do with some of his formulations themselves. Many of his essays were written to meet publisher's deadlines, before he had time to think through all of the implications of their arguments, and others were constructed with an eye to reconciling his theory of truth with his only slowly evolving metaphysics.

James's metaphysics, partially evolved or not, clearly shadows some of the claims he made about truth in *Pragmatism* and momentarily comes to the fore in his chapter entitled "Pragmatism and Humanism." In the latter, he contrasts the edition of the universe pragmatism provides—"unfinished, growing in all sorts of places, especially in the places where thinking beings are at work"[76]—with the edition rationalism or idealism affords—"the infinite folio, or *edition de luxe*, eternally complete; and then the various finite editions, full of false readings, distorted and mutilated each in its own way"[77]—only to conclude that the choice between them must inevitably have a good deal to do with temperament. The pragmatist, James cheerfully admitted, is no exception. In addition to being something of a happy-go-lucky anarchist, or at least an opportunist, the pragmatist is a pluralist who rejects the idea that truth is imposed on experience from a position outside in favor of the belief that truth emerges from within experiences that lean on each other without leaning on anything beyond them. "All 'homes' are in finite experience; finite experience as such is homeless. Nothing outside of the flux secures the issue of it. It can hope [for] salvation only from its own intrinsic promises and potencies."[78]

James had been interested in what holds experience together since his ruminations on "The Stream of Thought" in *The Principles of Psychology*, and he had returned to this theme in various essays on the same subject that he had published in the first decade of the new century. In the essay "Does Consciousness Exist?" for example, he had continued to challenge dualistic thinkers who severed the mind from the body and viewed consciousness as an entity rather than a function. Insisting that consciousness refers to an "external relation" rather than "a special stuff or way of being," James had asserted that "*the peculiarity of our experiences, that they not only are, but are known, which their conscious quality is invoked to explain, is better explained by their relations—these relations themselves being experiences—to one another.*"[79] But it was in the preface to *The Meaning of Truth* that James gave the most succinct expression to his metaphysics, or view of how the whole of life hangs together. He chose the name "radical empiricism" for his metaphysics because it starts with parts rather than with wholes, with particulars rather than unities, but then goes on to explain how the relations between parts relate to the parts themselves. Expanding on this series of assumptions, James said that radical empiricism consists of a postulate, a statement of fact, and a generalized conclusion. Its postulate is that philosophers can find the terms necessary to define all the things worthy of debate within experience itself. Its statement is that the relations between things are just as capable of being directly experienced as the things themselves. And its generalization is that the parts of experience are held together by relations that are no less real elements of experience than the parts themselves. From this James concluded that the universe as we know it needs "no extraneous trans-empirical connective support, but possesses in its own right a concatenated or continuous structure."[80]

James's commitment to radical empiricism did not deter him from writing at length about religion. As early as his essay "The Will to Believe," James had concluded that we have a right to choose for any options, religious or otherwise, that appear to be "live" as opposed to "dead," "forced" opposed to "avoidable," and "momentous" as opposed to "trivial" because, even if we can't prove them, we would lose the possibility of their being true at all if we postponed a decision about them indefinitely.[81] In *The Varieties of Religious Experience*, James had attested to the consciousness of a sense of a "More" that is continuous with the self, though operative outside the self, and capable of potentially saving the self from possible spiritual shipwreck. James was here at least prepared to call himself a "piecemeal supernaturalist" who "admits miracles and providential leadings, and finds no intellectual difficulty in mixing the ideal and the real worlds together."[82] Such a sense of the "More" is also close to what James described about the self in a later essay on "The Continuity of Experience," where he speaks of the margin or horizon of consciousness that surrounds its center and "shades insensibly into a subconscious more. . . . What we conceptually identify ourselves with and say we are thinking of at any given time is the centre; but our *full* self is the whole field, with all those indefinitely radiating subconscious possibilities of increase that we can only feel without conceiving, and can hardly begin to analyze."[83]

In both cases, James was careful not to step outside of experience to find the terms to describe something he sensed to extend beyond its conceptual boundaries. And so he resisted the temptation again, when he came to examine religion in the final chapter of *Pragmatism*. Here he utilizes the analogy of the relation our pets occupy to human life to evoke a religious sense of the relation that human beings occupy to the whole of the universe: "They inhabit our drawing-rooms and libraries. They take part in scenes of whose significance they have no inkling. They are merely tangent to curves of history the beginnings and end and forms of which pass wholly beyond their ken. So we are tangent to the wider life of things."[84]

James's critics, primarily from philosophy, who have based their case against him on problems with his theory of truth have clearly done him a disservice. Even if he thought of his contribution to philosophy as primarily epistemological, he put his theory of meaning and truth to work on an extraordinary range of issues that were by turns psychological, moral, social, political, historical, and religious. Nor did James see this as in any way an adulteration or betrayal of the essential pragmatist enterprise. James not only hoped that its adoption heralded a new dawn in philosophy but was unapologetic about the fact that pragmatism carried along with it certain intellectual entailments and predilections. We can perhaps best gauge the range and depth of his achievement by putting them in summary form.

To begin with, Jamesian pragmatism is, if not completely antifoundational, then at least thoroughly skeptical about neutral starting points for thought. Second, it is empirical not simply because of its stress on the concrete and the particular but because of its radical commitment to parts rather than wholes and its belief that the parts of experience must include feelings and ideas, as well as facts, whose relations can be experienced as fully as anything else. Third, it is pluralist in its affirmation of a universe whose parts are not only multiple and diverse but always changing and often untidy. Fourth, it is realistic in that it acknowledges that there are real gains and real losses in life and that what survives, as James's sister Alice once wrote in her *Diary*, are not the trials life brings to us but the courage with which we meet them.[85] Fifth, it is, to use Peirce's word, "fallibilist" in the sense that it regards all conclusions and certainties as open to further question even if not all at once. Sixth, it also holds with Peirce that philosophy needs to shift its model of argumentation from a chain that is no stronger than its weakest link to a cable whose strength derives from the multitude and interconnectedness of its fibers and thereby learn to trust in the number and variety of its arguments rather than in the decisiveness of any one of them. Seventh, and finally, it is democratic in that its central public aim is not only to dissolve the hierarchical protocols and formalities that define the topics and styles of traditional philosophical disputation but to enact in its own speech the informality, directness, and frankness of a conversation between equals. In short, by encouraging ideas to follow the irregular and unpredictable logics of dialogue rather than the more formal, systematic logics of disquisition and debate, James succeeded, as no other philosopher in the American tradition, in turning philosophy into a mode of answerable discourse.

Chapter 4

Pragmatism and *The American Scene*

Though William and Henry James have come in for their fair share of comparison, such comparisons have paid surprisingly little attention to the specific philosophical and methodological connections between William's pragmatism and Henry's critical theory and practice.[1] There are no doubt various explanations for this, ranging from the tendency still prevalent in some circles to see Henry and William as intellectual as well as temperamental opposites to the belief that pragmatism has always remained too crude a philosophical instrument to be entertained by a mind as aesthetically refined as Henry's. Such prejudices can be maintained, however, only at the expense of suppressing the admission, wrung from a surprised but elated Henry upon the completion of William's book on pragmatism, that in fact he himself, as he could now see, had always been a lifelong pragmatist. After finishing William's *A Pluralistic Universe*, Henry was even more emphatic in a letter to his brother:

> It may sustain and inspire you a little to know that I'm *with* you, all along the line—and can conceive of no sense in any philosophy that is not yours! As an artist and a "creator" I can catch on, hold on, to pragmatism and can work in the light of it and apply it; finding, in comparison, everything else (so far as I know the same!) utterly irrelevant and useless—vainly and coldly parallel.[2]

Such confessions might count for less if there was not such an abundance of textual evidence to support them. Yet even where such evidence has been placed in view, as in Richard A. Hocks's *Henry James and Pragmatist Thought*, we have been at something of a loss as to how to assess its significance for a rereading of the later work of Henry himself and for what it might tell us about Henry's relationship to the revival of pragmatism at the present time. Now, however, with the publication of Ross Posnock's recent *The Trial of Curiosity*, much of the uncertainty has been dispelled. Posnock argues that if the philosophical and critical pragmatism shared by both Jameses possessed any common thread, any overriding purpose, it was to develop in both of them a deep suspicion of the self-possessive individualism and obsession with cultural authority that marked the traditional bourgeois or Victorian conception of identity at the end of the nineteenth century, and to encourage in each a more relaxed, fluid, spontaneous, and pluralistic sense of self. A sense of self bent on dissolving the genteel boundaries between subject and object, detachment and commitment, self and other, it encouraged both to prefer, so Posnock maintains, exposure to control, vulnerability to power, contamination to propriety.

If this modernist project in pragmatic self-refashioning sounds a good deal more like the William of *Pragmatism, The Meaning of Truth*, and *A Pluralistic Universe* than the Henry of *The Lesson of the Master, The Sacred Fount*, or the critical essays, it was nonetheless Henry and not William, according to Posnock, who most successfully realized this modernist project in reconceiving personal identity. Thus, it was Henry and not William who anticipated, particularly in his final prose works, a new kind of immanent critique of the sort that we normally associate with the Frankfurt School. That is, it was Henry and not William who was best able to respond to difference, diversity, and contingency—what Theodor Adorno was eventually to term "the nonidentical"—and he did so through a process of self-fashioning that was first and foremost rhetorical. In the prefaces to the New York Edition, as in the later autobiographical works, *A Small Boy and Others, Notes of a Son and Brother, The Middle Years*, and especially in *The American Scene*, James assumes the persona that he calls the "restless analyst." This persona is a rhetorical figure whose discursive style is intended to loosen the intellectual, emotional, aesthetic, and sexual restraints placed on consciousness by Victorian, bourgeois culture and replace it with a more relaxed, at times almost reckless, curiosity and receptivity. What the "restless analyst" seeks is what Posnock calls an "exemplary immersion," what James termed "saturation."[3] What this rhetorical creation yields, on the other hand, is an image of an artist-critic who is almost the diametrical opposite of "the Master" celebrated by Leon Edel and so many others, a figure who is most inquisitive, tolerant, and modulated in his judgments at just those points where modern readers might have expected him to seem—and have consequently often judged James to be—most class-bound and fastidious. In addition to displacing the view that James was an "impeccably Olympian formalist and aesthetic idealist who, like his characters, turns his back on an impossibly vulgar modern world to cultivate what critics were fond of calling redemptive consciousness," this figure projects a model of criticism no longer determined exclusively by genteel codes of respectability and discrimination that is also desirous of encompassing the shifting, contradictory, enigmatic, and continuously disruptive contours of experience itself.[4] Indeed, by emphasizing the historicity and provisionality of such categories as individualism, consciousness, and identity in all the writings of his "second major phase," Henry expressed the hope that the United States might eventually develop social institutions and practices capable of dissolving the artificial distinctions between genders as well as classes so that new forms of agency, empowerment, and value might be explored.

Nonetheless, despite Posnock's success in providing us, in his analysis of these late works, with a James who is considerably more complex morally and more heterogeneous socially than the conventional portrait, he has surprisingly little to say about how, in the face of the obstacles that "the American Scene" presents to the inquiring mind, James managed to transform himself into this new rhetorical figure he calls the "restless analyst." What was there about the interpretive obstacles James confronted on his return to America, one wants to ask, that compelled him to create in response a new consciousness for the cultural critic that was fundamentally pragmatist and rhetorical? If *The American Scene* portrays experience, like the self, now almost everywhere rendered insusceptible to interpretation by traditional critical stratagems (this, indeed, is one of the text's most important subplots), what was there, in other words, about pragmatism that allowed it, when rhetorically transformed into the figure of the "restless analyst," to become an interpretive solution to the critical conundrums posed by modern American culture?[5]

The hermeneutic process by which James's "restless analyst" comes to his judgments in *The American Scene* is not incidental to the purposes of the book itself; indeed, it constitutes nothing less than one of the book's chief subjects and its principal form of connection with, indeed contribution to, the pragmatic method that Henry shared with William. To state that subject—and thus to define *The American Scene's* tie with William—in the simplest possible terms, we might say that Henry transforms pragmatism into an interpretive instrument no longer tied to the rhetorical procedures and premises of genteel (which is to say Victorian) cultural criticism by associating it rhetorically with the premises and procedures of a cultural criticism that is not only distinctively modern but proleptically postmodern.

The American Scene is based on a trip James made to the United States after a twenty-year absence that began at the end of August 1904. Following his arrival in Hoboken and a night spent at his publisher's in New Jersey with fellow guest Mark Twain, his travels commenced with an initial visit to scenes of his New York childhood at Gramercy Park and Washington Square. But this visit was cut short so that he could depart as quickly as possible for New England and Chocorua, New Hampshire, where William had a summer place. After several weeks spent in the New Hampshire hills taking in the full glory of an American autumn, James returned to other sites of family residence in Boston and Cambridge, with side trips to Concord and Salem, before descending finally to New York City again for a more prolonged inspection of what James was to call "the monstrous form of Democracy."[6] Continuing southward, he then proceeded to Philadelphia, where he stayed with the daughter of Fanny Kemble, before moving on to Baltimore and then to Washington, D.C., where his host was Henry Adams. After excursions to Mt. Vernon and other sites, James then proceeded into the deeper South, with stops in Richmond, Charleston, and various parts of Florida before returning north. In the spring of the following year, he undertook a second journey, to the Far West, that was to carry him to Indianapolis, Chicago, St. Louis, and finally on to California, though James was never to find the time or energy to write up the material from this second journey.

Despite these extensive movements throughout the country of his birth and the attention that James lavishes on so many representative sites and incidents, *The American Scene* is not essentially a work of travel literature. Travel is merely the pretext for what amounts, as so many of its admirers have attested—from Edmund Wilson, Leon Edel, and Alan Trachtenberg to Irving Howe, Lawrence Holland, and, now, Ross Posnock—to an extended essay (Auden called it "a prose poem of the first order"[7]) in cultural criticism. But *The American Scene* is unlike most other works in the genre of cultural criticism because of the radical character of its self-reflexivity; what sets it apart from so many other examples of this genre is the depth of its self-absorption with its own critical processes. (In one of the more remarkable treatments of *The American Scene*, Wright Morris has insisted that, in terms of its grasp of its subject matter, it is second only to *Democracy in*

America.) Travel in *The American Scene* is transformed into a trope for what the Victorian interpreter becomes in the American twentieth century: a kind of tourist or alien in his own country who is compelled to look for meanings in scenes or situations that by conventional or traditional critical stratagems refuse to produce or yield them. The cultural critic is therefore obliged to experiment or improvise methodologically by pragmatically converting such refusals into a key that will unlock the meanings those scenes conceal, disguise, or altogether efface. This is as much as to say that the meaning the interpreter naturally seeks in these scenes turns out to be related to the experience of its frustrated discovery, that experience of frustration itself, in turn, becoming the clue to the meaning of whatever was to be discovered in the first place.

Such pragmatic conversions carry with them, however, a corollary temptation. This is the temptation to condescension, a temptation that occurs when the critic correlates the need for such pragmatic conversions with a belief that they are occasioned by some deficiency in the material that requires them, and then goes on to presume that such deficiencies can be compensated for, as it were, only by the critic's own discriminations. Here criticism is seduced into taking on the role of cultural rehabilitation; what the culture can't provide for itself because of its apparent poverty of being, the critic can make up for through his or her sensitivity to cultural poverty. Much of James's accomplishment in this text, over and above the acuteness of his various judgments and the accuracy of his prophecies, derives from his twofold rhetorical ability to convert what looks like cultural deprivation into critical opportunities and to transform opportunities for critical rereading into incentives for developing a different kind of cultural interpretation altogether.

No one has perceived the complexities of this predicament, or James's response to them, more clearly than Wright Morris, when he concluded: "Caught between the past and the future, immersed to the eyes in the destructive element, [Henry] remained true to his genius—one on whom nothing, no, *nothing*, was lost."[8] Yet Morris's positioning of James's book between a past that is already over and a future that has not yet appeared is nowhere near as suggestive as the location he defines for James in the present. This is a present that is empty of registered significance, bereft of inherited content, a present that deprives the traditional critic of his or her subject. Such a present thus poses a grave crisis for criticism itself because it calls the critic's very identity into question. Left without any real subject to interrogate, the critic is forced back on the question itself, the question of his or her own identity in a situation now conceived to refute it. The only way of overcoming this situation is by somehow managing to turn the question itself inside out. If the absence or disappearance of a suitable subject raises new questions about the critic's identity, cannot the questioning of critical identity itself in the circumstances of its newly problematic status become a fresh stimulus for interpretive inquiry, perhaps even a new source of critical models?

This is precisely the "turn" that James himself negotiates when, in response to the way the American scene thwarts his traditional critical expectations, he, in effect, transforms Morris's "nothing" into a new subject of, as well as motivation for, cultural criticism itself. This "interpretive turn" amounts to seeing what can be learned from the failure of his materials to lend themselves to critical account. By converting what appears to be a failure of criticism into a new interpretive occasion, Henry finds himself in possession of a method, actually a cultural hermeneutic, that is prepared to view "nothing" heuristically as opposed to censoriously, that is, to take full account of, as Wallace Stevens writes in "The Snowman," "Nothing that is not there and the nothing that is."[9] A different way to put this would be to say that James elects to relinquish the intellectual shelter of the Victorian critic by turning the genteel ideology of critical superiority against itself.

At the beginning of *The American Scene* Henry seems prepared to adopt the mantle of genteel superiority. His visit had been arranged not solely to soothe sentiments of nostalgia but also to bring to bear upon the land of his origin the critical fruits of more than twenty years of expatriate critical experience. James knew that his gaze would be selective and that there would be many elements of his subject before which it would remain inert, but he was absolutely confident that the freshness of his eye after long absence, together with the acuteness of his judgments from long familiarity, guaranteed a heightened capacity for cultural perception and moral discrimination.

> I made no scruple of my conviction that I should understand and should care better and more than the most earnest of visitors, and yet that I should vibrate with more curiosity—on the extent of ground, that is, on which I might aspire to intimate intelligence at all—than the pilgrim with the longest list of questions, the sharpest appetite for explanations and the largest exposure to mistakes.[10]

Thus, when he announced his willingness to take a stand on his gathered impressions, stating that it was for them and them only that he returned, he was confessing to his belief in the complete reliability of his sense of his subject and of its aspects and prospects. He was prepared to go to the stake for his impressions, as he said, because as a critic he believed in their general validity and soundness. The confidence he invested in them was, as he put it, "a sign of the value that I both in particular and in general attach to them and . . . have endeavoured to preserve for them in this transcription."[11]

Whatever else Henry may have meant by this admission, it was also perfectly consistent with the aesthetic he had already developed as a novelist, an aesthetic that made the most of appearances not for their own sake alone but for the sake of the reality underneath. Believing that the artist's responsibility is to unfold all that is implicit in the "given case," James had found the chief challenge for the novelist to lie in creating conditions in which the potentialities of any "given case," its possibilities and extended implications, could most beautifully and instructively reveal themselves.

But what, in this instance, was the "given case," and how could it be represented? Henry defines the given case in *The American Scene* as the spectacle of a society seeking the shortcut of money to produce those things usually obtainable only through what he called" roundabout experience, . . . troublesome history, [and] the long, the immitigable process of time."[12] This was a case that could only be represented narratively, he decided, in the form of a drama whose *donnée* might then be described as "the great adventure of a society reaching out into the apparent void for the amenities, the consummations, after having earnestly gathered in so many of the preparations and necessities." Much of the interest in this drama, James reasoned, would naturally depend on whether the void was only apparent or actually real, with what did or didn't lurk beneath the appearance of this vacancy "to thicken the plot from stage to stage and to intensify the action." The task for the dramatist, then, was something more than "to gouge an interest *out* of the vacancy"; it was to "gouge it with tools of price, even as copper and gold and diamonds are extracted, by elaborate processes, from earth-sections of small superficial expression."[13]

To put this in slightly different terms, James was redefining his critical and artistic task as a determination of what the "vacancy," as it were, cost; of how much one was obliged to ante up—morally, emotionally, materially, and above all, aesthetically—to satisfy the needs of the spirit through the shortcut of money. What was this, however, but pragmatism with a vengeance? Henry was not interested in what the "vacancy" that constitutes "the American scene" amounted to in and of itself but in what Americans had been obliged "pay" for taking the shortcut of money to satisfy the needs of the spirit. Here was a subject that held promise "of the highest entertainment."[14]

But this was a promise that could be fulfilled, that would take on intensity, only as—and if—Henry could exploit the second element so crucial to his own aesthetic. This second element was the presence of one of those centers of consciousness that are endowed, as James had so memorably put it in the preface to *The Princess Casamassima*, with "the power to be finely aware and richly responsible."[15] Indeed, as James had said, "their being finely aware—as Hamlet and Lear, say, are finely aware—*makes* absolutely the intensity of their adventure, gives the maximum of sense to what befalls them."[16] Yet in reference to the new situation of American culture at the beginning of the twentieth century, such a consciousness was likely to find its greatest adventure not in delimiting or refining its range of discriminations, as Posnock points out, so much as in expanding and complicating them, really subtlizing them.

Thus, whatever was to be sacrificed by way of intensity, the intensity normally achieved through these centers of consciousness was to be more than made up for in a greater heterogeneity of perspective. In other words, to be "one of those persons on whom nothing is lost," as James noted in "The Art of Fiction," was in this instance to acquire a consciousness whose aesthetic vividness depended as much on gestures of self-dispersion as of self-containment, of self-pollution or at least of self-exposure as of self-refinement.[17] Yet this was still to ensure that the central consciousness, here defined as the "restless analyst," would contribute to a work of serious cultural critique some of the more obvious aesthetic effects of concentration and heightening that distinguish great art. Thus, like James's other, less discursive, writing, *The American Scene* would demonstrate not only how art makes life by creating the conditions in which life can be most ideally exhibited, but also how art enhances life by displaying, through such conditions, what is actualized within life and also what is merely potential to life. The realization of this project, then, would allow James to do more than refashion himself rhetorically; it would also enable him to delineate a dramatic structure in which he could fashion a literary performance of his own special kind of rhetorical pragmatism.

Nonetheless, when James attempted to employ this aesthetic on the situations, the objects, the events, that confronted him on his return to America, he immediately found himself faced with an unexpected interpretive dilemma. This dilemma was defined by the fact that the *donnée*, the "given case," resisted being read. James had encountered such difficulties before in the United States, as he had amply illustrated already in his book on Hawthorne, but here the problem was different. Here it was no longer a problem of finding his materials thin or opaque—or even, as his twenty years of European expatriation might have prepared him to feel, discovering them to be trivial and weightless—but instead of finding them hollow, empty, virtually blank. Seeking to discern the buried significance, the hidden meaning, behind appearances, he was immediately brought up short by the discovery that many of the appearances he most wanted to understand in America, that he most desired to fathom, lacked any buried significance or hidden meaning at all; and this created a critical crisis of the first magnitude:

> To be at all critically, or as we have been fond of calling it, analytically, minded—over and beyond an inherent love of the general many-colored picture of things—is to be subject to the superstition that objects and places, coherently grouped, disposed for human use and addressed to it, must have a sense of their own, a mystic meaning proper to themselves to give out: to give out, that is, to the participant at once so interested and so detached as to be moved to a report of the matter. That perverse person is obliged to take it for a working theory that the essence of almost any settled aspect of anything may be extracted by the chemistry of criticism, and may give us its right name, its formula, for use.[18]

Yet James was to discover again and again that instead of proffering such a sense, his material only confounded the exertions of the sense-maker. Appearances seemed to want for any intrinsic meaning, to be void of content; and from that moment, the critic "begins," James reasoned,

> and quite consciously, to go to pieces; it being the prime business and the high honor of the painter of life always to *make* a sense—and to make it most in proportion as the immediate aspects are loose or confused. The last thing decently permitted him is to recognize incoherence—to recognize it, that is, as baffling, though of course he may present and portray it, in all its richness, *for* incoherence.[19]

But James's critical difficulties did not end with his discovery of the apparent lack of a subject to interpret in America. If his problems had merely amounted to a sense of something absent, the critic could have been asked to supply the wanted element. But here the problem of absence had taken on a distinctly modern, even postmodern, connotation. Given that there seemed to be nothing behind or beneath the materials of American life by means of which the discerning observer might infer their significance, some more deeply interfused presence of the sort that used to be designated, say, by the term "tradition," one confronted in America a situation that struck

James as historically unprecedented, since "the living fact," he readily perceived, could now be made to stand for virtually almost anything.

James came to this realization almost at the outset of his visit, when he was confronted with what he termed "the New Jersey condition." The "New Jersey condition," which James was in truth to encounter again and again in his travels throughout the States, defined a situation in which material circumstances specifically designed for show, for display, for spectacle, were made to suffer the embarrassment of somehow being conscious at the same time of their own paucity of inner substance, their own dearth of supportive content. In New Jersey this situation was represented by an abundance of new homes of monstrous, indeed florid, proportions asking, even existing, to be admired but somehow, at the same time, waiting "for their justification, waiting for the next clause in the sequence, waiting in short for life, for time, for interest, for character, for identity to come to them."[20] Furnishing an instance of the expensive being converted into a power unto itself, but "a power unguided, undirected, practically unapplied," the New Jersey condition constituted an example of what money looks like "exerting itself in a void that could make it no response, that had nothing . . . to offer in return." All that could be accomplished pragmatically by a game like this which fell so far short of its goal was "the air of publicity, publicity as a condition, as a doom, from which there could be no appeal."[21]

Leaving aside the perspicaciousness of James's description of "publicity" in the very same terms that in the late twentieth century we might now use to define the condition of "celebrity," this display of money forcing itself upon circumstances that have no opportunity or reason, so to speak, to believe in themselves raised for James the all-important question of manners. Yet having just barely raised the question of manners, this display as quickly then proceeded to close off that very question by revealing that in the absence of any saving complexity, of any achieved protection, what is usually meant by manners couldn't survive, "and that nothing, accordingly, no image, no presumption of constituted relations, possibilities, amenities, in the social, the domestic order, was inwardly projected."[22]

James was able to risk such judgments this early in his book only because he could rely on his readers' knowledge of what more traditional societies normally do for their members, particularly for their more socially and economically privileged members. Designed to make the future as interesting as the past, they take great pains to provide forms, functions, customs, and continuities equal to any "massiveness of private ease," to make social relations, in other words, seem organic.[23] But in the United States, James felt, everything once associated with "the old conscious commemorated life" was being swept away by the "huge democratic broom," severing all the newer social practices and institutions from any structure of deeper meaning, from any cultural ground.[24]

Thus, the same "struggle in the void" that one encountered elsewhere in America was equally evident in the upper atmosphere of high society itself, where the entire "social organism" floundered "all helplessly, more or less floated by its immense good-will and the splendour of its immediate environment, but betrayed by its paucity of real resource."[25]

For James this impression—which he acquired at a New York dinner-party "of the most genial intention"—testified neither to the bankruptcy of values in America nor to their disappearance, so much as to what he called their "redistribution and reconsecration." While many European values were obviously missing, James had no interest in decrying their loss. Rather, the whole of his effort was to determine which values proposed themselves as "felt solutions of the social continuity."[26]

As James scanned possible options, it seemed to him that overriding all other values in importance was a marked unwillingness on the part of most citizens to consent consciously to any privation. James went on to describe this unwillingness as "the theory . . . of the native spirit," for which he found greatest evidence in the natives' desire for things of whose existence or even possibility they were as yet unaware.[27] In such a social world, James realized, the purpose of culture quickly becomes reduced to the service of these future awakenings, but this service can only be performed if the cultural medium itself is prepared to be stretched to an inordinate thinness. Thus, the elasticity of the cultural medium in America became itself a kind of marvel:

> One becomes aware . . . wherever one turns, both of the tension and the resistance; everything and every one, all objects and elements, all systems, arrangements, institutions, functions, persons, reputations, give the sense of their pulling hard at the india-rubber: almost always, wonderfully, without breaking it off, yet never quite with the effect of causing it to lie thick."[28]

While for James the interesting fact in this lay in how thinness seemed to do on this side of the Atlantic what thickness did—and, to some extent, does—on the other, the interesting fact for the contemporary reader is more likely to be found in how accurately James predicted the shift we are currently undergoing from a modern culture of consumption to something like a postmodern culture of simulation.

Reflecting on this dearth of interior connotation and implication that seemed to meet him at every turn in America, James was led to a double perception. The first had to do with the dependence of the scene, any scene, on its interpreter; before any situation would disclose even a portion of its possible meaning, one was compelled to read a good deal into it: "The observer, like a fond investor, must spend on it, boldly, ingeniously, to make it pay; and it may often thus remind one of the wonderful soil of California, which is nothing when left to itself in the fine weather, but becomes everything conceivable under the rainfall."[29] The second perception had to do with the necessity to be selective. If a single case could be made to speak for many others, the interpretive investor must exercise great care to find just those few whose "formed features," whose "signs of character," were "mature enough and firm enough to promise a savour or to suffer handling."[30]

Events and images in *The American Scene* thus tend to dispose themselves for James's perception very much in the manner by which he was struck with the culture of the hotel. While the outward elements of the American hotel were perfectly plain for anyone to observe and required no going behind or beyond them, as they would have in Europe, to infer the "multitudinous, complicated life" they concealed, the innerness of the American hotel struck James as nothing but "itself that life," an institution that comprised in its mere externalities, its manifest outward appearance, for a very significant majority of the people who could avail themselves of its benefactions, "the richest form of existence."[31] What in effect the hotel in America seemed to say is that its significance is written on its face and that, as a consequence, the "restless analyst" is free to "make of it what [he or she] can!" To this revelation, James could only reply:

> "Yes, I see how you are, God knows— . . . for nothing in the world is easier to see, even in all the particulars. But what does it *mean* to be as you are? . . . Distinct as you are, you are not even definite, and it would be terrible not to be able to suppose that you are as yet but an installment, a current number, like that of the morning paper, a specimen of a type in course of serialization. . . ."[32]

By seeing a representative American institution like the hotel as a text whose editions or versions have about them, almost necessarily, the air, like New York skyscrapers and Pullman cars, of the "perpetually provisional," James achieves here and elsewhere a certain interpretive as well as rhetorical leverage that keeps his inquiry going; it is as simple as noting in conclusion that "the particulars still to be added either to you or to them form an insoluble question."[33]

While this convinced Henry that America is a bad country to be stupid in, it also pointed him toward a way to "work" his impressions. Essentially, this critical or interpretive method amounted to a procedure well understood by his brother William but ill-appreciated by William himself in Henry's own practice of it. This was a procedure that recommended looking for the meaning of one's impressions not only behind or beneath one's experience of them but also within the tensions and frustrations, the transparencies and opacities, of that experience itself. So construed, the meanings of Henry's impressions were not be dissociated from the difficulties he suffered in obtaining them, in sorting them out, and in absorbing them. Indeed, his experience of those difficulties was intimately tied up not only with what they made him think but also with the way they made him feel. Thus, to record and convey those impressions, much less to appropriate them critically, involved something more than—and something different from—merely registering their sense and significance; it required as well an exacting expression of the alternations and ambiguities in his own developing felt awareness as he pursued their various and often contrary meanings. This kind of reflection called for what William had already defined as an "ambulatory" style, where one's movement toward a potential object of knowledge is dictated not by the content so much as by the impulse of the idea it communicates to us.

This is, of course, an almost exact description of the reflective style Henry had already perfected in his first major phase, in *The Wings of the Dove* and *The Golden Bowl* no less than *The Ambassadors*. Premised on the belief that reality is made, not found, constructed, not discovered, the ambulatory style that Henry shared with, but also carried further than, William holds "that the greatest threat to the inquiring mind is the temptation to interrupt the process of its own continuous constructions and reconstructions by arresting and isolating some moment from the ongoing process [of reflection] and taking it for an image of the whole."[34] Instead, Henry wanted a method capable of rendering the texture of the intellect feeling its way toward clarifications before they disintegrate again, as they usually do, into confusion and uncertainty; that is, he wanted—and he found—a way of representing the life of consciousness in the process of forming and dissolving and reforming itself again, of life in action.

One can discern a good example of this interpretive method and its ambulatory style of reflection operating in miniature in James's responses to the "queerness," as it seemed to him, of Cape Cod. Cape Cod's impression of "queerness" resulted from the fact that the buried life of the community appeared to hide itself entirely from the eye of the curious inquirer. As James reported it, what one saw was merely a facade of "little white houses" and "elegant elms, feebler and more feathery here than further inland" that disclosed nothing of the social existence secreted within. Constituting "a delightful triumph of impressionism" that reminded him of a "painted Japanese silk," Cape Cod nevertheless succeeded in frustrating all his efforts to read the scene more profoundly, to penetrate beneath its delightful facade, until he realized that part of the deeper meaning for which he was searching in the scene lay in the way it continually thwarted his attempts to find it. Hence the "story-seeker" in this scene was likely to discover the essential thread of his narrative precisely and concretely in the apparent lack of one; or, as James stated it more forcefully, "the constituted blankness was the whole business, and one's opportunity was all, thereby, for a study of exquisite emptiness."[35]

But this method is more than an interpretive technique in *The American Scene;* it is also a strategy of emotional survival that grows out of James's deepest personal anguish. Consider, for example, the scene of cultural aporia that confronted him on his return, for the second time within less than a month, to the house in Boston on Ashburton Place where he had spent two memorable years inaugurating his literary career. What he discovers on his return is not the facade of a house preserving the secrets, as he assumed it would, of its consecrated life, like "the scent lingering in a folded handkerchief," but "a gaping void, the brutal effacement, at a stroke, of every related object, of the whole precious past."[36] James likens this experience to the bottom falling out of his own biography and feels himself plunging "backward into space without meeting anything."[37] A most disorienting and, for Henry, deeply distressing, even tragic, experience, it also represents something else. The discovery of his own past under erasure signifies his personal connection with all that he sees going on around him in America, and he thus realizes that it provides, as he terms it, the "whole figure" for what his book is about: not just another interpretation of America, but an extended exercise in how, in circumstances of rapidly increasing, and self-induced, interpretive effacement, to go about reading the "nothing," or no-thing, that America had become, and perhaps in some sense always was.

Merely extend this hermeneutic procedure to many, if not most, of the interpretive sites James explores in his book and one can gauge something of the breadth and daring of James's method in *The American Scene.* Whether because of the constituted vacancy of the materials themselves or because they are merely gilded with a magnificence, a pretension, that awaits a legitimation that shall never come, James finds himself almost everywhere, like some proto-deconstructionist, confronted with rupture, absence, and vacuity exactly where he expected to find continuity, presence, fullness. This thematic becomes the more prominent as James travels southward. Moving into the "citronic belt," he discovers a land "all incongruously Protestantized," a "Methodism of the orange and the palm" whose very air, in its soft promise of no bruises, strikes him as distinctive, strange, even queer.[38] The only explanation he can furnish for this "softness" is an absence of friction that produces, in Baltimore and elsewhere, a false impression of safety concealing a cheerful emptiness underneath. This lack of discrimination bespeaks a desire for simplification that becomes, the longer one is exposed to it, inordinately monotonous.

Moving on to Mt. Vernon, James encounters what appears to be an extraordinary scene of presence rather than absence, a triumph, as he calls it, of "*communicated* importance." But the moment one asks in what this importance exactly consists, the impression it is supposed to make begins to fade. Mediated by the extraordinary beauty of the site, the impression has everything to do with the sense of Washington himself and is, on the face of it, easily read. It is the impression of "the resting, as distinguished from the restless, consciousness of public service consummately rendered."[39] But this impression proves so affecting only because the demonstration is made, albeit in a manner unconscious to the scene itself, on such a minor scale. Hence the "restless analyst" can detect in this scene something that, unbeknownst to itself, can be read out of it only because it can be read into it: namely, the touching spectacle of the "pale, bleeding Past, in a patched homespun suit," gratefully receiving the token appreciation of "the bloated Present."[40]

However, the most intricate and devastating exemplification of this disproportion between the modesty of the past's resources and the immodesty of the present's demands on them—as well as the most relentless and extended of James's pragmatic readings of the "Nothing that is not there and the nothing that is"—comes in his interpretation of Richmond, Virginia. As the capital of the Confederacy, Richmond is rich with associations both personal and historical. Two of his brothers had fought in the Civil War, and the city stood in what James could call, not without a little emotion, a "vast blood-drenched circle."[41] Yet as he contemplates the "tragic ghost-haunted city," what astonishes him most is the absence of any "registered consciousness of the past."[42] Rather, the scene indicates for James "no discernable consciousness, registered or unregistered, of anything." Richmond is simply a blank, a void; and yet it is with this impression, precisely, James notes, that "the great emotion was to come"[43] The meanness of reference, the poverty of recollected resources, not only belongs to the scene, but constitutes much, if not all, of its content, forcing James to ask himself whether this poverty was not, in fact, "the very essence of the old southern idea."[44] As James continues to meditate on the significance of this impression, he suddenly conjures up the image of a blighted or stricken figure seated uncomfortably in an invalid chair and fixing him with eyes that are half defiant and half deprecating. The whole impression is that of a person bent on maintaining appearances and, above all, a tone, "the historic 'high' tone, in an excruciating posture."[45]

James is initially at a loss to determine the full significance of this figure, so devoted to maintaining appearances in the midst of destitution, until later, when he visits the Richmond Museum and contemplates the heroism of its charming little curatrix. There amidst "the historic, the pathetic poverty of the exhibition"—"these documentary chambers . . . contained, so far as I can remember, not a single object of beauty, scarce one in fact that was not altogether ugly (so void were they of intrinsic charm), and . . . spoke only of the absence of means and of taste, of communication and resource"—James encounters a person who has survived one of the most "unrecorded and undepicted" social revolutions, in proportion to its magnitude, that ever was."[46]

Having suffered the disintegration of the old order and the indignities of defeat, this woman now gathers about herself a pitiful collection of faded tokens from the past to assuage her unrelenting sense of injury: "The sorry objects about were old Confederate documents, already sallow with time, framed letters, orders, autographs, extracts, tatters of a paper-currency in the last stages of vitiation; together with faded portraits of faded worthies, primitive products of the camera, the crayon, the brush. . . ."[47] Evincing everywhere something James describes—and later finds in Charleston as well—as "the nursing attitude," he notes that what makes it so remarkable is that it is so unavailing. This ritual "reversion of the starved spirit to the things of the heroic age" provides no permanent salve for the soul; here, in fact, the starvation of the spirit is unrelievable.[48]

Faced by the old curatrix with this spectacle of a "great melancholy void" that must be continuously repeopled and regarnished season after season, James finally comes upon the key that will unlock the historical riddle of blighted emptiness, of abject blankness, that first confronted him on his initial arrival in Richmond. James can now see that "it is the poverty that *is*, exactly, historic: once take it for that and it puts on vividness." And with the solution of the historical riddle of the poverty comes the clarification of the meaning of the melancholic void. For the despondency of the little curatrix is "more than the melancholy of a lost cause"; it is the melancholy "of a cause that could never have been gained."[49]

When James eventually moves on to Charleston, the feminized "charm to cherish" sedimented within this melancholy becomes even more explicitly linked to the promotion of "some eloquent antithesis" that seems almost to rise out of the Yoknapatawpha novels of William Faulkner: "just to make us say that whereas the ancient order was masculine, fierce and mustachioed, the present is a sort of sick lioness who is so visibly parted with her teeth and claws that we may patronizingly walk all around her."[50] This image, in fact, crystallizes a more precise impression not only of Charleston but of the secessionist South, as well as a kind of vacant cage, a cage once capable of emitting sounds of rattling bars that could be heard as far away as the North but now capable only of evoking the same kind of question one finds oneself asking at the end of *Absalom, Absalom!*: "How, in an at all complex, a 'great political,' society, can *everything* so have gone?"[51]

Severe as is this indictment, James's targets of censure in *The American Scene* are by no means restricted to the South. In New England, the depleted, forlorn look of "the undiscriminated, tangled actual" bears a striking resemblance to the portraits of desolation that Robert Frost would soon be painting in "An Old Man's Winter Night," "Bereft," and "Home Burial." In New York, he encounters desolation of another kind in the spectacle of conspicuous waste, of sham refinement, that seems to him so much of a piece with the American scale of enterprise, what he calls "the American postulate": "To make so much money that you won't, that you don't, 'mind' anything—that is absolutely, I think, the main American formula."[52] Philadelphia in its turn presents to James's imagination the double image of a sane society organized for civil discourse and discrimination and a pestilential city "organized all for plunder and rapine"; the interest of James's treatment derives from the way he sees these two aspects of Philadelphia existing so congenially alongside one other. In Washington, on the other hand, he discovers a city that pretends that nobody is in business, that the market doesn't matter, so that it can give itself over wholly to conversation about itself as, precisely, the "city of conversation."

In all this, James's judgments can be extraordinarily harsh, but his sentiments generally tend to move in the opposite direction. For interwoven with the evidence of distaste and disapproval in *The American Scene* is a generosity of judgment not at all inconsistent with James's overall pragmatic desire to give almost everything that comes within his notice, as Edmund Wilson long ago remarked, every benefit of the doubt. This is rather wonderfully dramatized when James gets to Florida and confronts an American type that might well have struck him as perhaps its most vulgar modern contribution to the human strand. This is the "drummer" or salesman who seems to stand out from all other kinds of Americans because of "the strange crudity of their air of commercial truculence, on being exactly as 'low' as they liked."[53] Yet as James contemplates their situation further, he quickly realizes that the distinguishing mark of their obviousness, of their transparency, is precisely their liability and the source of their pathos. At one and the same time more exposed than anyone else he had met in America, they are yet less capable of bearing it:

> For they hadn't *asked*, when one reflected, to be almost the only figures in the social landscape—hadn't wanted the fierce light to beat *all* on themselves. They hadn't actively usurped the appearance of carrying on life without the aid of any sort from other *kinds* of persons, other types, presences, classes. If these others were absent it wasn't *their* fault. . . .[54]

In the end, then, drummers are treated more like objects of pathos than objects of ridicule because they have to carry by themselves, like the American woman, so much of the burden of social intercourse while remaining "unrelated to any merciful modifying terms of the great social proposition."[55]

This is not to deny that James's observant eye possessed blind spots, even moral cataracts. Chief among them are some of his passages on African Americans which, even when they exhibit a measure of sympathy with the plight of Southern blacks, still display an all-too-familiar insensitivity not only to the suffering but also to the repression of former slaves in the South. Thus, while James can praise *The Souls of Black Folk* as the best book to come out of the South in many years, he never considers how Du Bois's book might have radically altered his own perspective on America's materialism. Hence what potentially could have been, as Kenneth Warren describes it, "one of the signal moments in American literary history" was lost.[56] Had he read Du Bois with greater care, he would have seen how his own repudiation of America's rampant commercialism must be coupled with a critique like Du Bois's of America's cancerous racism. James is quick to discern the hatred toward blacks that he detects in the smiling eyes of a young white Virginian: "It came to me that, though he wouldn't have hurt a Northern fly, there were things (ah, we had touched on some of these!) that all fair, engaging, smiling, as he stood there, he would have done to a Southern negro." But he is both obtuse and callous when he remarks on how little aptitude African American porters and waiters display for the civilities of personal service without ever wondering whether their indifference about the work might have had something to do with the fact that there was little else blacks could do in post–Civil War America.[57] Where his brother William had on several occasions gone on record to denounce lynching and other acts of violence against blacks, Henry's response to what he could readily and accurately sense to be the cruelty of white feelings toward black people was that there was nothing, given the horrors of the situation, that the nonresident could say or do to improve them: "the non-resident might well feel themselves indeed, after a little, appointed to silence, and, with any delicacy, see their duty quite elsewhere."[58]

Despite the fact that James took the trouble to visit Ellis Island and found himself genuinely disturbed by the way the experience of immigration itself seemed to bleach out of the native character of immigrant peoples so many of their most distinguishing and admirable virtues, his comments on America's most recent arrivals are scarcely less condescending. Yet it is in his various remarks about Jews, and the swarming life of the ghetto in New York City, that James's strongest sense of ambivalence about the effects of the melting pot become evident. In addition to observations at the beginning of *The American Scene* about the *nouveau riche* appearance of the homes of German Jews in New Jersey—"which was borne out by the accent, loud, assertive, yet benevolent withal, with which they confessed to their extreme expensiveness"—or his reaction to the smell of the Yiddish theatre in New York, the Jewish tenements remind him of a zoo full of squirming monkeys and squirrels. This impression leads him to ask, not without a trace of irony that carries more than a trace of anti-Semitism, whether the spectacle before him fits the description of what has been called the New Jerusalem. On the other hand, James remarks with apparent admiration on "the unsurpassed strength of the Jewish race," which makes "the individual Jew more of a concentrated person, savingly possessed of everything that is in him, than any other human noted at random—or is it simply, rather, that the unsurpassed strength of the race permits of the chopping into myriads of fine fragments without loss of race-quality?"[59] Or, again, when he contemplates what the "deeps and complexities" of this Yiddish world mean for the fate of the English language "as literature has hitherto known it," he can only recoil "at this all-unconscious impudence of the agency of future ravage."[60]

Yet when he measures the prospect of multiplying this much ethnic diversity and at the same time tries to imagine how it will be socially assimilated, then compares this to the economic "weight of the new remorseless monopolies," these reflections wring from him the tragically accurate observation that "there is such a thing, in the United States, it is hence to be inferred, as freedom to grow up to be blighted, and it may be the only freedom in store for the smaller fry of future generations."[61]

Given such mixed, and sometimes unattractive, reactions to America's experiments in what we now call multiculturalism, James's indulgence elsewhere of precisely those things that might have been expected to offend the values and tastes of a person who believed that "the highest luxury of all, the supremely expensive thing, is constituted privacy," seems only that much more remarkable.[62] And nowhere is this indulgence, though not unmixed with criticism, more apparent than in the closing pages of the text, where James finally attempts to take the full measure of his subject. His evaluation turns on what he calls the "Margin" in America, meaning that limitless perimeter "by which the total of American life, huge as it already appears, is still so surrounded as to represent, for the mind's eye on a general view, but a scant central flotilla huddled as for very fear of the fathomless depth of water, the too formidable future, on the so much vaster lake of the materially possible."[63] Not unlike the "mild, benignant" air of the South, the "Margin" represents a cultural horizon of "immense fluidity" "through which almost any good might come"—or any evil.[64] In its capacity to subsume all ethical categories, the "Margin" constitutes what James simply calls, in echo of his brother's use of the same term, the "looming mass of the *more*, the more and more to come."[65]

William meant by his own notion of the "More" something that is, or seems to be, continuous with the life of human consciousness itself but which may operate in the universe outside it, or at least is nonidentical with it; something that many of the more traditional religions associate with a personal god or gods but which other people merely link with some tendency assumed to be inherent in the fundamental structure of things as a whole. By contrast, Henry tends to identify the "More," at least in *The American Scene*, with the apparently infinite potential for the material expansion and enhancement of life in the United States—its "one all positive appearance . . . the perpetual increase of everything, the growth of the immeasurable muchness." A term equivalent to what other Americans have meant by the wilderness, the "Margin" serves Henry interpretively as the

American imaginary, "the deep sea into which [this] seeker after conclusions must cast his nets."[66]

When Henry finally gets around to casting his nets on his way back north from Florida, his almost instinctive reaction is to revert to traditional standards by arguing that the whole issue of evaluation can be reduced to a question of moral and aesthetic need. The need in America, he predictably senses, is simply for greater and different values than America itself can supply. But James knows that this perception can lead to very different responses. If some of America's citizens are likely to react to an inadequate supply of acceptable values in America by trying to create new ones, others are quite capable of reasoning that if no acceptable values are available in America their appearance must somehow be faked.

As it happens, much of what James reports himself confronting in the United States of 1904 and 1905 amounts to just such fakery, the simulation rather than the substance of values. Therefore, the question of evaluation tends to reduce itself to the devilishly ticklish issue of what to make of the charm of the "boundless immensity" that reveals itself from a Pullman car window when that very immensity is presumed by the culture to which the Pullman car itself belongs—and which the Pullman car is itself designed to represent—to exist solely for the sake of its pretensions to charm. The rumble of the Pullman's wheels, as if speaking for America as a whole, seems ready to plead, almost in apology: "See what I'm making of all this—see what I'm making, what making!"[67] But the connoisseur of appearances in James needs no reminders or directives. What America has in fact been making for so many years has administered only, as he says, "to the triumph of the superficial and the apotheosis of the raw."[68] Nor is James insensible of what all this making of the materially possible has done for America's original native inhabitants so cruelly dispossessed by it, who now have a perfect right, he adds, to indict America "for every disfigurement and every violence, for every wound with which you have caused the face of the land to bleed."[69]

But the modernist, or more accurately, the proleptic postmodernist, in James is not content to leave it at that. To comprehend America from the inside rather than the outside, to feel with America rather than simply to feel for it, and particularly for its disenfranchised peoples, he must place himself within the center of America's vision of itself, which amounts to repositioning himself rhetorically within the vision of the so-called "Margin." But to view America from within the perspective provided by the "Margin," from within the cultural imaginary it has created for itself, is to see a good deal more than simply what America has made, and is making, or even will make, so much of it hideous and banal; it is also to see what America has left unmade, if not still, perhaps, unimagined. At this point, however, America's "pretended message of civilization" is suddenly transformed from a history of "ravage," destruction, and displacement into "a colossal recipe for the *creation* of arrears, and of such as can but remain forever out of hand":

> You touch the great lonely land—as one feels it still to be—only to plant upon it some ugliness about which, never dreaming of the grace of apology or contrition, you then proceed to brag with a cynicism all your own. You convert the large and noble sanities that I see around me, you convert them one after the other to crudities, to invalidities, hideous and unashamed; and you so leave them to add to the number of the myriad aspects you simply spoil, of the myriad unanswerable questions that you scatter about as some monstrous unnatural mother might leave a family of unfathered infants on doorsteps or in waiting-rooms. . . . When nobody cares or notices or suffers, by all one makes out, when no displeasure, by what one can see, is ever felt or ever registered, why shouldn't you, you may indeed ask, be as much in your right as you need? But in that fact itself, that fact of the vast general unconsciousness and indifference, loom, for any restless analyst who may come along, the accumulation, on your hands, of the unretrieved and the irretrievable!"[70]

In shifting the basis of his evaluation from the sociopolitical and environmental offenses America has already committed to the historical debts it has yet to repay, James is attempting to assess America from a perspective that is internal rather than external to itself. To judge America not alone in terms of deformities already produced but as well in relation to obligations continuously deferred and possibilities recurrently postponed is to see America more nearly in terms of the inconsistencies, lapses, and contradictions inherent within its own imagination of itself than in terms of the failures, blunders, and transgressions visible to an outsider. James's immanent critique thus transforms a potential site of shame into an actual scene of solidarity and beyond. By converting the rhetoric of condescension into a discourse of answerability, James succeeds in the morally arduous task of feeling *with* America rather than merely feeling *for* it, and to feel for it though much of America doesn't seem to know how to, or even that it should, feel for itself.

PART THREE

Pragmatist

Rereadings

Chapter 5

Religion, Rorty, and the Recent Revival of Pragmatism

Religion, it must be said, has not played a very significant role, except perhaps negatively, in the recent renewal of pragmatism. There are no doubt many reasons for this, but none is more important than the responsibility that Richard Rorty deservedly bears for helping to promote this revival and the connection he has made between the development of pragmatism and liberalism's project of disenchanting the world religiously. Rorty has actually come up with two different genealogies for pragmatism, both of which narrativize its development as a secular coming-of-age story. In the first, which is to be found in *Consequences of Pragmatism*, pragmatism lies at the end of a process of de-divinization. The process began with metaphysical idealism's attempt to relocate the sphere of ultimate reality within human experience rather than beyond it, then led to Romanticism's claim that if ultimate reality is now immanent rather than transcendent, its meanings can be described in more than one vocabulary, and finally wound up with pragmatism's assertion that these different vocabularies are ultimately no more than different ways of expressing what we need and sometimes get.[1] In the second genealogy, which appears in his *Contingency, Irony, and Solidarity*, this sequence of historical transformations follows a course charted in Hans Blumenberg's *The Legitimacy of the Modern Age*. In this version, the love of God gave way, in the seventeenth century, to the love of truth, then the love of truth gave way, by the end of the eighteenth century, to the quasi-divinity of the self, and eventually the idealist or Romantic love of the self succumbed, toward the end of the nineteenth century and the beginning of the twentieth, to the realization, variously phrased by Nietzsche, Freud, and Wittgenstein, that we now don't need to worship anything at all as divine, whether God, the world, or our own spiritual nature, since, as we can now see, "everything—our language, our conscience, our community —is a product of time and chance."[2] In short, Rorty has traced a history linking the emergence of pragmatism with the arrival of a new antireligious dispensation in the West that has, in effect, emptied the world of intrinsic significance.

It should not go without notice that several of Rorty's own heroes within liberalism would have viewed his proposal to cure us of our dependence on metaphysics so that we can be freed to grapple with the real contingencies of our existence as going too far. Most conspicuous in this regard is, perhaps, Sir Isaiah Berlin who, while sharing Rorty's suspicions of religious authoritarianism, has nonetheless always conceded the validity of humanity's "deep and incurable metaphysical need" for greater moral and spiritual assurance. Using language similar to Rorty's but with a different intent, Berlin has acknowledged that this no doubt basic human desideratum often masks a deep and potentially dangerous "moral and political immaturity," but he has gone on to observe that this only makes it that much more incumbent on us to see to it that this immaturity doesn't get the better of us.[3] Berlin's pragmatic circumspection is a reminder, to paraphrase William James, that there are no intellectual methods to assist one in navigating between the opposite dangers of believing too little and of believing too much; there is only, he added, the intellectual responsibility to face such dangers and to try to hit the right balance between them.

In sounding this theme, James expressed what was to become, more than half a century later and in different terms, a leitmotif in the writing of a number of thinkers from Rorty's own generation, thinkers who struggled to prevent pragmatism from suffering a complete eclipse during the long period when linguistic analysis held complete sway in American philosophy. Easily effaced because the texture and tone of their work was conciliatory, generalizing, and melioristic in an academic environment where asperity, exactitude, and an uncompromising professionalism were much in fashion, philosophers like John E. Smith, Richard J. Bernstein, and John J. McDermott viewed pragmatism not only as a philosophical theory in need of defense but also as an intellectual method capable of keeping open the lines of communication between philosophy and some of the other departments of the intellectual life. Thus Bernstein, for example, sought to press "beyond objectivism and relativism," in the title of his third book, as he explored the ethical, political, and metaphysical horizons that defined the modern and the postmodern.[4] Smith, for his part, took it upon himself in *Reason and God* to stage encounters between philosophy and religion and also to historicize pragmatism by constructing a central place for it within a cultural narrative seeking to define, as he called his most widely known book, "the spirit of American philosophy."[5] And McDermott not only compiled important anthologies that became the chief resource for teaching James and Dewey (as well as Josiah Royce) but also produced two collections of his own essays designed to test the ontological and moral reach of a pragmatist notion of experience.[6]

Without such work—and this is only the tip of the iceberg—it would have been much more difficult than it has proven to be for certain contemporary thinkers to reintroduce the subject of religion into a discussion of pragmatism itself. Yet even now, when the wall of separation has been breached again and again, it still remains the case that many intellectuals continue to persist in the opinion that pragmatism is at the very least indifferent to religion and more likely inhospitable to it, if not downright incompatible with it. This is the argument that John Patrick Diggins has mounted about how pragmatism has betrayed its promise by contributing to the crisis of knowledge and authority associated with secular modernism. A crisis of spiritual disenchantment first identified by Max Weber, it has left us beached in a world of felt absences characterized by, in Diggins's language, "knowledge without truth, power without authority, society without spirit, self without identity, politics without virtue, existence without purpose, history without meaning."[7] Diggins is, of course, shrewd enough to know that this, as he views it, unpleasant, even repugnant, prospect—like the more relaxed and diffident, as well as cynical, postmodernist endorsement and exploitation of such evacuations—is not all that new or, for that matter, all that debilitating. Not only are we now unable to retrieve the epistemological or metaphysical certitudes that have been lost to us forever, but no one familiar with the thinking of America's seventeenth-century Calvinists or some of the Enlightenment thinkers in the eighteenth century needs to be reminded of how unstable and illusory many of those same spiritual certitudes were in the first place.

Diggins thus tends to speak out of both sides of his mouth. On the one hand, he is contemptuous of the antiabsolutist, antifoundationalist, antiessentialist world that secular modernism has brought us—a world where human beings, in their need for a kind of security they can never attain, fashion or refashion identities for themselves that are little more than expressions of the will to power and that can only be countered by a perspective that is suitably ironic, if not cynical. On the other, he has little difficulty reconciling himself to such a spiritually compromised, morally complex world because he believes that in all essential particulars its description has been available to us from the time of the Puritans nearly four centuries ago.[8] Interestingly enough, if Diggins thinks that there is no way of escaping the modern crisis of knowledge and authority into which the pragmatists, both wittingly and unwittingly, have helped thrust us, he is nonetheless confident that his own ability to pass judgment on this crisis—and on pragmatism's complicity with it—has remained uncompromised.

Diggins finds reinforcement for this view in a figure like Henry Adams, who not only assumed that the crisis of modernism was avoidable from the outset but then went on both to pass judgment on the moral and epistemological emptiness of the world it revealed and to anticipate the still more precarious, relativist, poststructuralist universe that Jamesian pluralism subsequently bequeathed to us. This is the universe which, on Diggins's reading, contemporary neopragmatism, principally in the form of Rorty's writing, is so ineffectual in addressing. Adams thus becomes the "quintessential modernist thinker" despite the fact that his extraordinary prescience about the modern crisis of authority and knowledge was matched only by stupefaction about what to do about it. While Adams found himself morally and spiritually stranded at the end of the nineteenth century by the new regime of forces that had rendered his eighteenth-century education, as he confessed, completely obsolete, his sometime friend and colleague William James was developing in the same historical moment a philosophical method and theory of truth designed to help negotiate some of the more hazardous intellectual challenges represented by this new constellation of forces. Diggins, however, will have none of this more conventional narrative. The point of his own story is rather to show that, while James and Dewey believed that rationalism and empiricism actually lead to meaning, clarity, and wholeness, Adams perceived that their true destination lies in the way of confusion, frustration, and negation.

As Diggins must know, Reinhold Niebuhr and his Puritan forebears (the case is rather different with the Founding Fathers) would have argued that the only way one can bring the things of experience under scrutiny is by positing the existence of some transcendental standpoint from which to view them. But Diggins discounts the need for this kind of transcendental perspective and simply argues that the Puritans and their descendants— along with various of the Founding Fathers and assorted "irregular metaphysicians," as R. P. Blackmur would have called them, from the nineteenth century (including Weber and Adams)—constitute a Calvinist tradition of finitude, irony, doubt, and inscrutability that in America still affords one the possibility of assuming a critical vantage point independent of this spiritual crisis from which one can weigh its mainly deleterious consequences. Hence Diggins concludes that the antidote to any attempt like James's or Dewey's to seek unity and coherence without the appeal to something transcendent is not to be found in shifting one's attention from problems of faith to problems of knowing and then staking one's future on the illusory belief that "all problems of knowing include the possibility of their [own] solution," but rather in contenting oneself with establishing the limits of the known and the limitations of the knower.[9]

Not least among the problems with this kind of revisionism is that when the classical pragmatists turned their attention, as they so often did, to the limits and limitations of knowledge, they were frequently brought up against all that apparently exceeds them. How else explain what James was doing phenomenologically in *The Varieties of Religious Experience* or what Dewey was undertaking aesthetically in *Art as Experience* or, for that matter, what Peirce was up to semiotically in essays like "A New List of Categories," "Some Consequences of Four Incapacities," and "The Architecture of Theories"? But communication between religious thought and pragmatic philosophy has been reviving since the 1970s when, quite apart from the work of such philosophers as Smith and McDermott, theologians like Bernard Meland, in *Realities of Faith,* Joseph Haroutunian, in *God With Us: A Theology of the Transpersonal Life,* and, later, Gordon D. Kaufman, in *An Essay on Theological Method,* began to reappropriate pragmatism as a model for testing the validity of theological and moral claims.[10] Kaufman put it characteristically by pointing out that if theology begins with images and notions of the world that are inherited from the past, it ends with the attempt to determine what difference a theistically revised notion of the world may make to the kinds of activity and forms of life that are possible within it. He thus concludes, "the criteria for assessing theological claims turn out in the last analysis . . . to be pragmatic and humanistic . . . not because theologians are necessarily committed to pragmatic or utilitarian conceptions of truth in general but rather because such considerations—when understood in the broadest possible sense—are the only ones by which a way of life, a worldview, a perspective on the totality of things, a concept of God, may ultimately be assessed."[11]

By the late 1980s and 1990s, intellectual commerce between religion and pragmatism had expanded still further. In *The American Evasion of Philosophy*, for example, Cornel West found it necessary to supplement the "prophetic pragmatism" he refashioned from Emerson, Du Bois, and Dewey with the personally meaningful Protestant neoorthodoxy he found in Reinhold Niebuhr.[12] At roughly the same time, the philosopher of religion Jeffrey Stout offered what he called a "moderate pragmatism" as his own candidate for, as his title phrased it, *Ethics after Babel*.[13] But perhaps the most dramatic rapprochement between religion and pragmatism was effected by the religious historian Henry Samuel Levinson who, in a book that succeeded in restoring George Santayana to the pragmatist tradition, produced a full-blown theory of what he called "pragmatism and the spiritual life."[14]

However, the recent story of pragmatism's associations with religion does not stop here. If, for example, one adopts a somewhat broader view of the historical development of pragmatism of the sort that, say, Joseph Brent brings to his biography of Charles Sanders Peirce, or that Alan Ryan takes in his biography of John Dewey, or, for that matter, that Bruce Kuklick assumed in *Churchmen and Philosophers*, one can easily see that religion played a not inconsiderable, if not always obvious, role in the thinking of the founding generation, and that it was also a factor in inducing others, such as Du Bois, and perhaps even Alain Locke, to embrace their own version of pragmatism.[15]

Indeed, by taking a less philosophical and more broadly intellectual and cultural approach to the evolution of American pragmatism, one can readily discern its inflections with the religious in the works of a long line of American thinkers and writers from Emerson and Thoreau to Wallace Stevens and Elizabeth Bishop. This is not, of course, to pretend that these exchanges have always been smooth or unvexed but merely to observe that, despite the widespread impression to the contrary that pragmatism is relentlessly secular created by the work of intellectuals like Fish, Smith, and, until recently, Rorty himself, pragmatism has not always proved insensible of, much less hostile to, religious interests. Nor should this come as much of a surprise. William James originally offered pragmatism as a way of settling otherwise endless metaphysical disputes, and there is no reason to think that we can't still employ pragmatism—precisely because in numerous instances it is already being so used—to sort out and assess the comparative merits of religious perspectives—or "world-formulas," as James elsewhere called them —in the new globalized world in which we now find ourselves, a world where none of us, as Clifford Geertz has pointed out, can any longer manage to get out of each other's way.[16]

With the recent appearance of Rorty's essay entitled "Pragmatism as Romantic Polytheism," it would appear that he may have begun to have second thoughts. While this essay hardly constitutes an apologetics for belief, it reflects a conviction that pragmatism and theism do, in fact, mix. Much depends on what Rorty makes of Matthew Arnold's famous prognosis that, as organized religion declined, poetry would have to take its place. Rorty thinks that this shift of authority—a transition that commenced with the Romantic poets a generation or two before Arnold began writing—eventually produced a pluralization of the ideals for life, a diversification of the notion of perfection, that can justifiably be called polytheistic. Rorty views this polytheism as wholly consistent with what William James meant in *The Varieties of Religious Experience* when he said that the divine in human life can never be reduced to a single quality, or set of qualities, but "must mean a group of qualities, by being champions of which in alternation, different men may all find worthy missions. Each attitude being a syllable in human nature's total message, it takes the whole of us to spell the meaning out completely."[17] Nietzsche came even closer, Rorty thinks, to spelling out what he means by polytheism when, in section 143 of *The Gay Science*, Nietzsche noted that the pre-Socratic Greeks encouraged individuality by allowing human beings "to behold, in some distant overworld, a *plurality of norms:* one god was not considered a denial of another god, nor blasphemy against him."[18] Polytheism of this sort does not compel one to believe in deities; it merely permits one "to abandon the idea that we should try to find a way of making everything hang together, which will tell all human beings what to do with their lives, and tell all of them the same thing."[19]

Describing this view of polytheism as Romantic utilitarianism by another name, Rorty sketches out in five interrelated theses "a pragmatist philosophy of religion."[20] Since this philosophy of religion is actually developed in relation to a discussion of how well its theses accord with what James and Dewey actually thought about religion, I want to take up the theses by which it is framed in light of Rorty's larger argument. That larger argument is itself shaped by certain problematic assumptions that have undergirded Rorty's writing at least since the publication of *Contingency, Irony, and Solidarity.*

The first of these assumptions has to do with the nearly absolute distinction Rorty makes between the individual and the social, between realms of personal choice and public responsibility. In addition to compelling Rorty to argue almost as though history and culture didn't matter—as though, in other words, people everywhere, and in all times, have been able to keep this distinction as pure as it remains in the pages of *On Liberty*—the wall he erects between the private and the public condemns him to repeat the same mistake that Alfred North Whitehead made when he maintained, against all evidence, that religion is chiefly concerned with what we do with our solitariness, not our sociality.

The second of Rorty's problematic assumptions in this essay is that the will to truth should be viewed as identical with the will to happiness and that their unity therefore leaves us with no way of differentiating either between the cognitive and the noncognitive or between the serious and the nonserious. But unless this sweeping claim is intended to reduce the will to truth to utter banality, don't we have to ask whether the history of religions, along with the history of art, haven't provided us with abundant testimony to the contrary? Don't they indeed both show us that under certain circumstances the will to truth decisively overrides the desire for happiness? Were that not the case, what sense could one otherwise make of the meaning of the Crucifixion for Christians, or of living in *galut* for Jews, or of the nature of suffering (*dukkha*) for Buddhists? The stock of happiness being, as it were, in such comparatively short supply, is not most of the rhetorical and ritual machinery of the world's great religions designed precisely, as the majority of their modern interpreters have informed us, to cope with this unpleasant fact? As in the mithridatic techniques of classical tragedy and modern psychoanalytic theory, the will to happiness in most religions takes a back seat to the will to truth in the hope that the homeopathic administration of the pain of truth will partially inure us to the greater truth of life's pain.

The third of the problematic assumptions that Rorty makes in this essay, as do other neopragmatist thinkers, has to do with the sharpness of the distinction he always wants to draw between outlooks that are religious and those that are secular. Quite apart from the brittle terms with which he usually makes this distinction and the prejudicial way he frames it, the distinction itself doesn't work very well in America. While it would not be quite accurate to say that America has never been secular, it would not be inaccurate to claim that the cultural formation known as "America" has always found ways to be religious in a secular age. This is not simply to say that America continues to valorize itself religiously but that, even when America underwent the experience of the Enlightenment, it appropriated the Enlightenment, as Henry May noted so definitively, in a decidedly religious manner.[21]

Nowhere is this residual religiousness more obvious, perhaps, than in what America has made, and continues to make, of the Christian scriptures, or Bible. In a manner that finds no exact parallel in any other nation, the Bible has become America's book. The Bible has become America's book not only because Americans like to think that they have read it more assiduously than any other people, but also because Americans like to think that the Bible is the book that they, more than any other people, have been assiduously read by. It is not surprising that these two beliefs complement one another. If Americans have long felt, and not without justification, that the Bible shaped their experience in decisive ways, they initially became compulsive readers of scripture in order to make certain that their experience did not betray or violate scriptural warrants and prohibitions. Either way, Americans have run the risk of hubris, and that willingly! They have cleaved to the Bible as though it were a national cultural possession for the sake of reassuring themselves that their own history was unfolding according to biblical prescriptions.

The dangers inherent in America's special claims upon the Bible have been obvious at least since 1702, when Cotton Mather first attempted, in his *Magnalia Christi Americana*, to fit our own experience into the Bible's epic structure. In the name of a sacred text that purports to define the ultimate design of all history, Mather presumed to find an explanation for the uniqueness of America's own history. In doing this, Mather was only following the practice of contemporary Puritan historiography. Mather's special contribution to the American theory of biblical interpretation was to suggest the possibility, quite without meaning to, of turning the coin on its flip side. If the Bible could be used to determine the exceptionality of America's origin and destiny, might not America be used to demonstrate the Bible's uniqueness? For example, it was easy enough to see how the evolution of American history represented a continuation of God's plan for all history as expressed in the biblical narratives. With only a slight change of perspective, was it not also possible to view the continuity between biblical history and American experience as a kind of confirmation of scripture? America might then be conceived not merely as an instance or exemplification of biblical patterns but also as a kind of legitimation of them.

Mather did not actually go this far, but others would not remain so theologically circumspect. And when they did not, as Sacvan Bercovitch has pointed out, then the relations between America and the Bible would acquire some disturbing dimensions.[22] The Bible would then be understood to belong to America precisely because it could be said that America already belonged, in a profound sense, to the Bible. If America was not itself the Bible's own text of experience, did it not represent a realization of the Bible's greatest promise? The result of this peculiarly American "interpretive turn" was to reduce both the Old and the New Testaments to a kind of National Testament, and then to convert the biblical *Heilsgeschichte*, or history of salvation, into the American salvation of history.

America's veneration of the Bible, which was eventually to give way to this biblistic veneration of America, all began quite innocently. It began during the years of America's earliest settlement among individuals who were keenly aware of the radical difference between the divine plan and human purpose. If the Bible expressed the Word that commissioned their "errand into the wilderness," the Bible was also a repository of the norms in relation to which that errand would have to be judged. The Bible, therefore, occupied an extremely ambivalent position in relation to the emergent culture of seventeenth-century colonial America. On the one hand, the Bible was viewed as creating a culture whose development it authorized and sanctioned. On the other, its cultural creativity was limited to supplying a rationale for the special mission that America was to accomplish and a set of guidelines for how to fulfill it.

Yet throughout the centuries of Western history, the Bible's relation to culture had become ambivalent in still other ways, and by nothing so much as the Bible's success in being disseminated throughout the rituals, the rhythms, the very fabric of cultural discourse. Even when people were able to preserve a sense of the Bible's authority over against culture, they were not able to resist thinking in its images, speaking in its language, feeling in its forms. And the situation has been no different in America, only exaggerated. The Bible has often been able to infiltrate culture as a form, or set of forms, in almost direct proportion to the distance it has been set apart from culture as a norm. Thus, one finds in America the same paradox that exists elsewhere in the West: the Bible has simultaneously furnished many of the most stable forms of consciousness in America, while at the same time serving as one of the chief sources of dissatisfaction with them. The Bible has at one and the same time furnished some of those basic continuities of American culture which, as Perry Miller put it, "underlie the successive articulation of ideas," while nourishing the forms of "sacred discontent," in E. H.

Gombrich's phrase, that such continuities have aroused.[23] Whichever the case, the Bible has not been abandoned even when its ideas have been rejected, any more than American culture has been secularized simply by virtue of having declared its spiritual independence from all forms of religious orthodoxy. Not to understand this paradox is to fail to comprehend how such texts as the First Amendment to the U.S. Constitution, which are often held up as testimony of the emergent secularization of America, are evidence of just the opposite. It is not merely that there is a contradiction between the "no establishment" clause of the First Amendment, which seems to promote secularism, and its "free exercise" clause, which offers implicit support to religion, but that both parties to the contradiction cleave to the Amendment with a zeal that is itself sacred.

These problematic assumptions have in turn created what appear to me to be several difficulties with the five theses that constitute Rorty's pragmatist philosophy of religion, and in the remainder of this chapter I want to examine three of them more closely. Let me begin with Rorty's preference for Dewey's view of religion over James's on the grounds that, if I understand Rorty correctly, Dewey defined pragmatism's relation to religion principally in terms of the notion of tolerance. Dewey, to be sure, often invoked the notion of tolerance to underline the fact that pragmatism views religion without prejudice, but the reduction of their relationship to one essentially of forbearance and sufferance clearly places it on too weak a footing even for Dewey himself. While it is true that Dewey never went as far as James did in the apologetic "Conclusion" to *The Varieties of Religious Experience*—where, as Rorty quotes him, he asserts that "the conscious person is continuous with a wider self through which saving experiences come"—James himself pulled back from this essentializing claim in *Pragmatism* and simply asserted that, except to morbid minds that desire nothing less than absolute religious certainty, a universe with a fighting chance of security is a more interesting, if not potentially a more uplifting, moral prospect than one without it. And in the famous pet analogy, James then went on to posit the high probability that our own relation to the universe may not be unlike the relation that our canine and feline friends presumably have to the things that go on in our own living rooms. Just as they participate with us in actions whose full meaning is completely beyond their ken, so we likewise probably take part ourselves in scenes of whose "cosmic" significance we have only the slightest clue.

In "The Will to Believe," written well before the religion sections of

Pragmatism, James had been even more circumspect about these matters by avoiding all talk of "higher powers," though Rorty rather curiously deflates the argument of this essay to the assertion "that we have a right to believe what we like when we are, so to speak, on our own time." We forfeit this right, Rorty continues, "when we are engaged in, for example, a scientific or apolitical project. For when so engaged it is necessary to reconcile our beliefs with those of others."[24]

Even if we could compartmentalize our lives so neatly, "The Will to Believe" actually refrains quite pointedly from privatizing or personalizing the religious will in this fashion, maintaining instead that belief becomes compelling only when it presents us with an option that strikes us as unavoidable, genuine, and serious. No mention here of, as Rorty implies, the right to believe anything we like so long as we don't let it interfere with the business of anyone else. By James's reckoning, any option that confronts us with a momentous choice that we can't put by because it is living and inescapable invokes what he might otherwise have called "the right to believe."

Long before his own summarizing remarks about religion and the religious in *A Common Faith,* Dewey gave some consideration of his own to those conditions that warrant "the right to believe." This topic comes up, for example, in *Human Nature and Conduct* in connection with a discussion of the mind's sense of the totality that surrounds it and that defines the horizon of meaning beyond the reach of current formulations and toward which the implications of any given act potentially extend. Confronted with the prospect of this unthinkable, nonrepresentable totality, Dewey postulated that the mind comes up against a sense of the whole which it cannot conceptualize but which it can nevertheless dimly imagine or conceivably intuit. But Dewey was not for long comfortable with the Hegelianism of these formulations and eventually exchanged them for the aesthetic idioms he adopted in *Art as Experience.* It is here, and not in *A Common Faith,* that Dewey makes his strongest case for the right to believe, but it is a case that holds little interest for Rorty because he sees Dewey's entire project to ground the aesthetic in the natural rhythms of ordinary experience as a form of outworn metaphysics.

Were Rorty not so quick to write off the whole of *Art as Experience* because of the traces of transcendentalism that shadow some, but by no means all, of its pages, he might well have found there a pragmatist attempt to reformulate the case for belief in relation to the nature of aesthetic drive, where obstacles and impediments to further growth are converted into instruments for the creation of a new, if only temporary, balance of forces.

That is, as Dewey understands it, art's juxtaposition of the actual with the imaginative, of the given with the potential, not only inscribes the critical within the aesthetic—"it is by a sense of possibilities opening before us that we become aware of constrictions that hem us in and of burdens that oppress"—but also opens the aesthetic to the possibility of continuously transcending itself by producing in response the desire to create more things like it.[25]

This leads to the second issue I want to raise in connection with Rorty's pragmatist philosophy of religion, which has to do with his desire to make religion more like art. Rorty intends to make religion more like art by dissociating his understanding of both from morality and from science alike. Thus, the pragmatist understanding of religion is less like morality and more like art, Rorty contends, in that it exhibits no interest in ranking needs, and it is less like science and more like art, he goes on, because religion is not involved in the prediction of consequences. But remove from art and religion alike the obsession with hierarchy, with ranking and valuation, as well as the preoccupation with projection, forecasting, and prognostication, and the question then becomes, Are you left with anything that can be recognized either as art or religion?

Rorty seems to be involved here in what can be described only as a kind of category mistake. As it happens, almost everything that goes by the name art—and this applies to most postmodernist art as well—is concerned with scarcely anything besides the ranking of human needs, though it refuses for the most part to undertake this task, as religion does, in a normative or prescriptive manner. And while all of the valuational procedures within art are equally dependent on the estimation of results, effects, and implications, most art goes about the business of predicting outcomes not on the basis of prophecy or proclamation, as in religion, but rather on the basis of inference, conjecture, hypothesis, and speculation. Art does not say that all families are always happy but that where "happy families are all alike," as *Anna Karenina* proposes, "every unhappy family is unhappy in its own way."

If Rorty were not so attached to a Romantic aesthetic that views art, as in John Stuart Mill or even Matthew Arnold, as a substitute for religion, he might see more clearly the virtues of a pragmatist aesthetic that views art, as in Henry James, Kenneth Burke, and, most recently, Richard Poirier, as a complement to, sometimes even a corollary or ally of, religion itself. In particular, art acts as a form of disruptive classification and reclassification in cultural experience, where the boundaries religion normally tries to defend, police and control—between the imagined and the real, the temporal and the eternal, the known and the unknown or unknowable—are shattered and redrawn by religion itself. Poirier's theory of literature is especially instructive on this last point just because its recent developments have occurred in such close conversation with poststructuralist theories of literature. Poirier has retrieved for us an Emerson who is the originator of a tradition of literary and intellectual pragmatism in American writing that, in addition to being underappreciated (where it has been recognized at all), constitutes an alternative to our conventional view of modernism and casts modernism's relation to postmodernism in an entirely different light. In his most recent book, Poirier associates this tradition with the discoveries afforded by a self-conscious linguistic skepticism.[26] This is a skepticism linked to the deconstructive mechanisms within language itself but one that also rethinks those mechanisms as tropological instruments capable of empowering language to resist the self-reflexivity of its own inherited meanings and thus point beyond those meanings toward possibilities for renewal that are at once personal and cultural as well as semiotic.

If this linguistic skepticism were merely another way of maintaining that "words," as T. S. Eliot said in "Burnt Norton," "will not stay in place,/ Will not stay still," such a demonstration would merely reinforce the appeal of deconstruction itself, with its summary rejection of the Eliotic quest for "the still point in the turning world" and its conviction that the instability of language points to the indeterminacy of its reference. But Emerson and James, together with Poirier, intend to say something quite different from this. Over against Eliot's attempt to evade such issues by positing the possibility of their transcendence in some larger "idea of order," and in contradistinction to deconstruction's frequent tendency to identify these problems with something flawed and treacherous about the nature of language itself, Poirier, William James, and Emerson—and, for that matter, Henry James, Gertrude Stein, Wallace Stevens, and Elizabeth Bishop—all insist that these obstacles that language places in the way of (what Dewey called) the "quest for certainty" afford significant opportunities, both cognitive and affective, for further knowledge, for the revelation of what Wallace Stevens meant by "ghostlier demarcations, keener sounds." William James himself formulated this proposition most simply when he somewhere stated that what "these [verbal] formulas express leaves unexpressed almost everything that they organically divine and feel." Poirier has in turn followed James by referring to this element of the "unexpressed" and the verbally inexpressible simply as "the vague" and by urging its recovery in criticism just as James urged its reinstatement in philosophy.

"The vague" and, for Poirier its cognate, "the superfluous" are to be associated with what James elsewhere called the "Sense of the More." This was James's rather crude, but nonetheless effective, description for that surplus of intelligibility that attends all acts of understanding, the remainder that is always left over, so to speak, when we try to calculate their sum. In this sense, vagueness is far more than a mere constituent of perception; it is also, as Poirier brings out more effectively than James ever did, the only guarantee that perception contains within itself a potential for criticizing some of its own cognitive deliverances. Requiring, as Poirier calls it, "a disciplined resistance" to the seductions of habit as well as to the desire for closure, vagueness functions simultaneously both as a kind of Burkean counterforce to dogmatization and as a Santayanean incitement to the exploration of new truths.[27] Often conveyed in writing by nothing more concrete than voice and sound, vagueness derives, so Poirier maintains, from the failure that language continuously experiences in its effort to represent its own understanding in words. If most postmodernist criticism typically reads this failure as the death knell of logocentricism, pragmatism reads it as representing potentially a "saving uncertainty."[28]

In this pragmatist understanding of language, the words are there—in Charlotte Perkins Gilman's "The Yellow Wallpaper" or Robert Frost's dramatic dialogues, Gertrude Stein's *Tender Buttons* or Wallace Steven's "The Snow Man"—to point to, or, better, to lead toward, insights, intuitions, intimations situated on the horizon of consciousness that would either be lost if in fact they were named or that lack any placement within our current hierarchies of understanding. Thus, for pragmatism art is important not because it designates, as in the monumentalist or hierarchic view, somewhere to get to but rather because it suggests, as in a more democratic or demotic view, somewhere to depart from. The arts, as Emerson said, are initial, not final. It is not what they achieve but what they aim at that matters. Hence, even when they claim to furnish their readers with what Thoreau described in *Walden* as "a hard bottom and rocks in place, which we can call *reality*, and say This is, and no mistake," that "bottom" or "*reality*"—as Thoreau characteristically added in further elaboration and as pragmatist critics like Burke, Trilling, Poirier, and Posnock would agree—is merely another "*point d'appui.*"[29]

Because it is difficult to imagine how human needs can be hierarchically rearranged, or at least imagined and represented as being amenable to such rearrangement, without producing some noticeable alterations in our sense of community (the community between text and reader, the community between one reader and another, the community between readers and non-readers), I want to take up as my third issue the definition of the ideal of human fraternity that pragmatism, like democracy, according to Rorty, supposedly takes over from Christianity. As Rorty phrases it, this is the belief that every human need should be satisfied unless doing so causes too many other human needs to go unsatisfied.

Here again I find that Rorty's preference for the minimalist case may encourage him to put the matter too weakly. If democratic pragmatism can be said to have inherited any conception of solidarity from Christianity, that conception has a lot less to do with the belief that we should get what we want so long as it doesn't prevent others from getting what they want and a lot more to do with the belief that no human being is an island unto itself because all human beings have to consider the needs of at least some others in order to satisfy their own. While this certainly does not go as far as someone like Emmanuel Levinas—and his claim that the self is thus constituted as a human being by means of its encounter with an "other" who is then experienced as the ground of the self's own ethicality—pragmatism does take over from Christianity a much stronger version of human fraternity than any with which Rorty seems to credit it—both in Dewey's theory of the Great Community (itself possibly influenced by Josiah Royce's theory of the Beloved Community) and in aspects of George Herbert Mead's social theory of the self.

Of particular relevance in this connection, since its influence on democratic pragmatism is less well known or fully appreciated than Dewey's, is Mead's understanding of the social nature of selfhood. Mead's theory presupposes that the self is capable of viewing itself as an object only because it is able to communicate with other selves. The possibility of such communication in turn depends on the gestural character of language and, indeed, of all symbolic exchanges. Gestures are premised on the expectation of a response, and they acquire meaning—and become what Mead calls "significant symbols"—only when they infer or assume the attitude of the response they are designed to evoke. Communication thus requires, as Dewey argued in his famous essay on the reflex arc, the coordination of patterned gestures or acts that are inherently symbolic. Mead, however, goes one crucial step further than Dewey in pointing out that communication thereby assumes that those who traffic in symbolic symbols must, of necessity, be able to internalize what others mean by them. But this in turn means not only that the communication between different selves depends on their reciprocal understanding of a shared system of significant symbols to whose gestural meanings they can respond; it also suggests that the individual self can only know itself as an object independent of others by taking the attitude expressed towards itself by those others with whom it is symbolically involved. To put this another way, significant symbols enable communication between and among individuals, according to Mead, by permitting the self to adopt the position of the other with respect to itself. In this model of social construction and interaction, then, democratic individuality is not based, as Rorty maintains, on the limited compatibility between the desires of the self and the desires of others, but on the practical intersubjective demands that require the self to adopt the point of view of the "other" in order to know itself, much less to communicate with anyone else.

Rorty's resistance to this kind of thinking could point to the fact that, despite his deep social conscience, he may in truth be more interested in liberty than he is in solidarity. This would help explain his preference, when it comes to religion, for freedom over commitment. But if Rorty remains a liberal (and a Romantic one at that) all the way down, he nonetheless runs the risk of forgetting that even the more socially radical of the Romantic liberals, such as Shelley and Whitman, were in the main less interested in the re-creation of the self than in the rebirth and reform of community.

Dewey, of course, was prepared to say exactly the same thing and even went so far as to define his own democratic and social ideal in *Art as Experience* in reference to Shelley's view of love, as "*a going out of our nature* and the identification of ourselves with the beautiful which exists in thought, action, or person, not our own."[30] But if Dewey's image of the democratic embrace of the actual and the ideal attested to the importance of mutuality and fellow feeling, his notion of the interpersonal as well as the transpersonal nonetheless suffered from certain lacunae of which Rorty remains curiously silent. Not only did Dewey fail to account for most of the complications of the subjective life, and particularly, as Alan Ryan has recently noted, for the whole realm of sexual relations, but he also paid comparatively little attention to the bureaucratic obduracy of large institutions and the mysteries of social change.[31] Lacking a sufficiently subtle theory either of the private or of the institutional, Dewey's theory of democracy may therefore prove too fragile a political foundation to support the edifice of Romantic polytheism without considerable shoring up. Such shoring up would require that Rorty look beyond the tradition of the "founders" of pragmatism to such thinkers in the pragmatist grain as Du Bois, Burke, Trilling, and Ralph Ellison, all of whom could suggest ways of complicating his Romantic polytheism with a richer sense of the duplicities of, and disturbances within, the self and with a deeper grasp of the dangers of bureaucratizing the imaginative.

But Rorty's Romantic polytheism creates further problems for a democratic pragmatist because of the way he conflates it with a celebrationist reading of America's religious destiny. By linking Dewey's pantheism with Whitman's—and thereby associating the unity of poetry and religious feeling with the creation of a community of free individuals—Rorty foresees Romantic polytheism completing itself in the construction of "the United States of America," an entity that, for both Whitman and Dewey, represented what Rorty calls "the possibility of as yet undreamt of, ever more diverse, forms of human happiness."[32] Over against this triumphalist image of American futurity, I would place a rather different religious prospect envisioned by a pragmatist, or at least a pragmatist sympathizer, of another stripe. When at the end of *The American Scene* Henry James was confronted with a similar temptation to link the nation with its visionary ambitions, he found himself thinking instead not of undreamt of forms of human felicity yet to be achieved but of historical obligations and commitments continuously deferred and of social and political potentialities habitually postponed. That is, when Henry James looked at his country pragmatically through the eyes of its own religious sense of itself, what he saw was not a blank check on the future that the United States of America had written to legitimate its present but rather the bill of arrears that the United States of America had already accumulated on its past. This bill of arrears revealed the inconsistencies, lapses, and contradictions inherent from the beginning within America's own religious imagination of itself, and it encouraged James to believe that this debt cannot, and will not, be settled without a full accounting of its costs to the treasury of national values and a full assessment of its consequences for a redefinition of national purpose. A task we have yet to fulfill, it is a project in which James could imagine the pragmatic serving as the perfect ally of the religious.

Chapter 6

Rhetorical Pragmatism and
the Question of the Historical

Pragmatism has not been notable for its contributions to the theory and practice of history. Although it has been the subject of extremely intelligent analysis by historians who could themselves be considered in some sense pragmatists—I am thinking in particular of David Hollinger, James Kloppenberg, Thomas Bender, Robert B. Westbrook, Joyce Appleby, Lynn Hunt, Margaret Jacob, and James Livingston[1]—pragmatism has never presented itself as an instrument designed primarily for historiographical work. This is not to deny that various pragmatist philosophers, Dewey preeminent among them, have been very good historians, nor that, like James and Bernstein, they have often argued for the importance of contextualization; it is merely to note that, whatever else pragmatism may claim for itself, it cannot pretend to have ever proposed that the historical should be the site of its most intensive investigations. All that has now begun to change, however, as historians have become more sensitive to what Hayden White, in a well-known book of some years ago, once referred to as *The Tropics of Discourse* and to what Robert Berkhofer, in the subtitle of his own more recent *Beyond the Great Story*, has called "history as text and discourse."[2]

That change is perhaps most evident in the work of those who have made what might be called the rhetorical turn in pragmatism. This is a turn signaled most dramatically in the writings of the literary critic Stanley Fish, who assumes that in a world without epistemological or ontological foundations, rhetoric carries the day in all disputes about truth. Or, as he prefers to put it, truth is a product of the conflict of views among various interpretive communities, communities that frame their appeals and make their assessments largely in relation to the persuasiveness of particular truth claims. We are thus imprisoned within systems of persuasion that prevent us from assessing our own beliefs and opinions against anything other than another set of beliefs and opinions. Even if persuasiveness is subject to pressure, leverage, and power, theory as such furnishes no independent position beyond rhetoric by which to evaluate the latter's competing claims. In effect, then, culture is a continuous, if not exactly seamless, whole composed of interpretations espoused by different communities, each interpretation vying with others to be accepted with no more to back them up than their suasive influence.

Walter Benn Michaels has perhaps done more than any other neopragmatist to lend such ideas historical application. One can obtain some sense of how this works from his latest book, *Our America: Nativism, Modernism, and Pluralism*, in which he turns his attention to an important paradox that developed in national self-consciousness during the 1920s. Noting that this decade witnessed an intensification of collective cultural interest in what it means to be an "American," Michaels asks how cultural identity could have been so drastically racialized at a time when in various discourses—literary, sociological, political—race itself was becoming increasingly acknowledged to be a limited, if not a fallacious, symbol of identity. Michaels' answer is brilliantly, if disturbingly and deceptively, simple. What many of the best known texts of American modernism achieved was less a rearticulation of race as a marker of cultural identity than a reconceptualization of cultural identity as inherently racial, even racist.

By means of this subtle shift of emphasis, Michaels turns American pluralism, whatever its stated intentions, into an ally of American nativism. Though modern American cultural pluralism may have sought to disarticulate racism from the white supremacism of the Progressives, it merely succeeded, he asserts, in reinscribing racism all over again by idealizing the notion of difference, thereby becoming for many intellectuals in the 1920s the dominant form of racism itself. This indictment of cultural pluralism in the interwar period is clearly intended, among other things, to challenge the grounds on which many today still press arguments for multiculturalism. In Michaels's judgment, such arguments reveal a hidden racist bias they assume they are countering, which thus transforms the ideal of cultural identity they espouse into something nonsensical and repellant.

Quite apart from the cleverness of this claim, which turns what might be considered a half-truth into a whole one, its chief problems stem from the ideologically seamless and, almost more important, ahistorical notion of culture on which it depends. Here, as in his earlier and widely admired *The Gold Standard and the Logic of Naturalism*, Michaels assumes, but never demonstrates, that cultural concepts possess a logic all their own, a logic that necessarily defines and regulates the sort of instantiation such concepts may achieve in specific historical moments and practices. Thus, in a book otherwise richly provocative, he runs the risk not merely of discovering an ontology that everywhere links race and culture in the era of American modernism, but also of reinforcing in his own discourse the same essentialism that ontology presupposes by insisting that the connection it represents must inevitably function rhetorically and ideologically in exactly the same way in all circumstances.

Given these difficulties with Michael's application of rhetoric to history, I want to look more closely at another pragmatist whose own coupling of rhetorical theory with cultural hermeneutics will better permit me to assess both the strengths and the weaknesses of pragmatism's approach to the historical. With strong affinities to Fish's antifoundationalism, if not to Michaels's, Steven Mailloux has proposed an unusually interesting marriage between pragmatic philosophy, hermeneutic criticism, and rhetorical theory.[3] Although this is not an altogether unfamiliar grouping—the precursor, of course, is reader-response criticism—his aim is to make that enterprise much more exacting and precise by isolating and then explicating the historically specific rhetorical tropes in relation to which readers presumably do their reading. Such tropes, and the constraints they are held to place on interpretation, embody, so far as literary interpretation goes, what might be called "the historical in history."

Interpretation theory thus becomes for Mailloux much more than a way of reading; in his culturally contextualized expression of it, interpretation theory is transmuted into a form of—or at least a way into a form of—history itself. To study the cultural conversations out of which readers constitute the literature of the past for themselves—particularly when the rhetorical practices that make up those conversations are embedded within the rich matrix of social forms, institutionalized disciplines, ideological frameworks, and empirical circumstances that made up American society at the time the text first appeared and was read—is for Mailloux to acquire at least one version, even if not the only version, of that past itself.

If I have gotten Mailloux's project more or less right, then the kind of question it inevitably raises is whether cultural rhetorical studies, here outlined still as a form of reception study, will furnish us with a sufficiently dense version, even if it remains but one version, of that past. Rephrased historically, this question might be put as follows: If we were to read *The Adventures of Huckleberry Finn* against the background of the cultural practices that legitimated, or at any rate bolstered, the famous ban on the novel— when the Library Committee in Concord, Massachusetts, decided in March 1885 to forbid the novel's circulation because of its association with "the 'Bad Boy Boom' of the mid-1880s, anxieties over gang juvenile delinquency, and the negative effects of reading crime stories and dime novels"[4] —would this give us, if not all, then at least enough of, what the novel meant in the rhetorically reconstructed moment of its first historical appearance, much less enough of what its supposed meaning in the moment of its initial historical appearance can mean to us now, in our own very different rhetorically constructed historical moment in the present?

This may merely sound like a variant on the question Mailloux himself asks about whether rhetorical hermeneutics, as he defines it, can escape the problems of its own rhetorical situation, but it is in fact a rather different question since it cannot be answered simply by saying, as Mailloux does several pages later, that rhetorical hermeneutics not only recognizes its own rhetoricity but also recognizes the rhetoricity of other interpretive situations. Even though such recognitions are not without significance, they also are not, as I see it, the main issue. The main issue, so far as interpretation is concerned, has to do with the density and opacity of that dimension known as the historical, a density and opacity that involves at the very least some sort of interpretive traffic—if not, in addition, some kinds of interpretive negotiations—between our by-whatever-means excavated and reconstructed sense of that prior historical moment and our by-whatever-means intuited and elaborated sense of our own contemporary moment. Yet for all of Mailloux's appreciation of his own rhetorically interpreted present, I find less support than I would have expected in his exposition either for undertaking such traffic or for conducting such negotiations, much less for puzzling out an assessment of the particular hazards and rewards that they afford in any given local instance.

As it happens, Mailloux would not object to this description of the process by which the "past" and "present" traffic with each other, but he would add that what I have described above is what in fact always occurs, not what should but rarely does occur. So this interpretive traffic and negotiation always already occurs because our senses of "past" and "present" are both equally fabricated, as William James reminded us, or "constructed," as we now say. Nonetheless, our notion of the historical depends to a large ex-

tent on our understanding of exactly how such constructions have been accomplished, who is responsible for them, what in any given instance they
are connected to or implicated in, where they lead, and what our own relationship to them is.

This is not to charge Mailloux with insensibility about such shadowy
matters—he is much too subtle a reader and much too careful a historian
not to appreciate their existence—but merely to note that they somehow
fail to make any real difference either in or to his account. Despite the differences between Mark Twain's time and our own, Mailloux's reflections
themselves seem to move confidently forward on the assumption that the
cultural reading practices of the 1880s did indeed constitute, for a majority
of Mark Twain's readers, pretty much the whole of their experience of his
most famous novel, and that therefore a recovery of these same practices,
when interpreted rhetorically as part of the larger conversation that defined
the culture of literacy in which the novel was received, will get us as close
to the past as any reading of *The Adventures of Huckleberry Finn* is likely to
take us.

If I nonetheless remain somewhat less confident about all this than Mailloux does, it is not because I lack sympathy with what he is aiming at. Analyzing the interpretive models by which readers are constituted as subjects
by the books they read, and the way they read them, is surely one way into
the historicity of a particular cultural moment, and just as clearly opens out
toward a deepened understanding of the relations between power and
knowledge in a particular society. I remain less confident only because I har-
bor reservations about some of the theoretical machinery Mailloux wishes
to employ to get himself there. These reservations, I should add, have nothing to do with the theoretical description he provides for his project—"doing history," as he calls it, by crossing rhetorical pragmatism and theories of
reading to produce cultural rhetorical studies strikes me as a perfectly legitimate enterprise—but only with the construction he has placed on several
of his key concepts. Yet these constructions entail real consequences.

In Mailloux's exposition of them, terms such as *pragmatism, hermeneutics,*
and even *rhetoric* seem, at least by my lights, to suffer a kind of slippage that
deprives them of some of their thickness, intricacy, and complexity of implication, and permits them too quickly to dissolve into, or be displaced by, one
another. As a result, someone unsympathetic with this attempt to reground
the historical study of literature in unprivileged, discursive terms might be
inclined to wonder whether rhetorical pragmatism serves any other central
function than to help him dismiss the claims of intellectual foundationalism,

whereupon rhetorical pragmatism becomes merely the license for a certain method of reading. But having licensed a certain method of reading, someone might again ask whether its densities don't tend to be thinned out when this new hermeneutics is then rhetoricized as the interpretation of those very tropes that are used to configure the social practices of literacy. Yet again, if the study of the social practices of literacy amount to no more than an examination of the rhetorical devices and conventions that discursively constitute the whole of the social and political world, then what are we to do with the kind of question for which philosophical pragmatism was in part originally conceived to pose rhetorically, the question about what gets communicated, as it were, beyond tropes, and what difference that makes?

Unless I miss my guess, this is precisely the kind of question that would least interest Mailloux because he would feel that it draws us furthest away from the realm of the historical itself. But one could just as easily argue that such a question—presupposing, as it does, that some people can think against and even outside the interpretive practices and intellectual frames of their own time—belongs to the very essence of the historical, and that to think otherwise—which is to think that the whole of the historical is to be delimited to, and identified with, those forms—is merely a prejudice of our own cultural moment. My own suspicion that Mailloux shares this prejudice is reinforced by the postmodernist spin that he puts on some of these same key terms. By "postmodernist" I mean only that he seems so quickly to buy into the Lyotardian vision of a world without metanarratives that relegates the notion of truth to the realm of consensus values and then reconceives interpretation as the study of those hermeneutic practices that legitimate and delegitimate various ways of reading. In this new dispensation, pragmatism, hermeneutics, and rhetoric all risk being eviscerated of important wider meanings through their association with a view of experience that, while acknowledging the historicity of all interpretive acts, including its own, in effect denies the possibility of critically comparing and evaluating them. This requires a complete acceptance of the Rortyan view that there are no criteria for deciding between what are, in effect, as all narratives or stories are, alternative metaphors. We are thus left hermeneutically with a conception of history as a conflict (where there isn't a consensus) of interpretations among which it is impossible to adjudicate.

Mailloux takes exception to this observation by saying that we do in fact make valid comparisons and evaluations all the time. His point, which is perfectly consistent with rhetorical hermeneutics, is that while "such evaluations take place within present assumptions and practices," we are not wholly constrained by those practices because presumably they are neither fixed nor completely consistent with themselves.[5] Judgment is possible, he claims, because change, and thus difference, are inevitable. My point, on the other hand, is that without some standards, however provisional or hypothetical or experimental, the conflict between interpretations, far from remaining potentially comparative, only becomes more pervasively meaningless. If it is really impossible in this relativist world to adjudicate among interpretations, can we actually say that we have any grasp of the historical itself, which traditionally carries with it a sense of the difference not only between our own time and another, but an appreciation of the difference it makes to perceive that difference? In the remainder of this chapter, therefore, I would like to explore several of the larger meanings that are in danger of being lost to Mailloux's key terms because of their postmodernist revisioning. The disappearance of these meanings may not only jeopardize the insights his key terms may provide into history itself but also diminish our understanding of the resources that pragmatism can bring to a discussion of such issues.

One such danger surfaces most clearly in relation to Mailloux's treatment of the notion of hermeneutics. While the author of such sophisticated studies as *Interpretive Conventions* and *Rhetorical Power* certainly doesn't need any lessons in the development of modern interpretation theory, I am still somewhat surprised that his own conception of it pays so little attention to one of the persistent concerns of that tradition from, say, Wilhelm Dilthey to Paul Ricoeur. The concern I have in mind is the distinction, perhaps most succinctly drawn by Ricoeur, between interpretation as explanation and interpretation as understanding and appropriation. As Ricoeur views it, explanation is employed most commonly in relation to phenomena that are intelligible in relation to a world allegedly composed of things like facts, laws, theories, hypotheses, verifications, and deductions. Finding its most congenial home in the natural sciences, explanation is, therefore, typically concerned with what Geertz calls a laws-instances rather than cases-interpretation reading of things. By contrast, understanding is more closely associated with what Dilthey was the first to designate as the human sciences, where the aim of inquiry is to gain access to the experience of subjects similar to but, at the same time, distinct from ourselves. Compelled as it is, then, to decipher forms in which these experiences of other subjects are expressed both directly and indirectly, understanding normally proceeds with its work of interpretation by a dialectical process of divination and validation.

The divinatory pole of interpretation is required to supplement the validational pole because, as Ricoeur sees it (other modern students of hermeneutics would put this somewhat differently), the discursive meaning of any text always surpasses the verbal intention, not to say the psychic experience, of its author, and thus necessitates a guess as to what the work or text in fact is in any one of its several modalities. Those modalities include not only what the text is in its wholeness—as a set of topics that reflect different hierarchies of significance—or in its singularity—as a more restricted repository of generic concepts and linguistic codes—but also in its potentiality—as a field of secondary as well as primary meanings whose possible horizon of significance can be actualized in a number of different ways. If this potential horizon of meaning that attaches itself to any text considerably complicates the divinatory process, turning that process itself into more of an art form than a scientific procedure, it also complicates, as various other hermeneutic theorists from Martin Heidegger to Hans-Georg Gadamer have pointed out, what texts can be said to express and in what ways they can be said to express it. Thus, even where such structural elements as generic codes, historical conventions, and literary topoi delimit the range of options from among which one can divine what the text both actually and potentially is, there are nonetheless, as Ricoeur points out, few rules of thumb in these matters for formulating good guesses and no scientific procedures for confidently confirming them. In all this interpretive guessing, where one depends on logics of probability rather than logics of verification, there inevitably remains a good deal of uncertainty, inconsistency, and sometimes ambiguity. In the natural sciences such qualities are often conceived as defects of the process of inquiry; in the human sciences, by contrast, they are more frequently viewed as its inevitable byproducts and even virtues.

There is no gainsaying that this tolerance for ambiguity and undecidability in interpretation makes the human sciences look somewhat anomalous both to specialists in the harder sciences and also to members of the general public. But their anomaly is further increased both by the way the human sciences resituate the object of textual, and specifically of literary, knowledge outside rather than inside the text itself, and by the special conditions they set for how, in the act of reading, that knowledge is made one's own. To revert to Ricoeur again, reading occurs in two basic but separate stages. In the first, reading effects a suspension or suppression of the text's ostensive reference in order to place the reader within what Ricoeur calls the "worldless place" constituted by the text's own systems of semiological production

—be they phonological, linguistic, grammatical, generic, or ideological.[6] In this stage of the act of reading, the text exists chiefly as form rather than function, as interior rather than exterior.

While this first stage of the reading experience is essential, and is the inaugural move in all structuralist modes of analysis, Ricoeur nonetheless believes with most other interpretation theorists that this stage must be followed by another if the hermeneutic arc is not to be short-circuited. This second stage of the reading process seeks to engage both the ostensive and the non-ostensive references of the text and to actualize them imaginatively in, as Ricoeur puts it, a new context, which is simply the existential situation of the reader her- or himself. Identifying the non-ostensive reference of the text with the kind of world opened up by the text, Ricoeur thus postulates that the sense of the text—or what it says—is to be found not wholly, or even primarily, within the text itself, or for that matter behind it, but rather in front of it, in the new possible way of looking at things that the text proposes or implies, the different, or at least distinctive, way of thinking and feeling about things that the text potentially enables.

Reading in this second sense is thus not completed until an interpretation is appropriated by becoming an event in the reader's own extended consciousness. Thus, in answer to the question of what is to be understood, and hence made one's own, in a text, Ricoeur replies:

> Not the intention of the author, which is supposed to be hidden behind the text; not the historical situation common to the author and his original readers; not the expectations of feelings of these original readers; not even their understanding of themselves as historical and cultural phenomena. What has to be appropriated is the meaning of the text itself, conceived in a dynamic way as the direction of thought opened up by the text. In other words, what has to be appropriated is nothing other than the power of disclosing a world that constitutes the reference of the text.[7]

This is as much as to say that appropriation marks the moment when the reader is in a position to understand the author better than the author her- or himself. By following the arrow of sense projected by, but not wholly inscribed within, the text, the reader acknowledges the power of the author's discourse to transcend "the limited horizon," as Ricoeur calls it, of the author's, or, presumably, the author's culture's, "own existential situation."[8] To make that discursive power one's own—that is, to follow the arrow of sense wherever it leads—entails an enlargement of mind that potentially enhances the reader's capacity for self-knowledge. Thus, the hermeneutic circuit is completed only when the reader has been able to reposition her or his reconstructed conception of the text's own self-understanding, itself a function of the text's projection beyond itself, within the expanded horizon of the reader's own new self-understanding.

From Mailloux's perspective, however, I think it would seem somewhat beside the point to resituate the reader's expanded self-understanding back within the loop of the interpretive process itself and to hold to the view that the hermeneutic arc remains abridged so long as there is no traffic or negotiation between the rhetorical recovery of the conditions of the text's historicity and the rhetorical refiguration of the reader's historicity. Rather, what he wants to urge is that we abandon the attempt to ground critical inquiry in general theories of interpretation and reconvert it instead into producing "rhetorical histories of specific interpretive acts."[9] And once this shift from hermeneutic theory to rhetorical history has been accomplished, then cultural rhetorical studies can take the place of pragmatist antifoundationalism and the way will be cleared for the interpretive employment of rhetoric, as Mailloux states in a memorable formulation, "to practice theory by doing history."[10]

At this point, the question to be asked is, What has been gained and what has been lost by this set of maneuvers? What has been gained is the ability to redescribe cultural studies as a form of rhetorical reception studies. So redescribed, cultural studies becomes an enterprise intent on showing how, when texts are resituated within the context of the cultural conversations that initially shaped their interpretation, the history of these conversations affords an instance of "interpretive theory as a form of rhetorical history."[11] Thus, the historical interpretation of *The Adventures of Huckleberry Finn* becomes an interpretation of the rhetorical tropes by which the text was read. What, on the other hand, seems to have been lost in this process of redescription is any way of determining whether one interpretation is finally any better than another, or how it would matter if it were. And this leads me to raise questions about Mailloux's view of pragmatism and his conception of rhetoric.

Mailloux's view of pragmatism, as he would be the first to admit, is strongly indebted to the postanalytic assault that Richard Rorty has made on philosophical foundationalism. This assault appears to leave the whole burden of argumentation in the hands of the field of rhetoric itself, where persuasion is achieved, in the Rortyan version, not through the refutation or subversion of ideas but rather through their displacement by more attractive alternatives. In Rorty this reduction is accompanied by a twofold claim. On the one hand, he asserts that if there are no absolute grounds for thought, if there are no Archimedean standpoints from which to make truth-claims, then there really are no grounds, no standpoints, for settling arguments whatsoever; there is merely, as Rorty calls it, "the practice of playing sentences off against one another in order to decide what to believe," a practice that "no more requires a 'ground' than the practice of using one stone to chip pieces off another stone in order to make a spearpoint."[12] This practice is ultimately resolved, at least for Rorty, by what deserve to be termed aesthetic factors. That is, we usually decide between competing versions of things, as Rorty notes in various places, in favor of what appears most attractive or appealing to us; essentially, what counts is desire, what we like or want. On the other hand, he maintains that since we lack any transcendental common vocabulary in which to weigh the alternative perspectives of different conceptual schemes and word games, we should abandon the attempt to argue between things that are to begin with inherently incommensurable and simply get on with the rhetorical business either of making our own positions look better by making those of our enemies look worse or by hunting for more inviting options.

Mailloux himself appears to be made uncomfortable by this last claim, acknowledging not only that new paradigms of understanding often emerge through the weakening of old ones but also that old paradigms often succumb to new argumentation. But if old paradigms can be weakened by new argument, old paradigms can just as surely be bolstered by better arguments, at which point Rorty's tactic of leaving the whole problem at the door of rhetoric, where the only relevant question becomes who has the more compelling tropes, becomes less convincing.

Less convincing still is Rorty's insistence that the possibility of comparing different paradigms or of arguing across them necessarily hinges on the existence of some transcendental common vocabulary. With assistance from Donald Davidson (a philosopher to whom Rorty also turns for support), I would propose on the contrary that such possibilities rest instead on something about the way we use language even in the absence of any universal discourse. As Davidson observes, we not infrequently do manage to make sense of assertions that are composed in different languages and that reflect conceptual schemes alien to our own without falling back on some global Esperanto. We make sense of them because we assume that there is one constant in the way that we, like other people, generally employ language. That constant is the common respect that we all pay to sentences that purportedly get things straight. In other words, the one condition that seems to operate across all languages—and to determine the possibility of having a language at all—is that all people everywhere attach a particular significance to those sentences that they regard as true. This is not, of course, to say that all people take the same things to be true but only to assert that at the most primitive levels of sense-making we all confer a special value on statements that we deem to be correct or valid.

On this view, truth is more than, as Rorty calls it, "a compliment paid to sentences that seem to be paying their way";[13] it is also a description of sentences that are alleged to hit the target. Such sentences work not only in the sense that they are, as William James maintained and Rorty echoes, "good in the way of belief," but because they render states of affairs that are assumed to be as they report them. These truth-conditions, as Davidson calls them, along with such things as rational constraints and procedures of logical inference, must hold, he believes, if the language or discourse in question, including fictive discourse, is to make any sense at all. Thus, despite the vast gulf between different cultures and orders of knowledge, a broad area of agreement exists between different communities of language that enables a fair amount of not wholly inaccurate translation to go on from one to another. Whether such agreement takes the form, in Davidson's words, "of a widespread sharing of sentences held true by speakers 'of the same language,'" or "in the large [is] mediated by a theory of truth contrived by an interpreter for speakers of another language," our shared presuppositions about what counts as evidence or plausible conjecture carry us a long way toward comprehending at least some of the utterances of people different from us because we begin in the position of already knowing a good deal about the way any language has to work.[14] Indeed, Davidson is prepared to go so far as to say that "whether we like it or not, if we want to understand others, we must count them right on most matters,"[15] which means that the precondition for understanding them, in Christopher Norris's rephrasing, is, first, that they make sense in ways not altogether dissimilar to our own and, second, that they place as high a value on sentences that get things right as we do.[16]

If this general semantic practice of honoring sentences that hold true constitutes a kind of linguistic universalism, it is nonetheless as far from traditional foundationalism, with which it could be mistakenly confused, as it is from cultural relativism, with which it is more typically (and disparagingly) contrasted. The contemporary form of cultural relativism derives from the belief that different languages and texts are products of the codes and conventions built into them, codes and conventions that prevent anyone not raised within the cultural world produced and framed by them from understanding anything they express. A position most forcefully articulated by those theorists who hold that the differences in languages are attributable to the differences between the essentially incommensurable conceptual schemes underlying them, it is reinforced in literary studies by Stanley Fish.

Fish, whose version of the new pragmatism has in turn strongly influenced Mailloux's, argues vigorously that since all interpretation occurs within the consensus of values and practices defined by some institutional or professional community, no theory attempting to call the terms of that consensus into question, or to revise them, can do so from a position outside their range of governance. But if the expressions of any culture or form of life make sense only in terms of the assumptions, practices, and consensual judgments that define it, then it is just as great a delusion, according to Fish, to think that one can criticize those expressions from some theoretical position independent of them as it is to imagine, to go back to Rorty again, that one can develop some neutral basis for deciding between their relative merits.

Yet this only raises all over again the issue of whether the notion of truth can simply be thrown out with philosophical foundationalism without depriving pragmatist hermeneutics of the possibility of engaging in any sort of cultural critique. Mailloux seems to suppose that with foundationalism out of the way, interpretation can simply be left to fend for itself "within the historical clash of opinion."[17] But one must then ask whether, without an acceptance of truth-conditions that obtain across as well as within opinions and interpretations and that afford us some measure of reciprocal grasp of their salient differences, we have any way of assessing those differences, much less of knowing where or how they might be at variance with our own.

Still another problem with Rorty's and Mailloux's summary dismissal of foundationalism lies in the alternative with which he thinks it leaves us. If the only alternative to being "objective," to achieving "a consensus on what we should believe"—a possibility for Rorty only when the debate occurs within a common or overlapping vocabulary—is "a willingness to abandon consensus in the hope of transfiguration,"[18] what kind of choice does this really amount to? Aren't the facts of the matter actually quite different, even contrary? For example, don't most of us act as though we have already been able, or should be able, to achieve a measure of consensus on what to believe, just as the vast majority of us behave most of the time as if "transfiguration" was probably not the main thing on our minds? Not that many of us wouldn't like to change our situation from time to time; only that most of us have no desire to couple this, as Rorty's trope suggests, with a fundamental change in ourselves.

But if in ordinary practice we in fact manage to reach certain kinds of agreement, even across broadly diverse ranges of experience, simply in order to converse, don't we also sometimes succeed in altering the way we think and feel without exchanging, or needing to exchange, whole conceptual frames or intellectual paradigms? The answer, of course, is yes, and the reason is the same in both instances. We succeed in securing a measure of consensus on what to believe—and, at the same time, occasionally abandon that consensus for the sake of adopting an alternative set of beliefs—because of our capacity to recognize that if many of the same truth-conditions operate within different vocabularies and worldviews, then we have some basis for comparing them and thus for changing our minds about which look better to us.

This suggests that the problem with Rorty's pragmatism may be identical to the problem with Fish's: both have been stripped down and modified to accommodate a postphilosophical view of culture in which all claims to truth or knowledge have been reconceived as rhetorical impositions made from within a body of currently acceptable beliefs, and all argumentation about their merits is in danger of being reduced to the performative level of their suasive effect. While this adjustment puts rhetoric back in the saddle, so to speak, this makes it all too easy to suppose that rhetoric, rather than conceptual schemes, is now what "goes all the way down," the form that rhetoric predominantly takes being interpretive tropes that are assumed not only to be culturally ubiquitous but also, at least for a certain class of readers, politically constitutive.

By this last assertion, I do not mean to suggest that there is anything problematic about the rhetorical study of the hermeneutic tropes that create and so often control habits of reading in any given era. Nor do I wish to challenge the contention that these tropics of discourse and interpretation, —located as they are at the nexus of a set of cultural conversations, institutional practices, and material circumstances—reflect such matters and also help shape them. Among all that Mailloux has accomplished here, he has nowhere been more successful than in showing how, in later nineteenth-century American literature, the tropes that associated reading with eating, mental discipline, and moral control managed to forge in the society of that era an amazingly "close connection among moral order, mental development, and bodily exercise."[19] All I wish to maintain is that by identifying these tropes so closely with the productive instrumentalities of meaning in this literature—and by assuming in addition that these instrumentalities extended throughout that part of the culture with which he is concerned—he tends to foreclose the question as to whether any writers were able to think against these tropes, or, for that matter, whether the tropes themselves, as Richard Poirier might propose, ever turned against themselves or took interpretive detours they were themselves supposed to prevent. Mailloux's close correlation of rhetoric with reading practices, and his view that these practices are deeply hegemonic, also tends to circumvent the question as to whether in "doing history" we are obliged to take any account of the many potential meanings, as they reveal themselves to our present historical position, that these same tropes apparently succeeded in glossing, effacing, or concealing.

The first issue comes up in relation to Mailloux's discussion of *Little Women*, a novel that, according to the traditions of the period, was both conventional and unconventional at the same time. While the novel is rich in sentimentality and moralism, using large doses of the *New Testament* and *Pilgrim's Progress* as rhetorical models both for self-control and for self-improvement, it is also obvious that the world of *Little Women* is distinct from the customs of the age: it is constituted not as a patriarchy but as a matriarchy; each of the novel's four heroines projects a somewhat different image of womanhood; and no matter how successful Jo's reading has been in creating a technology of the self that curbs her own anger, she, in particular, constructs herself as what, for her own era, was considered a new kind of "little woman," a tomboy ultimately unsusceptible to being disciplined within the conventional form of the female. Moreover, in Part II of *Little Women* and in its sequels, *Little Men* and *Jo's Boys*, Jo is handsomely rewarded for her pains not only with children and two careers but with a husband who does the dishes. "In contemporary terms," as Alison Lurie notes, "she has it all . . . : demand freedom and independence, and you may get it—and love as well."[20]

The second issue comes up in relation to Mailloux's treatment of *Pilgrim's Progress*, which he ably interprets as a gloss on the inner struggles of the girls and a model for their self-discipline. Reading *about* self-reform is here turned into reading *as* self-reform: "Consuming books like *Pilgrim's Progress* helps the girls re-figure the disorderly process of growing up as an orderly progression of moral development."[21] The question one is left with is what to do about the knowledge associated with a later and more sophisticated stage of development in the text's interpretation. This is a stage associated with our own historical moment, when we have now become convinced that to read Bunyan's text as representing any pattern of behavior to be imitated, any model of action to be appropriated, may well be seriously to misread it.

As reader-response criticism has taught us, the rhetorical tactics of *Pilgrim's Progress* are designed to erode the sense of certainty that there is some assured path to redemption, some reliable formula for salvation, and thus to prepare the reader to acknowledge, as Christian does, that nothing can be trusted as a moral guide, as an object of imitation, into the Heavenly City but that which is inimitable—namely, the absolute grace and sovereignty of God alone. Although this crisis of certitude has the paradoxical effect of at the same time throwing the self back on its own experience, it nonetheless erodes all confidence in the heuristic structure of mimeticism and thus modifies the function of rhetoric itself.[22] Learning to read the meaning of one's own experience, as Christian must, as a potential history of misreading only moves the self in the direction of an interpretive location where all the tropes by which its own situation might otherwise have been comprehended are shown to be inadequate and the self is left with no other alternative but to utterly entrust itself in faith to God's mercy.

While there is little evidence that any of the above enters the consciousness of the characters of *Little Women*, or even of its narrator, it is difficult to imagine how it could now be purged from our own. But this only points out that if our own historicized sense of any text is markedly different from that experienced by any of the characters in these texts, then recovering the literary past, or, in Mailloux's locution, "doing history," may well involve more hermeneutically than simply resituating the rhetorical processes of reading within the wider horizon of cultural dialogues that simultaneously framed and in part fashioned them. It may also have to do with determining what probable meanings, from among the various possibilities belonging to any text's potential horizon of significance, were rendered accessible to understanding and appropriation by those reading practices, and what meanings, from the perspective of our own later interpretation of that same text and its potential horizon of significance, were, for whatever reason, left unrealized, overlooked, hidden, or denied.

No doubt part of the meaning of the historical in any given situation, even the political meaning of the historical, can be reached through the study of rhetoric, as Mailloux rightly insists and so often demonstrates, when rhetoric is not viewed simply as "an expression or reflection of 'deeper' historical forces, whether psychological, social, political, or economic" but as "(at least partly) constitutive of these other historical categories." As Mailloux asserts, "A theoretically oriented cultural studies describes and explains past and present configurations of rhetorical practices as they affect each other and as they extend and manipulate the social practices, political structures, and material circumstances in which they are embedded at particular historical moments."[23] So far so good. But another aspect of the meaning of the historical is likely to be lost—and with it the opportunity to turn cultural rhetorical studies into a form of cultural critique—if we fail to build into our conception of it, with the assistance of more subtle notions of truth and more complex understandings of the process of appropriation, a more dialectical sense of the relation between the probable and the possible. Pierre Bourdieu says it perfectly: "the political task of a responsible social science [could we not say of a responsible human science?] . . . is to help define a rational utopianism by using the knowledge of the probable to make the possible come true."[24]

Chapter 7

The Pragmatics of the Aesthetic

> She would take him to faraway lands to observe foreign ways, so he could get closer to the strangeness within himself.
>
> Fatima Mernissi on Scheherazade

The correlation between the aesthetic and the pragmatic has been problematic ever since William James first hijacked—as Peirce later felt about it—the term *pragmatism* in his lecture on "Philosophical Conceptions and Practical Results" at the University of California at Berkeley in 1898. Indeed, despite recent work by various critics and scholars, conventional wisdom about pragmatism's sensitivity to the aesthetic remains pretty much where Lewis Mumford left it in *The Golden Day* in 1926.[1] "The Pragmatic Acquiescence," as he termed it, represented a particularly sorry moment in the history of American creative thought. Instead of effecting "an overturn in philosophy," as James himself had hoped, pragmatism simply "killed only what was already dead."[2] Amounting to no more than a bit of antifoundationalism here, a bit of social constructionism, relativism, and radical empiricism there, some individualism here, and some multicultural pluralism there, pragmatism betrayed the practical aesthetic mission of all genuinely innovative thinking: "to gather into it all the living sources of its day, all that is vital in the practical life, all that is intelligible in science, all that is relevant in the social heritage and, recasting these things into new forms and symbols, to react upon the blind drift of convention and habit and routine."[3]

While irony abounds in the fact that James himself could easily have accepted this definition of creative thought as the aesthetic mission of pragmatism itself—Mumford could have been parroting James when he said, "Life flourishes only in this alternating rhythm of dream and deed; when one appears without the other, we can look forward to a shrinkage, a lapse, a devitalization"[4]—Mumford's judgment at the same time reflects the depth of misapprehension from which pragmatism's interest in the aesthetic has suffered ever since. This misapprehension becomes only the more surprising if one remembers that the ultimate aim of Charles Sanders Peirce's "marvelously intricate universe," as Joseph Brent once described it,[5] was not merely to display the dependence of logic on ethics but also the dependence of ethics on aesthetics, and to demonstrate along the way how all logical inquiries require something like an aesthetic leap of faith to bring them to conclusion, as when we say "This fits" rather than "This is correct." It also disregards the fact that James himself installed the aesthetic at the very center of epistemological operations by reconstruing all mental calculations as a kind of art in which the "inferential" and the "possible" play at least as large a part as the "practicable." It entirely ignores the fact that George Herbert Mead subsequently constructed out of pragmatism a philosophy of the act in which thinking is undertaken and selves constructed by means of epistemological traffic in what Mead called "significant symbols." And, finally, it slights the all-important fact that Dewey later went further, perhaps, than all of his fellow pragmatists with his claim that, by permeating all experience, the aesthetic thus succeeds in making all experience art in potential.

To stay with several of the founders of pragmatism for a moment and draw this out somewhat further, it is worth recalling that James not only identified the meaning of ideas with outcomes and consequences; he also insisted that many of these outcomes and consequences cannot be verified and confirmed before we must act on them. We act for the most part not on the basis of confirmed facts but on the basis of surmises and conjectures. Thus, for James the imagination assumed a role in the operations of the intellect that was far from accidental or secondary, since so much of the life of the mind is devoted to determinations whose results we can never substantiate in advance but can only guess at or speculate before we have to respond to them. Dewey then took this same conception of the pragmatic method one step further in *Experience and Nature* by identifying what he called the "critical," by which he meant the intellectual, with a double movement that of necessity operates aesthetically in two directions at once. While one of the aesthetic movements of critical reflection inevitably carries inquiry back into the past to determine the probable, as opposed to certain, conditions from which something presumably emerges, the second inevitably carries inquiry forward by trying to figure out the potential, as opposed to the predictable or assured, outcomes in which something may issue.

In *Art as Experience*, Dewey ratcheted up still further his claims for the primacy of the aesthetic, arguing that, as the potential form and destiny of every experience, it is not merely one category among others but in fact the most basic category of all. Dewey had already stated as early as 1920 that "reconstruction in philosophy"—as he entitled the seminal lectures he delivered the year before in Japan—depends on relinquishing the search for an absolute and immutable reality and replacing it with an effort to enhance experience by exploring its possibilities for richer and more extensive fulfillment. This meant abandoning what he later called, in his Gifford lectures, "the quest for certainty" and supplanting it with a new philosophical practice in which "the creative work of the imagination" is understood to be merely the obverse of the "negative office" performed by philosophy's "critical mind. Where the latter is directed against the domination exercised by prejudice, narrow interest, routine custom and the authority which issues from institutions apart from the human ends they serve," the former points "to the new possibilities which knowledge of the actual discloses" and projects "methods for their realization in the homely everyday experience of mankind."[6] It was but a short step from thus reintegrating the imagination within the new practice of philosophy to reconceiving experience as itself a form of art in *Art as Experience* and then reformulating the purpose of art, in terms not unlike those that Nietzsche had invoked earlier, as the continuous revaluation and augmentation of life itself.

In the remainder of this chapter I wish to press these claims for the conjuncture between the pragmatic and the aesthetic still further. Let me begin by noting that insofar as the aesthetic can, at least under certain circumstances or conditions, be conceived as constituting, if not a realm apart, then at least a realm that is discriminable and distinctive, it has often been held to carry within itself practical dimensions with markedly ethical overtones. Support for this belief initally comes from a tradition that in America goes back at least to Ralph Waldo Emerson, Margaret Fuller, and Walt Whitman, and that has its sources in Europe in the thinking of everyone from Giambattista Vico, Johann von Herder, and Madame de Staël to Edmund Burke and Samuel Taylor Coleridge. Variously described most recently by Raymond Williams and Richard Rorty, this tradition possesses as one of its chief interests the meaning of culture itself when the chief business of culture now involves taking over and reshaping from theology and philosophy the task of deciding whatever is worth keeping in such various departments of contemporary experience as science, art, politics, social thought, literature, morality, humor, and religion.

In recent years, this same tradition has itself come under severe attack, where it has not been simply dismissed, for being no more than a reinscription of the traditional Arnoldian, or, if you prefer, Genteel American, theory of culture. Much of this attack has seemed by turns short-sighted and self-serving, since it could be plausibly argued that instead of having thoroughly broken with this theory of the work of culture, much less having successfully superseded it, we have merely decided in the present historical moment to reconceive what it is that culture actually seeks to repossess and reshape, how this process is effected, who in fact may be said to participate in or contribute to this process, and why it is that this project is deemed important in the first place.

Consistent with our more democratic, or at least less elitist, racist, or sexist views of such matters, we are now more likely to say that culture seeks to appropriate and redescribe what any given people have, if you will, learned from their experience. This is reflected not only in the specialized forms of their science, philosophy, religion, and so forth but also in their tales, songs, aphorisms, jokes, dances, riddles, oratory, and manners—in short, the strategies they have devised for answering, or at least for symbolically encompassing, the questions put to them by the problematics of their own existence. We still maintain, however, that one of the principal mediums in which such reflections occur is the realm of the aesthetic, which in alliance with its chief instrument, the imagination, provides the motive force for all those symbolic stratagems by which a culture's wisdom or ignorance is refracted and transmitted. We assume that the people who deserve most credit for contributing to and advancing this process are not simply those who, in response to questions posed by the problematic forms of their existence, have produced the most sophisticated symbolic answers to them, but also any individuals, far more numerous, who have had a hand in turning those answers into modes of ritual re-enactment and ceremonial self-realization for other people and later times. And, finally, we now take such cultural work to be important not alone because it reveals, as was once assumed, an essential unity of being underlying all its expressions but also because it suggests—or can suggest—something of the greater diversity of life forms that can now be comprehended and accepted as at once recognizably human and also ethically significant.

Culture in this sense, then, has in the interests of its own explication developed a kind of reading and writing—actually a kind of writing about reading—that we call criticism, a kind of writing that from the time of Goethe, Carlyle, and George Eliot to that of Hannah Arendt, Ralph Ellison, and Jacques Derrida has neither been, as Richard Rorty has put it, "an evaluation of the relative merits of literary productions, nor intellectual history, nor moral philosophy, nor epistemology, nor social prophecy but all these things mingled together in a new genre."[7] While the idioms in which this form of writing expresses itself have clearly changed over the last several decades, thanks in no small measure to the importation of a variety of new discourses from the Continent, the kind of task that this "new" genre of critical reflection has set for itself has remained more or less consistent. That task might be described as determining what to make of our customary ways of making sense when there is no longer any universally authoritative vocabulary in which to describe those ways, much less any universal agreement within such a vocabulary about how to evaluate their comparative advantages and disadvantages?

Here, again, the aesthetic is alleged to hold the key, a key that is both practical and ethical at the same time. As attested by a host of witnesses from Hans-Georg Gadamer, Paul Ricoeur, Wolfgang Iser, E. H. Gombrich, Annette Baier, and Clifford Geertz to Barbara Herrnstein Smith, the aesthetic emerges for this tradition at the point where, as Hayden White once put it, "our apprehension of the world outstrips our capacities for comprehending it, or, conversely, where canonized modes of comprehension have closed off our capacities for new experience." Either way, the aesthetic acquires a critical relation to what E. H. Gombrich refers to as a culture's mental set by appearing to breach, to return to White, "the conventional hierarchies of significance in which experience is presently order" and to project a new imagination or sense of things "which previously existed only as a perceptual possibility."[8]

While retaining the same practical and ethical mission for the aesthetic, Paul Ricoeur has expressed this somewhat differently by associating the aesthetic with the power texts possess to project a world of potential meaning and implication beyond the range of their own ostensive reference. In other words, texts become more aesthetic the less their range of potential meaning and implication is constrained either by the hierarchies of significance that define their wholeness or by the semiological and tropological mechanisms that determine their distinctiveness, and the more it depends on the vectors of sense they propel outward beyond themselves. It is these trajectories of meaning they project beyond themselves—and which can then be actualized and appropriated in any number of ways—that give to aesthetic as opposed to other kinds of texts the appearance of transcending themselves, of being able to invoke, or at any rate to insinuate, worlds of import not fully amenable to representation by their own expressive materials. But they transport us in imagination to distant places, to foreign topographies of the mind, to follow Scheherazade, only so that we may become better acquainted with the strangeness within ourselves.

Barbara Herrnstein Smith explains the aesthetic's, or, as she prefers to call it, the "fictive's," capacity for enabling this kind of flight and return in relation to the peculiar cognitive needs that it serves. On the one hand, human beings are unable to express or communicate everything they know, or feel, or desire, because, as she puts it, the motives, reasons, and necessities for human expression are far more plentiful than the opportunities for it. We all long for occasions to talk and be talked to that our society can never adequately provide, whether because the saying of it would expose us to contempt, hostility, danger, embarrassment, or incrimination, or because the persons with whom we would and must speak are, like dead relatives, absent friends, estranged lovers, divine beings, or jars in Tennessee, inaccessible to us, or because what we have to say is too complicated, subtle, ambiguous, self-contradictory, or offensive to put into words. Consequently, Smith notes, there are always sentiments we could express, ideas we would explore, and desires we might acknowledge if there were suitable occasions on which to do so, appropriate audiences to hear them, and available styles and forms in which to render them. On the other hand and at the same time, human beings are constantly subject to potential experiences, as Smith calls them, that pass them by, either because these experiences don't serve their most immediate cognitive needs or because, for whatever reason, human beings suppress them. Whichever the case, "much that is potentially knowable to us, because it is part of what has, in some sense, happened to us, slips by apparently unknown or at least unacknowledged."[9] Without some reason for acknowledging such prior experiences—"a perception never before quite articulated, an emotion we had sustained on the periphery of consciousness, a sense, barely grasped, of the import of some incident"[10]—they slip away from us, depriving us of what we didn't even know we knew.

Aesthetic or fictive texts seem eminently suited to help remedy these two problems by simultaneously furnishing occasions, with their necessary audiences and appropriate styles, when the unspeakable may be spoken, the potentially lost retrieved. However, inasmuch as aesthetic texts utter the unutterable not by actually bringing the dead back to life, rendering God visible, or recovering lost experiences, but rather by creating a re-presentation or imitation of such things, or at least by creating situations that trigger such memories and actions, there is much that is in danger of being missed, blocked, or misinterpreted in aesthetic transactions. If all the meanings of any text are at least potentially inferable, more of them in aesthetic texts are interpretively indeterminate and unstable; which is why aesthetic texts encourage, and indeed often compel, a greater degree of speculative play than other kinds of texts. In fact, that play itself constitutes a considerable part of their meaning. Not that the play is, as some poststructuralists believe, wholly speculative and free-form, encouraging readers to begin anywhere in a text and simply let their imaginations roam. Even the most experimental and nonconventional texts shape and direct such activity while at the same time provoking it: "Even as certain possibilities of interpretation are opened, they are also directed, lured, and redirected by the poet through the verbal structure he has designed."[11]

Perhaps the simplest way of explaining how the verbal structures of literary forms stimulate as well as direct the speculative play they encourage is by reminding us that they are generally constructed like conditional contrary-to-fact or "as-if" statements. Typically addressing aspects of human subjectivity that otherwise tend to be glossed, ignored, discounted, shunned, or mystified, aesthetic texts cast these aspects in forms that allow the feelings as well as the intellect to interrogate them. These forms are structured and motivated in such a way that within their confines we can accept as plausible, though not necessarily as inevitable, both the actions and the responses into which their initial situations—what Henry James called "the donnée"—are imagined to unfold. Grant me my initial assumptions, the aesthetic or fictive text states, assumptions that we can all accept as given with, or at least possible for, experience itself—in *King Lear*, let us say, that all fathers want gratitude from their children; in *Uncle Tom's Cabin*, that all mothers want to keep their families together; in *Moby-Dick*, that injustice perceived as divine must be answered for—and I will show you where those assumptions can lead.

As a suppositional or conjectural structure, then, what the aesthetic text takes from life are not its conclusions but rather the terms and substance of its original premise, which it then selects, rearranges, and develops on behalf of producing a purely hypothetical or speculative outcome, that is, a set of events that are not given at all with the original premise but which nonetheless follow from it as one set of alternatives within a variable range of conditions.[12] Aesthetic texts, we thus say, are less interested in confirming or interpreting the known than in extending the realm of the knowable. But the realm of the knowable they potentially extend is not one whose contents can be defined apart from the figures of its expression, and the figures of its expression allow for—and indeed invite—speculation as to their meaning precisely because of their critical relation to their own medium. And when literature reflects on its own discourses, it creates within those reflections an "internal distance" that ultimately results from what Pierre Macherey calls "the non-adhesion of language to language, the gap that constantly divides what we say from what we say about it and what we think about it." If this is the "the void, the basic lacuna on which all speculation is based," it not only prevents all speculation from becoming fixed on a single content but enables us, finally, to think and feel differently than we normally do.[13] Constituting an ironic relation between the aesthetic object and its own materials, this void or lacuna makes it possible for the aesthetic object "to erect a larger context of experience within which we may define and understand our own by attending to the disparity between it and the experience of others."[14]

In this conception, then, the heuristic value of the aesthetic is closely associated with its pragmatics, and its pragmatics are both critical and emanicipatory. Aesthetic texts are critical just insofar as they submit actual conditions and their presumed consequences to the contrasting prospect of potential experiences whose outcomes are merely plausible. On the other hand, aesthetic texts are emancipatory just insofar as the contrast they probe, or at any rate presuppose, between the actual and the potential leads to an extension, however minimal, of our sense of the knowable, just insofar as their technologies of projection alter, at least temporarily, how we think and feel.

From the perspective of contemporary critical fashions, this conception of the aesthetic and its heuristic potential may appear to concede too little to such current nostrums as the "death of the author," the self-deconstruction of the text, the intertextualization of culture, the relativization of cultural perspectives and standpoints, and the subsumption of all such processes in the struggle for power. Furthermore, each of these critical approaches amounts to a further erosion in the coherence, effectuality, or relevance of the category of the aesthetic itself. Its real vulnerability, however, may come from the greater likelihood that the aesthetic, far from being delegitimated, eviscerated, or extirpated in this postmodern moment, has now apparently breached all textual and nationalist boundaries and begun to circulate freely as, if you will, the main solvent of culture as a whole.

This last describes the altogether new efficacy and centrality attributed to the aesthetic by, among others, Arjun Appadurai. Appadurai attributes this alteration in the fortunes of the aesthetic to the development of a post-electronic world, together with recent, unprecedented movements of people worldwide, that have created new opportunities for the making of imagined selves and invented worlds:

> Thus, to put it summarily, electronic mediation and mass migration mark the world of the present not as technically new forces but as ones that seem to impel (and sometimes compel) the work of the imagination. Together, they create specific irregularities because both viewers and images are in simultaneous circulation. Neither images nor viewers fit into circuits or audiences that are easily bound within local, national, or regional spaces. Of course, many viewers may not themselves migrate. And many mass-mediated events are highly local in scope. . . . But few important films, news broadcasts, or television spectacles are entirely unaffected by other media events that come from further afield. And few persons in the world today do not have a friend, relative, or co-worker who is not on the road to somewhere else or already coming home, bearing stories and possibilities.[15]

Nonetheless, even if technological advances in the global reach of communications and the increased movement of peoples have now somehow altered the role of the imagination, and with it the practical work of the aesthetic, it seems on the face of it a bit exaggerated to claim that this has fundamentally altered the role of the imagination in the modern world. Ever since the age of print capitalism, as Benedict Anderson pointed out some time ago, the imagination has been busy creating—and revising—collective senses of identity among people lacking any personal knowledge of each other, people defined by boundaries other than geographical or territorial, boundaries that can nowhere be accurately or adequately represented, even through the instrumentalities of the law. These same collective senses have also always been reinforced for people in the age of print capitalism by an unsubstantiable belief in the sovereignty or integrity of what those boundaries mark, a sense of sovereignty that has in turn afforded them a feeling of solidarity with others that is more or less self-validating.[16] And long before the age of printing, as everyone from the brothers Grimm, Max Mueller, and Sir James Frazer to Jane Harrison, Northrop Frye, and Italo Calvino have reminded us, narrative structures that were originally transmitted orally, such as myth, legend, folktale, and even anecdote, accomplished roughly similar feats.

Appadurai's point, however, is that this is the first age when, as he puts it, "the imagination has broken out of the special expressive space of art, myth, and ritual and has now become a part of the quotidian mental work of ordinary people in many societies." The imagination has not only, as he says, "entered the logic of ordinary life from which it had largely been successfully sequestered" but in its role as the producer and reinforcement of fantasy work has now also acquired a new and more collective sense of agency.[17] Whether as catalyst or as intoxicant, the imagination helps potential young freedom fighters and their antagonists dream, so to speak, in "Rambo"; at the same time it enables women separated by oceans as well as cultures to share with their sisters all over the world senses of common oppression and empowerment. In instances such as these, the imagination is more than a place of escape; it is also an inducement to action and a site of contestation.

While much of his analysis is persuasive, Appadurai's claim that until very recently the imagination has been largely sealed off from the logic of ordinary life—and thus presumably has been unable to perform its role in the pragmatics of daily existence—is quite possibly overstated. Even if the scope of the imagination—and perhaps as well its ethical governance, or at least its ethical influence—has never extended wider than it now does in our new digital era, it has always been deeply sedimented in the logics—and what Ralph Waldo Emerson called the "precincts"—of the ordinary. Let me turn to three somewhat different accounts of how the aesthetic has found its way into the precincts of the ordinary, the first social and political, the second epistemological and ethical, the third literary and cultural.

The first account comes from the writings of Hannah Arendt and in certain respects parallels the thinking of John Dewey. Arendt's theory about the ethical dimensions of the aesthetic emerges from her discussion of Kant's *Critique of Judgment*, and particularly the first part, entitled "Critique of Esthetic Judgment." In this section, Kant tries to distinguish between the kind of thinking we associate with pure reason, which requires that the thinker be in agreement with him- or herself, and the kind of thinking called judgment, which requires that the thinker come to some kind of agreement with, as it were, everyone else. Assuming that the positions of all others are at least potentially open to inspection, this second kind of thinking is decidedly social, even political:

> the power of judgment [as of interpretation] rests on a potential agreement with others, and the thinking process which is active in

judging [or interpreting] something is not, like the thought process of pure reasoning, a dialogue between me and myself, but finds itself always and primarily, even if I am quite alone in making up my mind, in an anticipated communication [or conversation] with others with whom I know I must finally come to some agreement.[18]

The thinking known as judgment, then, is made possible by the imagination and seeks insofar as possible to liberate itself from purely personal or subjective factors and enter into the place from which others think, thereby achieving what Kant called an "enlargement of the mind."[19]

But this raises a serious question as to just what thinking in the place of others amounts to. As Arendt clarifies in her "Excerpts from Lectures on Kant's Political Philosophy"—which are attached as an appendix on "Judging" to the second volume, called *Willing*, of her *Life of the Mind*—it does not amount to thinking what others think. Complete empathy is neither desirable nor possible, since it would prevent one from thinking for oneself even as one tries to move into a space that is more public than private, a space, as Arendt describes it, "open to all sides."[20] Kant says at one point that thinking in the place of others entails "comparing our judgment with the possible rather than the actual judgment of others, and by putting ourselves in the place of any other man"[21]; Arendt says at another point that it "means you train your imagination to go visiting."[22] In either case, the object is to move toward a perspective that is more general without being abstract. As the thinker moves from standpoint to standpoint, his or her thinking expands. But this expansion is not achieved at the expense of subsuming all of the particular standpoints that the thinker encounters along the way: "It is on the contrary closely connected with particulars, the particular conditions of the *standpoints you have to go through* in order to arrive at your own 'general standpoint'" (my italics).[23]

As it happens, Kant's reflections on judgment would have proved less interesting to Arendt if he had not made these discoveries in the process of examining the subject of taste. For Arendt, this remained a relationship of the greatest significance because it demonstrated that taste, which has always traditionally been thought of as the most private and idiosyncratic of senses, is in fact the most public and political of human faculties. Arendt elucidates its public as well as political dimensions by pointing out that if arguments about taste cannot, as she believes, be adjudicated, much less resolved, without appeal to the sentiments and sensibilities of others, such disputes also possess the inevitable effect of drawing individuals out of themselves and into a wider world of meanings that they can share, or at least contest, with their fellows.

The effect of the exercise of taste, then, is to extend the public world of meaning, of interpretation, of significant experience we share with others by compelling us to join with them in a debate about what things are most worth valuing in that world and what attitudes shall be taken with respect to them. Without the constant and relatively free exercise of taste, Arendt believed that this world of publicly acknowledged and variously interpreted meanings and values we call culture would eventually disappear. With its assistance, on the other hand, she felt that this public world of culture could be continuously expanded and enriched, because questions of taste, like all other matters of individual judgment, can never be resolved through coercion or the appeal to authority, but only through moral argument, or, as Arendt was fond of quoting Kant to say, "by wooing the consent of everyone else."[24]

In this view, taste is not, as proverbial wisdom has it, the one thing that is altogether beyond dispute but rather almost the only thing, as Dewey noted, about which we ever do dispute. Dewey's statement is worth quoting entire:

> The word "taste" has perhaps got too completely associated with arbitrary liking to express the nature of judgments of value. But if the word be used in the sense of an appreciation at once cultivated and active, one may say that the formation of taste is the chief matter wherever values enter in, whether intellectual, esthetic or moral. . . . Instead of there being no disputing about tastes, they are the one thing worth disputing about, if by "dispute" is signified discussion involving reflective inquiry. Taste, if we use the word in its best sense, is the outcome of experience brought cumulatively to bear on the intelligent appreciation of the real worth of likings and enjoyments. There is nothing in which a person so completely reveals himself as in the things which he judges enjoyable and desirable. Such judgments are the sole alternative to the domination of belief by impulse, chance, blind habit and self-interest. The formation of a cultivated and effectively operative good judgment or taste with respect to what is esthetically admirable, intellectually acceptable and morally approvable is the supreme task set to human beings by the incidents of experience.[25]

To complete the circle with Arendt, all that Dewey omits to say here, but expressed elsewhere, is that by being formed in relation with, and always in dialogue with, other people, taste, which is but the handmaiden of the aesthetic, not only presupposes community but actually generates it.

The second account of the sedimentation of the aesthetic in the precincts of the ordinary comes from what philosophers like Martha Nussbaum and Mark Johnson have taught us about the role of the imagination in ethical reflection and understanding. Nussbaum's models come almost entirely from fiction, particularly from Henry James's view of the novel as a moral form devoted to showing us how to live and Marcel Proust's conviction that certain truths can only be examined and expressed in the form of stories. Her central point is that literary forms evoke certain kinds of practical moral reflection that cannot be evoked in any other way. She asserts that this practical thinking is most adequately expressed in complex narrative structures, by which she means everything from Samuel Beckett's novels to classical tragedy:

> ... we can say provisionally that a whole tragic drama, unlike a schematic philosophical example making use of a similar story, is capable of tracing the history of a complex pattern of deliberation, showing its roots in a way of life and looking forward to its consequences in that life. As it does all of this, it lays open to view the complexity, the indeterminacy, the sheer difficulty of actual human deliberation. If a philosopher were to use Antigone's story as a philosophical example, he or she would, in setting it out schematically, signal to the reader's attention everything that the reader ought to notice. He would point out only what is strictly relevant. A tragedy does not display the dilemmas of its characters as pre-articulated; it shows them searching for the morally salient; and it forces us, as interpreters, to be similarly active. Interpreting a tragedy is a messier, less determinate, more mysterious matter than assessing a philosophical example; and even when the work has once been interpreted, it remains unexhausted, subject to reassessment, in a way that the example does not. To invite such material into the center of an ethical inquiry concerning these problems of practical reason is, then, to add to its content a picture of reason's procedures and problems that could not readily be conveyed in some other form.[26]

If one of the reasons narrative deserves to be invited into formal ethical inquiry is because of the contribution it can make to our understanding of "reason's procedures and problems," a second is because aesthetic forms put the emotions to uses they are usually not given in nonaesthetic, more discursive forms. As Nussbaum says with particular reference to narratives (though I don't see why this doesn't apply to all forms of the aesthetic), the practical utility of the emotions as an aid to reflection is a direct result of the way they not only stimulate cognitive activity but also represent it. Indeed, far from merely arousing emotion in the reader, narratives—and, I would argue, other aesthetic forms—exist in themselves, Nussbaum rightly notes, as models, paradigms, examples, archetypes of what, in certain instances, feeling or emotion actually is. Hence the emotions are not sensational only but also cognitive, and the ideas they represent are so closely related to various of our beliefs and opinions about the world that when we change the one we alter the other.

Nussbaum's claims for the moral validity of the study of stories rests a good deal of its own validity on the belief "that the concrete judgments and responses embodied in stories are less likely to lead us astray, in the sense that they will contain what is deepest for us, most truly expressive of our moral sense, and most pertinent to action, by comparison with the abstractness of theory."[27] Yet at the same time, she admits that this does not overlook the fact that stories originate from the same fields of experience as do our other theories and beliefs and they therefore deserve to be treated with the same kind of suspicion, of interpretive skepticism and wariness, that we bring to our study of any other social constructs. This admission seems to render her argument for the moral utility of the aesthetic somewhat circular, but its circularity may simply be a function of how closely she ties the moral dimension of the aesthetic to the supposed inherency of narrative as a structure of the human mind itself. In point of fact, Nussbaum never veers very far from a notion of narrative associated with the nineteenth-century European and English novel; she has little to say about forms where such notions have been challenged (Sterne, Diderot, Broch, Musil, Kafka, Gombrowicz) or where narrative has itself been mixed with and transmuted into other forms, such as music, painting, architecture, industrial design, even fashion.

Mark Johnson seeks to back his own claims for the imaginative structure of moral understanding—and hence for the ethical implications of the aesthetic—by seeing narrative as only one of five components of moral reasoning, each of which contains a figurative component. Employing second-generation cognitive science, Johnson argues that the exercise of the moral imagination requires the ability not only to construct and interpret narratives but also to recognize and be able to think with the help of prototypical structures, to employ and manipulate semantic frames, to develop and extend conceptual metaphors, and to identify and reflect on "basic-level experience."

To think at all requires that we employ categories and concepts, but categories and concepts do not reflect, as is popularly supposed, sets of properties belonging to things in the world; rather, they describe what cognitive science thinks of as resemblances between things that seem to be of a similar type no matter what their properties or features. Thinking prototypically rather than strictly categorically thus enables reflection to become more ambulatory and less rigidified, just as, according to cognitive science, our terms and concepts acquire much of their referentiality and specificity by means of the larger frames or schemas within which we understand them. While such frames or schemas are not infinitely variable, they provide much of the scaffolding and orientation for thought that is then free to undertake more precise mappings with the help of the tropological operations afforded by metaphors.

Metaphor contributes to the moral reflection in several ways, according to Johnson. In addition to generating different ways of conceptualizing particular situations, metaphor furnishes "different ways of understanding the nature of morality as such (including metaphorical definitions of the central concepts of morality, such as will, reason, purpose, right, good, duty, well-being, etc.)," and it provides a mechanism or technology "for analogizing and moving beyond the 'clear' or prototypical cases to new cases."[28] However, there may well be experiences which have no known prototypes, which disrupt, break through, or simply recompose our traditional frame and schemas, and defy metaphorical comparisons or analogies. Johnson calls these "basic-level experiences" because they refer to such elemental phenomena as pain, fear, harm, pleasure, and humiliation, phenomena that may, or may not, be universal but that nonetheless put great pressure on the felt legitimacy or effectuality of all the other imaginative or aesthetic components of moral reflection.

At the end of this series, Johnson situates narrative itself, not because he views it as any less important than the other components of the moral imagination but rather because he seems to believe that its operations can only be understood in relation to them. If narrative is the way we organize the other components of moral reflection into a meaningful structure, it is also the way we make sense of these other ways of making sense. While no one of these modes of thinking is by itself capable of enabling the imagination to overcome the protocols of reason in moral reflection, working together they help the imagination to transform morality from a rational search for immutable laws to guide our life into a continuously aesthetic and, at the same time, practical exploration of possible solutions to the problems with which life confronts us.

The third account of the way the aesthetic has sedimented itself into the precincts of the ordinary comes from the literary critic Richard Poirier and his explicit efforts to reprise Emerson as the source of an American tradition of pragmatic reflection about poetry, language, and culture generally. Emerson is most famous aesthetically, perhaps, for his claim that the poet "uses forms according to the life, and not according to the form."[29] A statement frequently taken to license a vaporous, diffuse, unstructured subjectivity of which, as poet and even essayist, Emerson himself has often been held to be guilty, it has been used by Poirier not only to retrieve for us an Emerson who, while relaxed, digressive, and recursive, is anything but undisciplined or disengaged but also to reposition this Emerson as the source of a tradition of literary and intellectual pragmatism in American writing.

This tradition of pragmatism originated with Emerson, the elder Henry James, and his sons William and Henry, and includes Whitman, Frost, Stein, W. E. B. Du Bois, and Stevens, while also conceding a place to a host of other writers from Thoreau, Dickinson, Pound, and Dewey through Ernest Fenollosa, Alain Locke, Marianne Moore, William Carlos Williams, and Kenneth Burke to Ralph Ellison, Elizabeth Bishop, and Frank O'Hara. It has shared a suspicion of metaphysical certainties, a delight in novelty, fluidity, and action, a respect for the ordinary and the local, an absorption with the relational and transitional, and a conviction that the thinness of American cultural life—which so many critics, including Henry James, have decried as one of America's greatest cultural deficiencies—is actually one of America's genuine cultural assets.

American pragmatist writers have characteristically responded to this condition of putative cultural poverty in one of several ways. The first of these ways, even if not named as such, has received more attention in Poirier's *The Performing Self, Norman Mailer,* and *Robert Frost: The Work of Knowing,* while the second is addressed more in his *The Renewal of Literature* and *Poetry and Pragmatism.* In its vernacular and sometimes ironic or, borrowing a term from the title of Poirier's first book on Henry James, what might be called its "comic" mode, Emersonian pragmatism seeks to make a virtue of America's cultural deficiency by evincing a wary but often bemused, if not ironic, skepticism toward anything that can be associated with what the sociologist Peter Berger once called "the noise of solemn assemblies."[30] Assuming that in an economy of moral and intellectual scarcity cultural forms will always rush to fill the vacuum, the comic or vernacular strain in American pragmatism typically attempts to resist the development of a certain moral pretentiousness by rhetorically negotiating a kind of transcendence "downward" in order to restore the hard edge of proportion to the overblown values that otherwise threaten, as Mailer writes in *Armies of the Night*, to engulf each small human existence. In its comic dimensions, then, whether in the form of Mark Twain's fables or Marianne Moore's poems, American writing in the pragmatist tradition tends to view "the world's rich store of error as a genuine aspect of the truth" and therefore urges us, in the face of the way "the troublous genius of symbolism" is always tempting us to misjudge and inflate reality, to spy on ourselves with "pious yet sportive fearfulness."[31] Hence, Poirier dismisses claims about "the prison-house of language" as a critical soap opera and he recurrently chides contemporary critics for their inflation of theory.

On the other hand, in its more elevated, less antic mode, American literary, and particularly poetic, pragmatism has turned America's cultural poverty into a kind of asset—and often found its own most intense consummations—by examining moments, instances, situations where the ordinary, without being reduced to allegory or ideology, is transcended, so to speak, "upward" because it is imagined, as Poirier has written in *The Renewal of Literature*, "as if it were not less but, because extemporized within and also against existent forms, immeasurably more than the result of some 'arrangements of knowledge.'"[32] Here rhetoric seeks not to deflate, subvert, exaggerate, or ridicule the subjects of its discourse but rather to submit to the tropological behavior of language itself when those capacities that enable language to resist the technology of its own traditional associations are seen not as sources of human dispersion but of human consolidation and empowerment. In the tropological moment when words jump the tracks of their own institutionalized usages, the performative behavior of the writing calls attention to the presence of a human self even in gestures of its own disruption and effacement.

In *The Renewal of Literature* this literary practice of self-erasure is called "writing off the self."[33] In *Pragmatism and Poetry*, where attention seems to shift from what, in the earlier book, Poirier described as "the deed of writing" to something closer to what might be termed "the deed of reading," this process of self-evacuation is revealed instead in the discoveries afforded by a self-conscious linguistic skepticism, when the arrow of sense released by the deconstructive mechanisms within language itself actually enable language to point beyond skepticism, toward possibilities for personal and cultural renewal. Still more recently, in "Why Do Pragmatists Want to Be Like Poets?" Poirier identifies this same process specifically with the action of poetry: "In the category of serious poetry I of course include prose, any kind of writing in which the words speak to one another, sometimes across great textual expanses or among several texts; they clarify, inflect, argue among themselves; they merge into metaphoric or tonal concentrations, then self-divide and branch out toward other concentrations and developments."[34] To follow this movement by which language branches out, crosses over, infiltrates, and even moves, as it were, beyond itself requires that we begin to think differently about words and the things that can be done with them. Where the conventional way of thinking about such matters associates words with, as Coleridge referred to them, "fixities and definites," language with reference, verbal signs with substantives, Emerson argued, anticipating the nomenclature that William James would later employ to give this linguistic skepticism its first American philosophical elaboration, that words have more to do with actions and events, language with processes and power, verbal signs with transitives and connectives.

Poirier takes this fact and shows how language can veer away from its "inherited structuring"[35] without losing either its momentum toward further articulation or its rootage in the soil of ordinary discourse. This turning back upon itself, which we usually describe as troping, is, according to Poirier, language's gift of itself to itself, a reminder, if we ever needed one, that we need not look outside of language for whatever language can tell us of, in Dewey's phrasing, "the better life to be lived." Such clues as it affords to sublimity, perfection, and consummation are inscribed within the machinery of its own odd being, which, as Poirier has always been quick to add, is animated by "a form of energy not accountable to the orderings anyone makes of it and specifically not accountable to the liberal humanitarian values most readers want to find there."[36] To follow up such clues as it affords to "a better life," we must merely attend to those Emersonian and Poirierian moments of transition, of redirection, where the familiar is defamiliarized, the stable unsettled, the commonplace made uncanny, the legible rendered illegible without becoming unintelligible.[37]

This is reminiscent of what psychoanalytic criticism sees as the dialectic or oscillation that structures all desire and that in particular determines the function of fantasy. According to Slavoj Zizek's reading of Lacan, fantasy breaks the deadlock that desire finds itself in by constructing a scene in which the pleasure that is otherwise lost to us is relocated in the supposed "other" who deprived us of it. Fantasy thus provides a screen that shields the self from the radical threat of the "other's" own desire. To the pragmatist, on the other hand, this oscillation or dialectic merely suggests the excess, exuberance, and uselessness—what Poirier calls, thinking of Emerson, the "superfluousness"—that attends all desire and that colors all perspectives, thus encouraging the critic, like the poet, to reread and revise him- or herself. Hence Poirier's willingness not just to return to old readings and amend them but, as in the case of T. S. Eliot, for example, to formulate essentially different estimates. Thus, from a poet whose work Poirier admired for its willingness, as he put it in *The Performing Self*, to decrease its own certitudes, to a poet, as Poirier said in *The Renewal of Literature*, whose imperious preference for an aesthetics of crisis and difficulty is overwrought, self-protective, and snobbish, to a poet, as he more recently notes in *Poetry and Pragmatism*, whose imperfectly unacknowledged but still proleptic relation to a more pragmatist aesthetics of density, vagueness, and provisionality is now clear, Eliot has become for Poirier a poet he is willing to rethink because in reading himself reading Eliot he has found ways, like any good fallibilist, to be reeducated.

In an age of high theory orthodoxy, Poirier's pragmatist criticism thus represents a challenge to a variety of contemporary critical shibboleths that are at once historical, literary, cultural, political, and religious. Historically, it amounts to the recuperation of one of America's still unexhausted canonical icons by, so to speak, making him and the "tribe," as Poirier refers to it, that comes after him strange again; by, in other words, making Emerson and his pragmatist descendants once again interpretively elusive, disconcertingly strange, and critically available. Literarily, it proposes that the tradition of pragmatist literary experimentation that Emerson helped inaugurate in America offers a fundamentally different way of conceiving the intellectual and moral problems associated with linguistic and philosophical skepticism, problems that are now assumed in our postmodernist moment to define the legacy of modernism itself. Culturally, it breaks with the view that literary production has primarily to do with overcoming the burdens of inherited culture or transcending the crises of historical dissociation by claiming that the work of writing and reading spring from the same grammar of motives as a number of those other beneficial human activities with which they bear close analogies, such as parenting, lovemaking, gardening, statesmanship, and sports. Politically, it maintains that the processes by which language in particular and culture in general are currently imagined to thwart, and even to disable, human agency are paradoxically the very instruments by which human agency is in fact further enabled and empowered. Religiously, it coincides with the view that vagueness is not only a pre-condition of wisdom but a component of all warrantable belief.

Such observations notwithstanding, it may be difficult for some readers to square the critic who once associated his ideal society in *The Performing Self* with, among other things, "the disruption of conformity, the revelation of differences, [and] a tensed variety that makes every element aware of every other and especially of itself,"[38] with the critic whose sense of rhetorical wariness in a public culture currently suffering from a case of symbolic overdetermination compels him to claim, in *Pragmatism and Poetry*, that the only changes pragmatism effects are changes of language that occur wholly within language. Even if this is no more than a way of saying that pragmatism works, as Poirier notes in the same passage, in a manner similar to poetry, readers may fail to see the congruence between this conviction and the view that Poirier expressed in one of the several chapters in defense of the young in *The Performing Self*. There he contended that only through the promotion, and not just the allowance, of difference among its parts, "only by the encouragement of eccentricity," will American society "be able to locate, scrutinize, and periodically shift its center."[39]

Poirier's explanation of how changes within language altering the nature of language itself can affect something other than structures of discourse might be clearer if he could be persuaded to draw more heavily from time to time on the formulations of Dewey rather than on those of James or even of Emerson. For Dewey realized, as Emerson and James never quite managed to, that if pragmatism's relations to the structures of power and the hierarchies of culture are, on the analogy with poetry, more oblique than direct, more disguised than overt, they are no less explicit and sometimes even effective for all that. Allowing for differences of expression, Dewey found the key to their relationship exactly where Poirier now does: in the tensions and resistances of their forms, which not only open up spaces for reflection and feeling that those forms cannot contain but disclose within those spaces, as Poirier agrees with Dewey, possibilities never before apprehended.

If this turns culture itself into what Satya Mohanty calls "a moral testing ground," that moral testing ground is for Poirier, as it was for Arendt, Nussbaum, and Johnson, something more than, or at least something different from, the almost infinitely fluid, changeable, and redescribable medium that it becomes for Appadurai, where the global movement of people and information now permits the imagination to infiltrate and inflect even the most routine structures of daily life. Appadurai's view of culture bears a strong resemblance to the readily familiar postmodernist image, where aesthetics tends to subsume all other categories, including ethics, in a realm in which everything is presumed to be constructed and thus contingent, relative, and redescribable. But if everything is constructed, and hence susceptible to redescription, including our discriminations and judgments, then no matter how diverse its elaborations, aesthetic or otherwise, there is no way of explaining, as Mohanty reminds us, "what difference different kinds of construction make."[40] Diversity then exists, or at least exists for us more and more in contemporary life, not as a heuristic instrument but merely as a theatrical entertainment or a source of diversion. Hence, whether we phrase the ethical question in Dewey's terms, as which life would be better to live, or in Mohanty's terms, as why the oppressed may know something the rest of us need to understand, we cannot learn anything necessary to, or propaedeutic for, the reform of conduct or the revision of practice from any theory that severs the aesthetic from the pragmatic, that divorces the imaginary from the empirically consequential.

This leads Mohanty back in the direction of Kant in the belief that the only way that we can secure the lessons that aesthetics, among other disciplines, teaches us about cultural diversity is by grounding them in a limited kind of moral or humanistic universalism. Yet such a move is not without its difficulties. The problem is not that such a moral universal inevitably leads to an idealization of Enlightenment reason or freedom—to my mind, Mohanty successfully shows that it does not, and, in any case, belief in the dignity of reason and an autonomous human agent capable of a measure of free choice is not, as Amartya Sen has recently demonstrated with great eloquence, either an invention of the French Enlightenment or a Western bias[41]—but rather that it raises a spectre of one of the more invidious forms of essentialism, one where the definition of humanity in all its inconceivable variety is reduced to a set of shared and sharable traits.

Mohanty is by no means unmindful of this difficulty and therefore bases his claims for such universalism not on the positive features that human beings exhibit in all cultures and at all times—who could know such things?—but rather on those needs that human beings have revealed over the course of human history, needs that are inscribed, at least negatively, in the world's various declarations of human rights. These rights constitute what might be thought of as the world's estimate of those minimal requirements for human welfare that no culture or society should be permitted to deny its members. Elsewhere Mohanty associates those features "which are not purely cultural or conventional but are shared by all humans across cultures" more positively with people's ability to determine their own lives.[42]

If this still sounds like too Western a sense of universalism—isn't it, really, the disputes we have about which rights to call human rights, and how far such rights extend into the life around us, and not the consensus we ever reach about how many such rights there actually are, which reveal our commonalities, or at least our resemblances, as human beings?—the conclusion that Mohanty draws from this assertion is unassailable: "It is from such radical claims that all anticolonial movements of our times have drawn their best arguments, and it is these universalist moral and political positions that have been behind the demands for socialism, for the equality of women or the abolition of slavery—in short, behind so many of the struggles to extend and deepen democracy which constitute our modernity."[43] It is also difficult to believe that any theory of aesthetics or ethics grounded on something very much less general, or, at any rate, less widespread than this kind of humanism can provide a sufficiently convincing explanation either for how aesthetics can render diversity educative or for how consciousness can thereby be altered.

But what happens if we test this against the most difficult cases? How can consciousness be altered when the diversity in question is so alien or repellent to our experience as to be almost unrecognizable? How does aesthetics educate in the face of those experiences that challenge to the limit, if not exceed, or, rather, defeat, its own powers of representation? To answer these questions, we must turn to sites of the most extreme alterity to see how the imagination grapples not simply with what it views as the not-self but with what it experiences as inhuman, with what defies the very notion of solidarity.

PART FOUR

Beyond

Solidarity

C h a p t e r   8

Beyond Solidarity

If virtually all of the terms in which the sense of human solidarity was once expressed have now either lost much of their credibility or become obsolete, where besides the global economy do we look for possible models of its reconception and reconstitution? In this chapter, I want to examine three literary and cultural sites where a move beyond solidarity has been achieved, without precipitating a fall back into dependence and subordination, through the discovery of a certain kind of kinship with "the enemy." The first of these sites is to be found in the literature we call "postcolonial." To invoke the names of several of the figures who currently dominate its criticism, such as Edward Said, Homi Bhabha, and Gayatri Spivak, along with several of their shrewdest critics like Aijaz Ahmad and Benita Parry, is, of course, to be reminded that postcolonial literature is far from easily classified or summarized, but there still seems some agreement that this is a literature committed to resisting, if not subverting and supplanting, all those formal and informal discourses that seek to naturalize colonial power and to legitimate the perspectives that support it.[1] Such discourses are resisted in this literature through a process that is at least twofold. If the colonized "self" is to avoid the surrender of its identity to the terms dictated by the colonizing "other," it must not only forgo the temptation simply to demonize that "other" but also contrive, at least at some moments, to transcend the discursive oppositions that currently define their relationship. Demonizing or merely even stereotyping the colonizing "other" tends to reinscribe the totalizing structure of domination and subjugation even in the process of reversing its applications. Transcending such discursive oppositions altogether raises questions first voiced by Albert Memmi about how stable the distinction between colonizer and colonized is in the first place.[2]

This is not to say that postcolonial theorists are prepared to rewrite the history of colonization itself as a narrative whose purpose was something other than domination, exploitation, and oppression; it is only to acknowledge that with increasing sophistication postcolonial critics and theorists have mounted a challenge to the notion that the postcolonial subject is or was simply colonization's casualty. If the master texts of colonialism, from Christopher Columbus's *Journal,* Daniel Defoe's *The Adventures of Robinson Crusoe,* Ernest Renan's *The History of the Origins of Christianity,* Gérard de Nerval's *Voyage en Orient,* and Gustave Flaubert's *Salammbo* to Rudyard Kipling's *Kim* could not have been constructed, as Spivak maintains, without portraying the colonized as victims, their very fixation on the structure of victim-victimizer at the same time reveals, as Bhabha has noted, their insecurity about its boundaries and stability. Either way, colonizing power is no longer seen as completely hegemonic. Just as in "othering" the primitive, the European fetishization of the African reflected anxiety and fear as well as mastery and suppression, so in mimicking masters, native behavior had the effect, as V. S. Naipaul and, before him, Herman Melville, noted of menacing as well as amusing colonials. Thus, the whole process of colonization, as well as, of course, the opportunities for resistance to it, has come to be seen as extremely complex, varying from country to country and almost from decade to decade. As a result, one must be careful about asserting structural uniformities under colonialism, as the colonial subject was, even in his or her dependence, the unacknowledged source, as Spivak has pointed out, of the self-construction of colonialism's master texts; and the hybridization colonialism produced, as Bhabha maintains, merely repeated with a difference certain inconsistencies, fractures, and contradictions within colonial power itself that threatened its own legitimacy and opened up sites for possible opposition.

Indeed, Bhabha has gone farther, perhaps, than any one but Sara Suleri in dissecting the "ambivalence" of colonial discourse, showing how its struggles with its own distortion and displacement produce something that is often hybrid and unstable, and also quite different from the rhetoric of colonial authority from which it is alleged to proceed. Suleri has in turn extended this shift of the colonial model from a structure of domination to something closer to a structure of interaction by claiming that "colonial facts," being "vertiginous," often seem to be without "a recognizable cultural plot": "they frequently fail to cohere around the master myth that proclaims static lines of demarcation between imperial power and disempowered culture, between colonizer and colonized. Instead, they move with a ghostly mobility to suggest how highly unsettling an economy of complicity and guilt is in operation between each act on the colonial stage."[3] Created at the intersection of numerous boundaries that were irregular and mobile from the beginning, the distinctions between colonizer and colonized, then, should be thought of less as totalized formations in opposition to one another than as "constructions of a common, complexly interacting system."[4]

Such a system, whose oppositional formations resist being totalized because of their complex interactions, is brilliantly evoked in a text like J. M. Coetzee's *Waiting for the Barbarians* or, even better, his *Foe*, where the discursive terms that define the relations between, in the first instance, torturer and victim, or in the second, colonist and colonized, are converted upward without necessarily either viewing as diabolical the first of the terms in each pair or inevitably denigrating the second. Friday's amputated tongue, and the muteness it creates, enacts one version of the problem that the colonized typically confront: the problem of making meaning at all when others control the technology as well as the materials of its production.

Yet Friday's responses to his own muteness—dancing in a circle, playing a single note on his flute, writing and rewriting the letter "O"—all dramatize far more than his exclusion from the circles of interpretation that shut him out. They also make up a counter-representational mode designed to escape the force of the discursive polarities still operative in his resistance to, and rebellion against, the practices that prevent his participation. By in effect turning those practices against each other, Friday succeeds in transforming the signs of his own silencing into symbols by which to signify it. But he also achieves, indeed enacts, something more. In addition to exhibiting a political agency that his former status as a colonized subject purportedly denied him, he manages to illumine the ambivalence of the cultural instruments that were used to mute colonial subjects like himself by showing how they can also be employed almost as effectively to give him voice as to muffle him.

Foe is, of course, a rewriting from the perspective of the colonies of one of the great fables that inaugurated and help reinforce the colonial enterprise. Robinson Crusoe joins Christopher Columbus, John Smith, and Pocahontas, along with Caliban and Kurtz, as one of many "inaugural figures," as Edward Said calls them, who, with their initial Western texts, now not only constitute one of the most active sites of anticolonial and postcolonial reinterpretation but also furnish excellent examples of the way senses of kinship develop among strangers, rivals, opponents, and even foes.[5] This is particularly evident in the way two of my earlier literary examples have offered themselves for use in postcolonial reconstruction.

Shakespeare's "The Tempest" may represent the more celebrated case simply because its reinterpretation has afforded opportunities for postcolonial resistance in the Caribbean as well as in Africa. In the West Indian C. L. R. James's *The Black Jacobins*, the Barbadian George Lamming's *The Pleasures of Exile*, the Martinican Aime Cesaire's *Une Tempete*, the Cuban Ferdinand Retamar's *Caliban*, and the Barbadian Edward Kamau Braithwaite's "Caliban," no less than in the Kenyan Ngugi Wa Thiong'o's "Towards a National Culture" and the South African David Wallace's *Do You Love Me Master?*, Caliban serves as a figure who galvanizes opposition to the hegemony of the West. Caliban is moreover seen as a figure whose spirit of defiance has been faithfully represented by a host of historical figures—Retamar lists no less than thirty-five successors—from José Martí and Touissant L'Ouverture to Fidel Castro and Frantz Fanon. Whether one views Caliban as accepting his mongrel nature without necessarily jeopardizing his chances for future development or sees him instead as a figure capable of casting off his deformities and exchanging his present bondage for his former precolonial self, the role he has played of oppressed slave to an outside master has found its echo in subjugated communities throughout the world.

Strange as is the sense of fundamental kinship between Shakespeare and newly empowered victims of colonialism, then, the master-slave trope inscribed within "The Tempest" may well be, as Said says, "the founding insight of anti-imperialist nationalism."[6] And while the spirit of liberation that this trope has helped to energize in colonial countries can easily lead, as V. S. Naipaul has argued, to new orthodoxies and repressive tyrannies if one set of nationalist functionaries is simply replaced by another, it can also continue to serve as a source of continued liberation if, as Said adds, "Caliban sees his own history as an aspect of the history of *all* subjugated men and women, and comprehends the complex truth of his own social and historical situation."[7]

Rewritings of Conrad's *Heart of Darkness* provide, in certain respects, an even more dramatic instance of the way the sense of fundamental kinship operates across oppositions in postcolonial writing. The most celebrated example is afforded by Chinua Achebe, whose *Things Fall Apart* was written, with Yeats in mind, explicitly to challenge the distortions of Joyce Cary's comic novel *Mister Johnson* and to respond to Conrad. Achebe's target is a racism that expresses itself most egregiously in the way Conrad, like Cary, as Achebe notes in an essay of 1989, dehumanizes native people.[8] Achebe's response is to produce the portrait of a society that, for all its potential tensions, contradictions, and vulnerability, was coherent and creative, not to say complex, long before the coming of the Europeans. The arrival of missionaries, district commissioners, and other functionaries may shatter the once-stable balance of this intricately organized traditional world, but the tragedy of its collapse in no sense supports notions of African "simplicity," "childishness," "naïveté," or "innocence." Africa here, as in Ngugi wa Thiongo's *The River Between*, which invokes the spirit of Conrad's text from the beginning, is a land of complex traditions and conflicts whose future, as also depicted in Nadine Gordimer's "The Congo River," is shrouded in uncertainty and mystery.

V. S. Naipaul's *A Bend in the River* provides another instance of Conradian revision, this time, as in Achebe's *Anthills of the Savannah*, in the form of an African society in the throes of trying to reconstruct itself following the revolution against white imperialism, when rule of the country has now been assumed by an African nationalist government whose policies are just as repressive and cruel to native peoples as those of the white colonialists that they replaced. Naipaul views this postcolonial society as one whose very success in achieving independence has turned against it by depriving anyone of the capacity either to resist the new state or to confront, much less untangle and settle, the numerous conflicts left over from colonialism itself. As copper prices rise and fall, the community at the bend in the river is subjected to periods of prosperity, followed by periods of chaos, while the President of the country, known simply as the "Big Man," first employs Western imitation and then native violence to retain his own control and privilege. Naipaul's Marlow is an Indian Muslim from an East African coastal region who moves into the interior of the country to the town at the bend in the river to avoid being washed away by the tides of history that recurrently sweep over Africa as a whole and give credence to the opening line of the novel: "The world is what it is; men who are nothing, who allow themselves to become nothing, have no place in it." To avoid becoming the victim of such a pitiless, if not cynical vision, the narrator escapes one dying community only to take up residence in a community even more terminally afflicted, where time seems to run forward and backward simultaneously, as the myth of progress serves only to pull people back into the darkness of the past. It is a world whose basic rhythm is to build and destroy, to inspire and prey upon. Thus, the rage of those who take out their anger "against metal, machinery, wires, everything that was not of the forest and Africa" is as futile and pointless as those who use language to bypass the bush and the villages to create hollow edifices out of words like the "Domain," the newly established university city and research institute whose purpose is to produce the new African, which by the end of the novel is on the verge of being taken over by the jungle. All these gestures of making and unmaking are themselves struggling against what is depicted as a historical process of entropy that, like the "tall, lilac-coloured" water hyacinth that mysteriously appeared a few years before Salim arrives in the interior, is slowly but relentlessly taking over the river itself.

An Indian from Trinidad who has long lived in England, Naipaul's bitter disillusionment with nationalist movements, both political and religious, that swept through much of the Third World in the second half of the twentieth century is evident here as in much of his later writing (*Among the Believers* is a critique of Muslim fundamentalism; *Guerrillas*, an exposé of corrupt politics; *India: A Wounded Civilization*, a study of a country suffering from various disabilities). That disillusionment has earned him a good deal of disapproval from many students of the postcolonial who believe that his own status as an outsider and exile has made him too diffident to the plight of the ordinary African and too censorious of the struggle for independence. Yet it should be noted that, even if Naipaul has taken some ironic pleasure in pointing out the ways that postcolonial nationalism has mimicked Western colonial practice, he has also spared no pains in showing how postcolonial nationalism so often contains within itself a minatory design on its own people.

Still another instance of rewriting Conrad—and one that deserves to be more widely known in the West—is to be found in Tayeb Salih's *Season of Migration to the North*. This novel reverses the action of *Heart of Darkness* almost exactly, by recording the story of an extraordinary African, actually Sudanese, named Mustafa Sa'eed. Mustafa emigrates to London for purposes of conquest not unmixed, as in the case of Kurtz, with idealism. Upon returning to the Sudan to take up the life of a peasant farmer living along a great river, this time the Nile, he passes his story on to a fellow countryman who has shared his European exile and who duplicates his journey back to Africa following Mustafa's death. The Conradian doubling of Mustafa's odyssey with the narrator's allows Salih to establish a necessary critical distance between the extraordinary cultural mission of his own protagonist and the moral assessment he wants to make about the complexities of post-colonial existence in a still traditional world.

Mustafa's migration north carries him to one of the great centers of Western imperialism, where he lives out some of the roles that Europeans have cast him in. Miming the aspiration that British liberals have to pretend that Mustafa is, in Conrad's phrase, "one of us," he becomes a successful academic whose reputation as a liberal who has made his name by his appeal to humanity in economics is matched only by the suspicion that he has actually served as an agent of the British in the Sudan and a traitor to his own people. In parody of the identities that his British women foist upon him, he becomes an African sex god whose bedroom turns into a theatre of seduction that eventuates in the suicide of two women, the destruction of the life of a third, and the murder of his British wife. Living with the economic theories of Tawney and Keynes in the daytime, he inhabits Sodom and Gomorrah at night.

Mustafa, is described as all intellect and no feeling—"You're not a human being," as a female friend in Cairo had said to him, "You're a heartless machine"[9]—and enacts a kind of anticolonial revenge of the mind against those twin citadels, really corpuses, of European sanctity, the cultural canon and the white female body. The books that crowd the shelves of Mustafa's secret room, every one of which is in English, like the women he seduces (one of his English wives actually relinquishes her Christianity to worship him as a deity), serve as trophies of a lust that has its analogue, if not its source, in the heart of European as well as African darkness. During his trial for murder, Mustafa explains himself to the judges with the words: "In that court I hear the rattle of swords in Carthage and the clatter of hooves of Allenby's horses desecrating the ground of Jerusalem. . . . Yes, my dear sirs, I came as an invader into your very homes: a drop of poison which you have injected into the veins of history."[10]

This, too, however, needs to be qualified. As Mustafa realizes in recalling his entry into the world of Jean Morris, his British wife, everything before he had met her felt like a premonition, while everything after felt like an apology not for murdering her but for living a deception. One of the witnesses at his trial tries to turn it into a tale of conflict between two worlds where the West broke Mustafa's heart. But he is not Othello, he protests, but the "desert of a thirst, a lie." Mustafa's *hegira*, as it has been called, his journey to the North, is not only, like Mohammed's from Mecca to Medina, an escape from persecution—in Mustafa's case, the persecution of colonization—but also a flight towards a fabrication that can only end in self-destruction. Mustafa is as much the victim of colonialism as its avenger and can only break through this cycle by recreating a traditional life that includes taking a Sudanese wife, becoming a farmer, and accepting responsibility for his Islamic neighbors. That *hegira* also furnishes the narrator with the material to retell the story of the struggle against colonialism in both its imperialist and traditionalist dimensions from the perspective of those who have had to define their sense of fundamental kinship with it in terms that are not self-deprecating. If the victims of colonialism cannot expunge their past, they can at least reclaim and revise the readings of it that the colonizers have always advanced in their own interests. Anticolonial resistance is enacted in the ability to see in narratives of oppression the potential to rewrite them as stories of liberation. This, in effect, is how the narrator recasts the tale of Mustafa's Sudanese wife, Hosna Bint Mahmoud, who responds to her forced remarriage to one of the village patriarchs who attempts to rape her by killing him and herself.

But oppression and liberation become, in effect, two sides of the same truth, the truth that the past is now inscribed within the present not only as curse, injury, and disfigurement but also as material for what is potentially, but far from assuredly, a different future. Put another way, the past can be rewritten only if the narrator of Mustafa's tale, Marlow's equivalent, can purge himself, as Marlow cannot, not only of Europe's obsession with Africa but also of Africa's obsession with Europe. Thinking back on his own sojourn in London, when on a summer night the voices of the English could sound like those of his own people and he would imagine them as black or brown so that they would resemble the faces of Sudanese, he moves toward realizing a sense of kinship beyond solidarity by noting what separates as well as unites him with the British:

Over there is like here, neither better nor worse. But I am from here, just as the date palm standing in the courtyard of our house has grown in *our* house and not in anyone else's. The fact that they came to our land, I know now why, does that mean that we should poison our present and our future? Sooner or later they will leave our country, just as many people throughout history left many countries. The railways, ships, hospitals, factories and schools will be ours and we'll speak their language without either a sense of guilt or a sense of gratitude. Once again we shall be as we were—ordinary people—and if we are lies we shall be lies of our own making.[11]

In addition to postcolonial writing, one can find evidence of a move beyond solidarity precipitated by a similar recognition of fundamental kinship with the enemy in the literature that has been created in response to the Holocaust, or *Shoah*. Such literature—I am thinking, say, of the fiction of Primo Levi or the poetry of Paul Celan, both of which strive to make us believe, as Paul Celan says in his poem "Threadsuns," that "there are/still songs to be sung beyond humankind"—positions itself analogously to that tenuous light referred to in Celan's poem. This is a light that hangs over the waste and void before (or is it after?) Creation and yields, as in Celan's more famous poem "Death Fugue," images composed out of the words of the victims themselves and the language of his own memories. These are images— milk that is black, graves dug in air, hair of ash, dances fiddled for gravediggers—that simultaneously render the abomination in all its horror and, as John Felstiner says in his wonderful book, somehow find a voice to detail what happened.

Part of the miracle of this poetry is that its voice is created out of the language of those who sought to silence its speaking. As Shoshana Felman states, "This radical, exacting working through of language and of memory at once, takes place through a desperate poetic and linguistic struggle to, precisely, reappropriate the very language of one's own expropriation, to reclaim the German from its Nazi past and to retrieve the mother tongue— the sole possession of the dispossessed—from the Holocaust it has inflicted."[12] The poems thus enunciate, in the tongue of their oppressor and nemesis, a relation, at once cognitive and affective as well as linguistic, of strange and terrible consanguinity.

In his lecture of thanks for receiving the Literature Prize from the Free Hanseatic city of Bremen, Celan speaks of how language was the one thing that loss couldn't destroy: "But it had to pass through its own answerlessness, pass through a frightful falling mute, pass through the thousand darknesses of death-bringing speech. It passed through and yielded no words for what was happening—but went through those happenings. Went through and could come into the light of day again, "enriched" by all that."[13] His poems, like those of other, younger poets, are thus "efforts of someone . . . shelterless in a sense undreamt-of till now and thus most uncannily out in the open, who goes with his very being to language, stricken by and seeking reality."[14] Shelterlessness thus becomes a mode of accessing as well as bearing reality, of giving "reality one's own vulnerability, as a condition of exceptional availability and of exceptionally sensitized, tuned in attention to the *relation between language and event*" (italics Felman's).[15]

Later in the same speech, Celan tries to explain what, as language and because of its language, is at stake in such poetry, in any poetry. What is at stake is nothing less than dialogue, communication, communion with an approachable "other" who may never be reached but toward which the poems continue to proceed, like letters in a bottle cast out to sea in the hopes of reaching some, as Rosmarie Waldrop in her translation of the Bremen Literary Prize calls it, "shoreline of the heart."[16]

But who, then, is the "other" toward which the poem is *en route*? In his great lecture entitled "The Meridian," delivered on the occasion of receiving the Georg Büchner Prize in Darmstadt, Celan first describes it, thinking of Büchner's *Lenz*, as the self unaware of its own being, moving into the realm of the strange and uncanny in order to free itself of its obviousness, to encounter itself as strange. He is speaking here of the experience of Büchner's character but also of the experience produced by Büchner's art, which moves toward an otherness it intends, an otherness it means to bespeak. But this in turn permits Celan to shift his focus to the fact that by its very nature poetry—indeed all art—wishes not only to speak in its own behalf but, for that very reason, "also on behalf of the strange." Yet Celan immediately corrects himself to say: "no, I can no longer use this word here—on behalf of the other, who knows, perhaps of an altogether other."[17] The poem does not speak from the perspective of that "altogether other," for this would be to give up its own ground, actually "the ground of its own margin." The poem occupies a position that is in effect "still-here," not "already-no-more," but "intends another, needs this other, needs an opposite" if only because its life, its very being, is predicated on what Celan calls "the mystery of encounter."[18]

Even if Celan quickly gave up the more musical, explicit treatment of such mysteries that made his early "Death Fugue" so famous and eventually so widely anthologized as well as powerful, this aesthetic made his work vulnerable to Theodor Adorno's charge that every effort to write lyric poetry after Auschwitz is somehow barbaric. Celan's poetry acknowledges the logic behind that charge but at the same time contests, indeed repudiates, it on the same grounds that Adorno himself later repudiated it. Those grounds are based on the paradox that art alone is capable of witnessing to that which makes of it a mockery, of celebrating life while commemorating its annihilation. As few others, then, Celan realized that experiences such as the Holocaust force poetry into silence, but he also realized that the temptation to silence deriving from such experience must itself be given voice. Hence the breaks, jumps, distant allusions, and deconstructions that make much of his later poetry so difficult to follow, so quick to descend into the depths of its own unspeakability; and his willingness to confront his former enemy in the person of Martin Heidegger, in the hope that the great German philosopher, who never retracted a single word he had written or spoken in support of the Nazi regime, might one day—"today, . . . a thinking man's/ coming/word/in the heart"[19]—acknowledge, if not the crimes Nazism committed against humanity, then the suffering it brought to survivors like Celan.

Jewish and Christian myths of origin attest that the world may once have been washed by God and made immaculate, but Celan believes that God has now been annihilated, his annihilation bringing with it a terrible new ambiguity, what we might call a fresh new spectre of comparisons. The light that was in the present *of* that God, and that was as well present *in* that God, is, like the past tense of the verb "to be" and salvation, too, simply gone. What is left is merely the haunted darkness still lit by the memory of that earlier fable.

Once
I heard him,
he was washing the world,
unseen nightlong,
real.

One and Infinite,
annihilated,
ied.

Light was. Salvation.[20]

The world of suffering and abjection that Primo Levi brings before us knows of no such myth even as it testifies to all that has been annihilated with it. But Levi's world, like Celan's, nonetheless invokes through images of its absence another possibility. This is the possibility that the God of "Once" was both infinite and evil, that the divine and the demonic are merely, as certain radical thinkers from Irenaeus to Paul Tillich have maintained, if not different sides of the same thing, then the difference between the presence of the divine and its withdrawal. "If the visible spheres were formed in love, the invisible spheres," Melville's narrator in *Moby-Dick* writes as if for every death camp inmate, "were formed in fright."

Traditional Christian theology argues that religion colludes with the demonic only when it allows itself to furnish the forms and legitimation for idolatrous faith, that it serves as a counterforce to the demonic so long as it remains true to its own Christological inversion of the terms of empowerment and redemption. On the other hand, certain strains of Jewish mysticism concede that the demonic may have to be construed both as destructive and, in ways that controvert many of our customary ways of making sense religiously, creative. Still other traditions—tragic theodicy, according to Paul Ricoeur; feminist theology, according to Rosemary Ruether—actively entertain the possibility that God, at least as He has typically been conceived, is indeed radically evil. What, then, is meant by the demonic, whether conceived as "other" to the divine or as a component of it? To revert to Christian theology again, evil is usually associated in this tradition with hubris, selfishness, pride, concupiscence, but such terms seem weak surrogates for the kind of malevolence we hear in the words of Shakespeare's Aaron in *Titus Andronicus*, whose monstrous villainy, as he remarks, "Doth fat me with the very thought of it!" By beseeching Hell to let his murderous deeds be witness to his worth, Aaron seems to commit evil, like Flannery O'Connor's Satanic figure in "A Good Man Is Hard to Find," solely for the sheer pleasure of it.

But this leads us back to the ambiguity inherent in the Western notion of a divine that is at once potentially treacherous, evil, and pitiless as well as pure and good, an ambiguity no one can confront without risk of somehow being implicated in its doubleness. Here, finally, is where the hazards of the self's attempt to understand God's indifference to, or absence from, events of extreme suffering and viciousness at least partially lies, the hazard to which Holocaust writers such as Celan and Levi must so constantly and radically expose themselves. In seeking to represent the morally unthinkable, they run the risk, almost too disquieting to contemplate, of becoming potentially complicitous with committing the unspeakable.

It is in *The Reawakening* that Levi finds for himself some of the terms to render what was lost to the victims of the Nazi work and death camps. It is related to the sense of shame that the prisoners see reflected in the eyes of the Russian soldiers who ride up to the camp to liberate them. The soldiers approach as if to a funeral scene, "oppressed not only by compassion but by a confused restraint" that the inmates know so well and that drowned them every time they had to witness or suffer some outrage: "the shame the Germans did not know, that the just man experiences at another man's crime; the feeling of guilt that such a crime should exist, that it should have been introduced irrevocably into the world of things that exist, and that this will for good should have proved too weak or null, and should not have availed in defense."[21] The moment of liberation is thus stained with remorse and anguish as well as joy—remorse (Levi's word is "a sense of pudency" or "modesty"), because "we should have liked to wash our consciences and our memories clean from the foulness that lay upon them"; "anguish, because we felt that this should never have happened, that now nothing could ever happen good and pure enough to rub out our past, and that the scars of the outrage would remain within us for ever, and in the memories of those who saw it, and in the places where it occurred and in the stories that we should tell of it."[22]

In *Survival in Auschwitz* (originally and more appropriately entitled *If This Be a Man*) Levi is compelled to describe the source of this "incurable offense" as "an inexhaustible fount of evil" that encompasses everyone touched by it: "it breaks the body and the spirit of the submerged, it stifles them and renders them abject; it returns as ignominy upon the oppressors, it perpetuates itself as hatred among the survivors, and swarms around in a thousand ways against the very will of all, as a thirst for revenge, as a moral capitulation, as denial, as weariness, as renunciation."[23] This "fount of evil" first makes itself known almost from the very moment the inmates enter the camp, where they are stripped of everything betokening their humanity— possessions, clothes, shoes, hair, name—so that their life in the camps will not awaken in those to whom they must answer even the slightest sense of human affinity: "if we speak they will not listen; if they listen they will not understand." In a crime that threatens to silence the capacity to explain, the perpetrators of this regime, and all who conspire to make it work, seek nothing less than, as Levi calls it, "the demolition of a man."[24] That demolition is most completely accomplished in the "musselmanns," as they are called in the camp, what Levi refers to as the "drowned," who fall to the bottom. These are the anonymous, endlessly renewed, mass of men and women who through bad luck, some misfortune, a stupid accident, or a basic incapacity are defeated before they can learn how to resist and live out their allotted time before being exhausted or selected for the gas chamber as "non-men, . . . the divine spark dead within them, already too empty to really suffer."[25]

But the demolition of man was also achieved among many of those lucky enough to be saved, such as the Jewish prominents who were given some authority over other inmates. In order not to lose that authority by having someone more suitable replace them, they were given natural inducements to be cruel and tyrannical. But to these natural inducements was added the fact that without any outlet for the hatred all prisoners felt toward their oppressors, that same hatred was bound to double back, "beyond all reason," against the unfortunates under their control. Thus, Jewish prominents, or, for that matter, anyone victimized by this system of degradation, could receive satisfaction only by unloading onto their "underlings the injury received from above."[26]

Seeking words for the barbarity that is enacted in Auschwitz, Levi turns for analogies to the world shared by camp inmate and common reader alike:

> Consider what value, what meaning is enclosed even in the smallest of our daily habits, in the hundred possessions which even the poorest beggar owns: a handkerchief, an old letter, the photo of a cherished person. These things are part of us, almost like the limbs of our body; nor is it conceivable that we can be deprived of them in our world, for we would immediately find others to substitute for the old ones, other objects which are ours in their personification and evocation of our memories. Imagine now a man who is deprived of everyone he loves, and at the same time of his house, his habits, his clothes, in short, of everything he possesses: he will be a hollow man, reduced to suffering and needs, forgetful of dignity and restraint, for he who loses all often easily loses himself.[27]

But if the enormity of this lethal enterprise of dehumanization defies the power of language to express, the moral depravity of its authors does not. The guards and their superiors are not so much inhuman to Levi as subhuman: "Their humanity is buried or they themselves have buried it, under an offense received or inflicted on someone else. The evil and insane SS men, the Kapos, the politicals, the criminals, the prominents, great and small, down to the indifferent slave *Haftlinge*, all grades of the mad hierarchy created by the Germans, paradoxically fraternize in a uniform internal desolation."[28] No one more completely epitomizes that internal desolation—and the demonically absolute indifference to others that it spreads like a contagion in its wake—than Doktor Ingenieur Pannwitz. Pannwitz is one of the three German physicians in charge of the Polymerization Department in the factory, as large as a small city, called the Buna to which Levi, along with all the other camp inmates, is assigned to work. Named after a type of rubber, the Buna never produced a pound of synthetic rubber before the war was over. When Pannwitz raises his head to glance at Levi for the first time during their interview, Levi is brought face to face with a gaze so pitiless it seems to come from another order of life:

Because that look was not one between two men; and if I had known how completely to explain the nature of that look, which came as if across the glass window of an aquarium between two beings who live in different worlds, I would also have explained the essence of the great insanity of the third Germany. . . . The brain which governed those blue eyes and those manicured hands said: "This something in front of me belongs to a species which it is obviously opportune to suppress. In this particular case, one has to first make sure that it does not contain some utilizable element."[29]

The modern process by which human beings are reduced to the level of things in the eyes of others may well have begun with the industrialization of the body, which started in the West with the Marquis de Sade and the rise of pornography, but the Nazis took the degradation of the human to lengths perhaps never before contemplated, much less accomplished, in human history. They were out not simply to crush other people but to extinguish them entirely because they were viewed as inferior. Hence, the great danger of this degradation comes not from what the prisoners suffer in the eyes of their oppressors but from what they suffer in their own eyes. They are rendered of absolutely no human account by an ""other" who views its own cruelty and indifference as natural and inevitable. Here is no monster like that depicted in Francisco Goya's painting of *Saturn Devouring a Son*, a figure who looks out from the painting in amazement and horror at what he is doing and cannot stop doing, but a creature like the God in Comte de Lautreamont's "*Les Chants de Maldoror*" who feeds himself, as is his right, on his victims for all eternity.[30] Nor is it coincidental that the behavior of Lautreamont's God, who constantly repeats himself, resembles that of a machine. Such mechanical responses deprive him of the possibility of being considered simply criminal. Instead, his evil, like that of the authors and administrators of the Holocaust, is truly demonic because it is predicated on the desirability of creating a world where cruelty and normality, barbarity and ordinariness, are the same thing.

One's only defense against this diabolical form of world-making or, rather, world-unmaking is the capacity to see it as unwarranted, as inhuman. Levi makes no bones about the fact that he would have lost this capacity himself if it had not been for his two friends, Lorenzo and Alberto, who manage to live outside this world of abomination. What saves them from its contamination—and, together with a considerable degree of luck or the good fortune of health and illness occurring at the right moment, enables Levi to survive it as well—is not any residue of natural goodness within the human soul, goodness though there occasionally is, so much as the thing that such goodness presupposes and requires to persist: the belief "that there still existed a just world outside our own, something and someone still pure and whole, not corrupt, not savage, extraneous to hatred and terror; something difficult to define, a remote possibility of good, but for which it was worth striving."[31] This is what, at another fateful moment in Levi's odyssey, permits him to see in the canto from Virgil's *Ulysses* a set of images that suggest a life elsewhere in which the human body is not rendered thoroughly dispensable like a used tissue, where the human spirit is not treated, insofar as it is acknowledged at all, as no more than an object of ridicule, humiliation, and torment.

Even in moments of greatest extremity, then, Levi never loses the ability to see German behavior as not only a radical deformation of the human norm but also, improbably, as something from which he and others can, and if they are to survive must, learn. The Nazis are never understood as acting so far beneath or so far beyond the human norm that Levi can't find, within the terms of his own experience of them, ways to hold them accountable for the enormities they commit and to express his and other's own terrifying sense of their radically attenuated and almost inconceivable but still problematic kinship with them. This becomes clearest to Levi only toward the end of his ordeal, when the irony slowly dawns on him that the Germans come closest to succeeding in their project to demolish the human in the very moment of their own defeat.

By the end of the tenth day following their departure, the camp had been reduced to a world of dead bodies and spectral, emaciated human beings. The degradation that the Germans had begun when they were in control has now, as the last vestiges of civilization within as well as around the prisoners simply vanish, been very nearly consummated in their collapse. It is the moment when the prisoners, now free of their captors but without anything within remaining to fall back on, lose all forms of something like Conradian restraint: "It is man who kills, man who creates or suffers injustice; it is no longer man who, having lost all restraint, shares his bed with a corpse. Whoever waits for his neighbour to die in order to take his piece of bread is, albeit guiltless, further from the model of thinking man than the most primitive pigmy or the most vicious sadist."[32]

If this bestiality symbolizes one pole of human degradation and Pann-witz's inhuman gaze another, both represent potentialities for the human soul that, in addition to being distantly related, must also evoke, as they do for Levi, something like a saving curiosity. For all their horror, they are not so alien to the human as to permit Levi to dismiss or discount them as non-human, much less as nondiscussable. Such potentialities can and must be interrogated because no human experience, no matter how much it challenges our moral faculties, can be assumed to be "without meaning or unworthy of analysis." Also, as Levi continues, "fundamental values, even if they are not positive, can be deduced from a description of the world of the camps."[33] The fundamental values are in this case inhuman or subhuman rather than nonhuman because their historical exemplifications, so blameless in the first instance and so cruel and heartless in the second, elicit in response an intuition, however imprecise but still somehow inviolate, of those boundaries of the human imaginary that have in both cases been stretched to the breaking point but must in neither ever be allowed to dissolve.

Levi keeps such boundaries in sight by writing with such unaffected simplicity and candor about those prosaic details whose clear perception, along with good fortune and good friends, was needed to survive. Yet it is one of the tragic ironies of Levi's experience, and that of other survivors, that the Nazi's may have prevailed more completely than they could have appreciated precisely because of the odium that became attached to surviving itself. In *Survival in Auschwitz*, Levi was compelled to describe surviving as morally inadequate: "We survivors are not only an exiguous but also an anomalous minority: we are those who by their prevarications or abilities of good luck [*fortuna*] did not touch bottom. Those who did so . . . have not returned to tell about it or have returned mute, but they are . . . the complete witnesses, the ones whose depositions would have a general significance."[34] Many years later, in his last and most tormented book, *The Drowned and the Saved*, Levi struggled with the fear that it was the murdered who deserved to survive as the survivors themselves did not:

> The saved of the Lager were not the best, those predestined to do good, the bearers of the message: what I had seen and lived through proved the exact contrary. Preferably the worst survived, the selfish, the violent, the insensitive, the collaborators of the "gray zone," the spies. It was not a certain rule (there were none, nor are there certain rules in human matters), but it was nevertheless a rule. I felt innocent, yes, but enrolled among the saved and therefore in permanent search

of a justification in my own eyes and those of others. The worst survived, that is, the fittest; the best all died.[35]

The last of the sites I want to examine, where a move "beyond solidarity" may have been encouraged by a paradoxical recognition of kinship with one's adversary or enemy, has been created over a much longer period of time. It is represented by the literature and thought, and particularly the folk art and folk religion, of African American slaves and their descendants. A tradition, or rather assemblage of traditions, that has hardly suffered from any scarcity of brilliant interpreters from a range of disciplines—including folklore, religious studies, sociology, ethnomusicology, social and cultural history, and literary criticism—this tradition has also elicited a fair measure of consensus on how African Americans managed to survive the ideological, emotional, and physical depredations of the slave system and of the system of institutionalized racism that replaced it. This survival was enabled—and, from the testimony of numerous recent commentators, often still is—by the refusal on the part of a substantial number of African Americans either to accept, or simply to invert, the Manichean regime of racial polarities that oppressed them. What they did instead was to create out of its gaps, ruptures, and inconsistencies a series of imaginative spaces located, so to speak, between the white world and the black where, as Lawrence Levine has written, "legal slavery" could be prevented "from becoming spiritual slavery."[36]

Levine's claim belongs to a long history of important revisionist challenges to a liberal tradition of misinterpretations that begins, perhaps, with Gunnar Myrdal's *An American Dilemma* in 1944 and continues in, among other odd places, E. Franklin Frazier's *The Negro in the United States* (1957), Nathan Glazer and Daniel P. Moynihan's famous study of 1963 on American ethnic groups entitled *Beyond the Melting Pot*, and even Frantz Fanon's *Toward the African Revolution* (1988).[37] This liberal tradition holds that, in the face of the massive attack launched by the antebellum South on virtually every aspect of the cultures brought to the New World by African American slaves, black culture in America has never really achieved a distinctive identity independent of white culture and that wherever black culture has departed from dominant patterns, those departures should merely be understood as divergences from, and possibly deformations of, its white parent.

Along with many others—from Alan Lomax, Herbert Gutman, C. Eric Lincoln, Nathan Huggins, Eugene Genovese, and Albert J. Raboteau to Elizabeth Fox-Genovese, Henry Louis Gates, Jr., Thadious Davis, and

Trudier Harris—Levine undertakes to prove, to the contrary, that many elements of African culture, including religious beliefs, survived the horrors of slavery through their re-creation as a series of mainly folk practices intended to furnish their participants with a sense both of psychic relief and of personal mastery.[38] Levine and others also insist that these same folk practices and beliefs, of which "the dozens" or "signifying" may be the most famous, far from representing a slavish imitation of white culture, in fact constituted a series of highly inventive and resourceful, if also subtly disguised, adaptations and expressions of resistance to the recurrent degradation of black experience by white Americans. As a result, this revisionist tradition of scholarship rightly maintains that black Americans have not, as Glazer and Moynihan alleged, lost most forms of group pride, group history, or group solidarity, but rather have succeeded in fashioning for themselves, often against staggering odds, a complex and resilient culture capable of giving expression to many of their most characteristic dreams, fears, and achievements.

To isolate and critically recuperate such expressive forms, much less to find a way of describing what goes on in the imaginative spaces they have created, has required of many scholars a shift in traditional historical perspectives and methods. If the historian's normal tracking devices were not—and often still are not—designed to consider material such as humor, oratory, music, jokes, songs, aphorisms, tales, and other reflective forms as legitimate sources of historical insight, much less of religious meaning (especially when, as in these African American forms, the line between the religious and the secular is so vague and uneven), still less were they originally designed to explore the intellectual component of such forms. Yet it is just here that much of the most important revisionist scholarship has staked its claim and mounted its argument. Its contention is not simply that folk materials provided the forms in which over the years African Americans most frequently and most candidly represented themselves to themselves but that these same forms also furnished many of the vehicles in and through which African Americans conducted some of their most serious intellectual as well as affective business.

For all of the creativity and significance of the new revisionist history, it can scarcely be maintained that Lomax, Huggins, Lincoln, Genovese, Raboteau, Harris, or Gates were the first students of such matters to assert that folk forms represent perhaps the richest repository and distillation of American black experience, or to argue that through such forms black experience has developed its own insights into the human condition and produced its own strategies for survival. This proposition is defended and elaborated with great eloquence, for example, in the essays Ralph Ellison had been writing since the 1940s, and that were gathered in 1964 in his *Shadow and Act*. This conviction is also in evidence in the work that Albert Murray, Ellison's friend, began to publish in books like his far-too-little-known *The Omni-Americans* of 1966. It found expression two decades earlier in such texts as Saunders Redding's *No Day of Triumph* in 1942. Doubtless owing its origin to, among others, W. E. B. Du Bois and his pioneering study *The Souls of Black Folk*, as well as to the subsequent discoveries made by the writers of the Harlem Renaissance, this proposition has been a staple of revisionist criticism for the better part of a century.[39]

The originality of the new revisionist history, then, lies not in the way that it views African American folk culture as a more or less coherent, or at least comprehensible, system but rather in the way that it links the study of folk forms to an understanding of the distinctiveness of African American modes of mentality, including religious mentality, and then uses their symbiotic relationship to correct some of the most serious misreadings to which black history has been subjected. Measuring these folk forms, and their historical importance for the formation of a distinctive African American culture, not in terms of their relationship to white culture but instead in light of what they made of the opportunities afforded them, it has attempted—and largely succeeded—in demolishing the image constructed by previous historical portraiture. The scholarship that depicted African American slaves "as inarticulate intellectual ciphers, as objects who were continually acted upon by forces over which they had no control" has been largely replaced by one that more accurately and truthfully perceives them "as actors in their own right who not only responded to their situation but often affected it in crucial ways."[40]

I am quoting from Levine's *Black Culture and Black Consciousness*, which for several reasons warrants somewhat closer inspection. For one thing, it is as successful as any work of recent revisionism not only in repossessing historically something like the whole of a subject peoples' mental and emotional life but also in demonstrating how the creative resilience of that life carried them beyond solidarity, as I am phrasing it, toward newer forms of inter-subjective reciprocity with the "other" that originally sought their enslavement and, later, their subjugation. Levine's book thus serves to exemplify what other texts have likewise asserted. For another, however, Levine secures this argument by exploiting a theory of symbolic action first developed by the pragmatist cultural critic Kenneth Burke.[41] Reviewing his argument somewhat more closely, therefore, will allow me to show how an explicitly pragmatist approach to cultural interpretation can be employed more widely to flesh out a transnational theory of cultural criticism.

Burke's theory posits that all critical and imaginative forms, including folk forms, are expressly, if not always obviously, constructed as answers to questions posed by the problematics of the situations in which they first arose. To be sure, such forms are designed not as simple answers but rather as stylized answers, essentially as strategic answers. That is, they are designed not merely as responses to situations but as responses intended to encompass critically the questions posed by those situations. Therefore, Burke wants to distinguish clearly between "situations" and "strategies." Situations represent problematic experiences of a representative kind. Strategies represent ways of dealing with such situations by sizing up the problematics that compose them, analyzing those problematics into their component parts, and defining the situations as a whole in a way that contains an implicit attitude towards them, a way that, in essence, conveys an interpretive perspective on them.

This is what Ralph Ellison was driving at in his famous review of *An American Dilemma* when he asked rhetorically whether any people can "live and develop over three hundred years simply by *reacting?* Are American Negroes simply the creation of white men, or have they at least helped to create themselves out of what they found around them?"[42] Designed to point out the absurdity of what several generations of liberal condescension had covered up, Ellison's questions in effect answer themselves. People can only "live and develop" over three hundred years of deprecation at the hands of others—and because of being compelled to see themselves so continuously through those "other" eyes, of self-deprecation also at their own hands— only by creating an entire arsenal of symbolic strategies that not only afford them ways of taking the measure of the representative situations that confront them but that also supply them with the motive force to address those situations intellectually and emotionally.

This is the Burkean perspective that Levine brings to his analysis of everything from African American oratory, song, and humor to slave religion. In the case of slave religion, he deftly subverts the standard view that the slaves simply grafted African meanings onto white forms by showing how the entire propulsion of their religious experience actually encouraged them to move in the opposite direction, by adapting the forms of white religion to the very different structures, meanings, and needs of their own experience as blacks. This amounted to nothing short of a religious reversal.

Instead of converting themselves to the Christian God, African American slaves and their later descendents set about converting God to themselves, as W. E. B. Du Bois first described in *The Souls of Black Folk* and as the anthropologist Paul Radin later put it more formally: "The ante-bellum Negro was not converted to God. He converted God to himself. In the Christian God he found a fixed point and he needed a fixed point, for both within and outside of himself, he could see only vacillation and endless shifting. . . . There was no other safety for people faced on all sides by doubt and the threat of personal disintegration, by the thwarting of instincts and the annihilation of values."[43] The chief instruments of this conversion were ritual reenactments of the divine acts of creation and salvation through which, in song, dance, oratory, narrative, and prayer, slaves were able not only to extend the boundaries of their own world backward, so to speak, until it fused with the Old Testament narratives of deliverance and support amidst suffering, but also to project it upward until it became one with the New Testament narratives of beatitude and the fulfillment of Time.[44]

In creating out of their worship a world that did not seek to adjust itself to the white world that oppressed them but instead sought to reabsorb within itself all the elements from that "other" world needed to satisfy their own negotiations with the divine, black Christians in the South accomplished spiritually what southern white Christians could not. This is not to say that white Christians didn't try as well to convert God to themselves, but their own efforts in this respect were crippled from the start. Because of their systemic racism and ethnocentricity, their ability to feel or enact the spiritual deliverance offered by the Christian faith, or as Donald Mathews has written in *Religion and the Old South*, "to sense the agony and alienation of the cross and therefore to understand the Gospel as a truly liberating force," was fatally blocked. While they may have been moved occasionally by sentimental evocations of the redemption of the "captives" (always black), the general run of white Christians knew almost nothing, Mathews points out, of what their black fellow Christians understood immediately about the power of faith to transform the most benighted of conditions: "Enslaved, they sang of freedom; defeated, they awaited victory; powerless, they exercised the power of the 'righteous remnant'"[45]—all the while demonstrating a more mature grasp than their white counterparts of the vindication promised by a God whose power lies in the assumption of powerlessness. Even before Gabriel's trumpet had sounded, black Christians had experienced a miraculous transformation: "The trumpet sounds within-a my soul," they could sing; "I ain't got long to stay here."[46]

The Negro spirituals thus constitute a move beyond solidarity. They are the testimonial of a people whose sense of fundamental kinship with the enemy enabled them to find, as Levine puts it, echoing Du Bois, "the status, the harmony, the values, the order they needed to survive by internally creating an expanded universe, by literally willing themselves reborn."[47] But the spirituals are evidence of much more than what Nelson Goodman once called "ways of world making."[48] They also show that religious world-making was not inconsistent with political critique, that black folk culture in general often provided African Americans "other—and from the point of view of personality development, not necessarily less effective—means of escape and opposition."[49]

Such arguments are part of Levine's avowed purpose, along with that of other revisionist historians, not simply to examine modes of consciousness formerly ignored but to expand the moral consciousness of his readers. His aim is at once to recover "the richness of expression, the sharpness of perception, the uninhibited imagination, [and] the complex imagery" of African American folk thought and to help us rethink its ethical significance.[50] In this, the trick is always to avoid what Lionel Trilling long ago diagnosed as one among the more frightening paradoxes and greatest dangers of the moral imagination by which, "when once we have made our fellow men the objects of our enlightened interest, [we] . . . go on to make them the objects of our pity, then of our wisdom, ultimately of our coercion."[51] Levine avoids this trap by everywhere keeping before his reader the two central facts that for him, as for other students of these matters, constitute the moral value of African American folk thought and experience: first, that no matter how massive the psychic assault of the slave system or the system of institutionalized racism that replaced it, neither the slaves nor their descendants ever permitted these systems to insinuate themselves into all the interstices of mind and feeling; and, second, that African Americans were able to create from within these gaps and crevices of mental and emotional life modes of expression and reflection and communal affirmation that were not only culturally distinctive and psychologically empowering but that remain for people everywhere emblematic of the way the human spirit can sustain itself in the face of, and imaginatively at times even surmount and transcend, the most invidious forms of human bondage.

Here, then, as in much postcolonial and Holocaust literature, alterity is not one element of identity among others, nor is it merely that over against which identity supposedly constitutes itself. Alterity is, rather, represented as that in relation to which identity must somehow, even at the risk of its very existence and often under the most unimaginably arduous conditions, still hold itself in tension and, to that degree, accountable. While this can require a moral discipline of almost superhuman proportions, its expressions nonetheless hold clues not easily reducible to paraphrase, much less translatable into political programs, for how to reverse, or at least to interrupt and deflect, those symbolic processes that associate the formation of human identity with the denigration of human difference. Alterity in this case *is* the difference that makes a difference, the difference that allows the self to become corrigible to the other without reducing the other to a cipher of the self. Alterity is that which enables cultures, like selves, to learn from each other, to become constituents of each other's identity. Reconceiving identity in relation to notions of difference rather than of sameness, therefore, need not accentuate division, estrangement, stigmatization, enmity. Rather, it is one way—and perhaps the only way—that division, estrangement, stigmatization, and enmity may be controlled, if not actually overcome.

When policy analysts try to establish the normative ideas that might influence the restructuring of global governance, they typically resort to notions such as "human rights," "the common [environmental] heritage of mankind," "sustainable development," the "global commons," and "future generations."[52] These are all notions that reflect the ethical claim of the "other," that resist reductionism or essentialism even where, as in the case of human rights, they seek to formulate those minimal standards of human welfare, including the right to self-determination, that should apply to everyone. They are predicated on the belief that solidarity is not similitude and that the only possibility of actualizing anything remotely resembling it in what most people most often experience, despite its globalized description, as "a world in pieces"[53] is by incorporating into our definition of it more and more of what I have called the pragmatics of otherness. This amounts to thinking beyond solidarity in the direction of a world where the hope of consensus is replaced by the need for "comity."[54] This would be a world where the relations between self and "other," rather than being suffered as discursively deforming or dangerously destructive, could be accepted as dialogically, even ethically, enhancing.

The symbolic refiguration of such a world is one of the central tasks that a "multiculturalist" and transnational or, indeed, a global, criticism, as it might be called, has yet to fulfill, but I am persuaded that it can do so only by remaining true to its original pragmatist impulse. That impulse presupposes with Dewey and, before him, with James that if many of "the goods of life are matters of richness and freedom of meanings" and "a large part of our life is carried on in a realm . . . to which truth and falsity as such are irrelevant,"[55] then aesthetics may provide us with more viable models for some kinds of reflection than the natural sciences and the conceptualization of, if not a common human nature, then at least the nature of a common, or, in any event, a sharable human world may be a job for which the imagination is better equipped than the analytical intellect, the artist than the political scientist. At any rate, the challenge for both is the same: to determine what difference difference makes in a world increasingly defined under the sign of the global.

Notes

Introduction

1. Quoted in Richard J. Bernstein, *The New Constellation: The Ethical-Political Horizons of Modernity/Postmodernity* (Cambridge, Mass.: MIT Press, 1992), 43.

2. Quoted in Bernstein, *New Constellation*, 45.

3. John Dewey, *Democracy and Education* (1916; New York: The Free Press, 1966), 87.

4. See *Deconstruction and Pragmatism*, ed. Chantal Mouffe (London: Routledge, 1996), particularly Jacques Derrida, "Remarks on Deconstruction and Pragmatism," 77–88.

5. Jacques Derrida, "Dialogue with Jacques Derrida," in *Dialogues with Contemporary Continental Thinkers*, ed. Richard Kearney (Manchester: Manchester University Press, 1984), 118.

6. Jacques Derrida, "Afterword," *Limited Inc.*, ed. Gerald Graff (Evanston, Ill.: Northwestern University Press, 1988), 112.

7. Bernstein, *New Constellation*, 219.

8. Cornel West, *The American Evasion of Philosophy: A Genealogy of Pragmatism* (Madison: University of Wisconsin Press, 1989); Ann Douglas, *Terrible Honesty: Mongrel Manhattan in the 1920s* (New York: Farrar, Straus & Giroux, 1995); Ross Posnock, *Color and Culture: Black Writers and the Making of the Modern Intellectual* (Cambridge, Mass.: Harvard University Press, 1998); Nancy Fraser, "Another Pragmatism: Alain Locke, Critical 'Race' Theory, and the Politics of Culture," in *The Revival of Pragmatism: New Essays on Social Thought, Law, and Culture*, ed. Morris Dickstein (Durham, N.C.: Duke University Press, 1998), 157–76.

9. Charlene Haddock Seigfried, *Pragmatism and Feminism: Reweaving the Social Fabric* (Chicago: University of Chicago Press, 1996).

10. Charles Sanders Peirce, "How to Make Our Ideas Clear," *Philosophical Writings of Peirce*, ed. Justus Buchler (New York: Dover Publications, 1955), 30.

11. Clifford Geertz, "The Uses of Diversity," *Michigan Quarterly Review* 25 (Winter 1986): 120.

12. Derrida, "Afterword," *Limited Inc.*, 112.

13. Homi Bhabha, "The World and the Home," in *Dangerous Liaisons* (Minneapolis: University of Minnesota Press, 1997), 448.

14. Nadine Gordimer, *My Son's Story* (London: Bloomsbury, 1990), 241.

15. Johann Wolfgang von Goethe, *Goethe's Literary Essays*, ed. J. E. Spingarn (New York: Harcourt, Brace, 1921), 98–99; cited in Bhabha, "The World and the Home," 449.

16. Bhabha, "The World and the Home," 445.

17. W. E. B. Du Bois, *The Souls of Black Folk* (New York: New American Library, 1969), 44.

18. Richard Rorty, *Contingency, Irony, and Solidarity* (Cambridge: Cambridge University Press, 1989), 6.

19. Richard Rorty, *Consequences of Pragmatism* (Minneapolis: University of Minnesota Press, 1982), xliii.

20. Among those who most readily come to mind, I would cite Hilary Putnam, Nancy Fraser, Richard J. Bernstein, Charlene Haddock Seigfried, John McDermott, and Cornel West in philosophy; Clifford Geertz and Renato Rosaldo in anthropology; Jerome Bruner in education; Lynn Hunt, Joyce Appleby, James Livingston, James Kloppenberg, and David Hollinger in history; Richard Poirier, Barbara Herrnstein Smith, Henry Louis Gates, Jr., Ross Posnock, Peter Carafiol, Steven Mailloux, and Jonathan Levin in literary and cultural studies; Richard Posner and Thomas C. Grey in law; and Gordon Kaufman, Henry Samuel Levinson, and Jeffrey Stout in religious studies; along with such intellectual fellow travelers as Stanley Cavell, Martha Nussbaum, Charles Taylor, and, from an earlier generation, Nelson Goodman.

21. Salman Rushdie, *In Good Faith* (New York: Granta, 1990), 3–4.

22. Richard Rorty, "On Ethnocentrism: A Reply to Clifford Geertz," *Michigan Quarterly Review* 25 (Fall 1986): 534.

23. Morris Dickstein, "Introduction: Pragmatism Then and Now," *The Revival of Pragmatism*, ed. Morris Dickstein (Durham, N.C.: Duke University Press, 1998), 17.

24. John Diggins, *The Promise of Pragmatism* (Chicago: University of Chicago Press, 1994), 370.

25. Van Wyck Brooks, *America's Coming-of-Age* (Garden City, N.Y.: Doubleday Anchor Books, 1958), 3.

26. Brooks, *America's Coming-of-Age*, 3.

27. John Dewey, *Reconstruction in Philosophy* (New York: H. Holt, 1920)

28. John Dewey, *Experience and Nature*, 2d ed. (La Salle, Ill.: Open Court Publishing, 1971), 9–10.

Chapter 1

1. Edmundo O'Gorman, *The Invention of America* (Bloomington: Indiana University Press, 1961).

2. Several of the paragraphs that follow are drawn from my introduction to *Early American Writing*, ed. Giles Gunn (New York: Penguin Books, 1994), xvi–xxi.

3. Quoted in Gunn, ed., *Early American Writing*, xviii.

4. For a helpful discussion of these issues, see Gari Laguardia and Bell Gale Chevigny, introduction to *Reinventing the Americas: Comparative Studies of Literature in the United States and Spanish America*, ed. Bell Gale Chevigny and Gari Laguardia (Cambridge: Cambridge University Press, 1986), vii.

5. If this amounts to arguing that higher education in the United States should become more accessible and accountable to a wider spectrum of Americans that, in particular, includes women and minorities, this does not necessarily mean that the American academy has recently, for the first time, suddenly fallen into politics. American higher education has always been linked to politics, and specifically the politics of class, gender, and race, since its origins as an institution created principally for the training of white males for the clergy. And long before the controversy over political correctness arose, American education acquired the essential rudiments of its present form of politicization when, during the period following World War II, a marriage of convenience was arranged between the American university system, Big Business, and the Federal government.

Thus, the argument that education ought to remain apolitical, disinterested, and objective sounds more than a little disingenuous to most of those on the left in this debate, especially when that argument is made by many conservative critics like the late Alan Bloom, or Dinesh D'Souza, or Roger Kimball, who are, or were, anything but apolitical, disinterested, and objective themselves. Nonetheless, these same critics on the right have an undeniable point when they assert that political correctness has given way at various moments to a new social self-righteousness that is potentially not only anti-intellectual but discriminatory in reverse. This occurs when the politically valid desire to protect individuals from the abuse of their rights under the First Amendment encourages some to imperil the rights of everyone else by legislating not only what constitutes permissible discursive practice in higher education, as well as the wider society, but also how the general education curriculum, like the political sphere as a whole, should be restructured.

6. Frederick Crews is particularly acute on this point. See Frederick Crews, *The Critics Bear It Away: American Fiction and the Academy* (New York: Random House, 1992), especially pp. xiii–xvii.

7. Louis Menand, "Being an American," *Times Literary Supplement*, October 30, 1992, 3–4.

8. Kenneth Burke, *Counter-Statement* (Berkeley and Los Angeles: University of California Press, 1968), 183.

9. Menand, "Being an American," 4.

10. Antonio Benítez-Rojo, "The Repeating Island," in *Do the Americas Have a*

Common Literature?, ed. Gustavo Pérez Firmat (Durham, N.C.: Duke University Press, 1990), 85–106.

11. Clifford Geertz, *The Interpretation of Cultures* (New York: Basic Books, 1973), 3–32.

12. Renato Rosaldo, *Culture and Truth: The Remaking of Social Analysis* (Boston: Beacon Press, 1989), 207.

13. Gloria Anzaldúa, "Towards a New Consciousness," in *Borderlands/La Frontera* (San Francisco: Aunt Lute Book Co., 1987), 77–91.

14. Rosaldo, *Culture and Truth*, 103

15. Rosaldo, *Culture and Truth*, 202.

16. James Clifford, *The Predicament of Culture* (Cambridge, Mass.: Harvard University Press, 1988), 25.

17. Clifford Geertz, *Local Knowledge* (New York: Basic Books, 1983), 16.

18. For a fuller delineation of these strategies, see the excellent discussion of them in David Spurr's *The Rhetoric of Empire* (Durham, N.C.: Duke University Press, 1993), 187–89.

19. José David Saldívar, *The Dialectics of Our America* (Durham, N.C.: Duke University Press, 1991), 17.

20. Carolyn Porter, "What We Know That We Don't Know: Remapping American Literary Studies," *American Literary History* 6 (Fall 1994): 451.

21. Peter Homans, *The Ability to Mourn: Disillusionment and the Social Origins of Psychoanalysis* (Chicago: University of Chicago Press, 1989).

22. Judith Butler, *The Psychic Life of Power* (Palo Alto, Calif.: Stanford University Press, 1997), 167–98.

23. Paul Ricoeur, *Freud and Philosophy: An Essay on Interpretation* (New Haven, Conn.: Yale University Press, 1970).

24. Henry James, "Is There a Life After Death?" in F. O. Matthiessen, *The James Family* (Knopf, 1947), 613.

25. Mitchell Breitwiesser, *American Puritanism and the Defense of Mourning: Religion, Grief, and Ethnology in Mary White Rowlandson's Captivity Narrative* (Madison: University of Wisconsin Press, 1990), 302.

26. Nicolas Abraham and Maria Torok, *The Wolf Man's Magic Word: A Cryptonymy* (Minneapolis: University of Minnesota, 1986).

27. Jacques Lacan, quoted in Breitwiesser, *American Puritanism and the Defense of Mourning*, 325.

28. Breitwiesser, *American Puritanism and the Defense of Mourning*, 41.

29. Rosaldo, *Culture and Truth*, 7.

30. Peter Brooks, "The Proffered Word," *Times Literary Supplement*, November 9, 1991, 11.

31. For a slightly fuller explanation of this process, which I paraphrase here, see Giles Gunn, *Thinking Across the American Grain* (Chicago: University of Chicago Press, 1992), 12–13.

32. Homans, *Ability to Mourn*, 273–76.

33. Christopher Miller, quoted in John Guillory, *Cultural Capital: The Problem of Literary Canon Formation* (Chicago: University of Chicago Press, 1993), 53.

34. Carlos Fuentes, *Myself with Others: Selected Essays* (New York: Farrar, Straus, & Giroux, 1988).

35. The reference is to an observation of the poet James Merrill, which Clifford Geertz reversed in the title of a well-known chapter from *Local Knowledge* entitled "Found in Translation: On the Social History of the Moral Imagination," pp. 36–54.

Chapter 2

1. David Hollinger, *Postethnic America* (New York: Basic Books, 1995), 1–2.

2. Hollinger, *Postethnic America*, 86, 120, 124. Henry James was, of course, far from consistent in these sentiments, expressing elsewhere, and with considerable candor, his aversion to various effects of the process of immigration.

3. Hollinger, *Postethnic America*, 117.

4. Michael Sandel, quoted in Hollinger, *Postethnic America*, 117.

5. Hollinger, *Postethnic America*, 118.

6. Hollinger, *Postethnic America*, 116.

7. In regards to Derrida's interest in the importance of difference and alterity, Bernstein says, "Derrida 'speaks to' many of 'us' because the question of otherness (in all its variations) has become a 'central'—if not the central—theoretical/practical question of our time. How can we hope to be open to, and respond responsibly to the terror of otherness and the singularity of the Other? This is primarily an ethical-political question for which there is not and cannot be a 'final solution.'" Richard J. Bernstein, *The New Constellation: The Ethical-Political Horizons of Modernity/Postmodernity* (Cambridge, Mass.: MIT Press, 1992), 219.

8. Bernstein, *New Constellation*, 66.

9. Jacques Derrida recorded the depth of that relationship in a funeral oration he delivered for Levinas on 28 December 1995, which was published as "Adieu," trans. Pascale-Anne Brault and Michael Naas, *Critical Inquiry* 23 (Autumn 1996): 1–10.

10. Jacques Derrida, *Writing and Difference* (Chicago: University of Chicago Press, 1978), 104.

11. Derrida, *Writing and Difference*, 125.

12. For Mikhail Bakhtin, *transgredient* refers to those moments when we see ourselves from the point of view of other people; *exotopy* names the principle by which, particularly in aesthetic activity, after seeking to put oneself in the place of another through an effort of empathy or identification, then one returns, in a reverse secondary movement, to oneself (one's own position) and finds oneself, as it were, outside, transformed into a self-other.

13. Rorty does not believe that the terms *identity* and *difference* can be made relevant to political discussion. See Richard Rorty, *Philosophy and Social Hope* (New York:

Penguin Books, 1999), 234–39. In this belief he is challenged not only by me but also by other pragmatists such as Richard J. Bernstein, Nancy Fraser, Ross Posnock, and Charlene Haddock Seigfried.

14. See William E. Connolly, *Identity/Difference: Democratic Negotiations of Political Paradox* (Ithaca, N.Y.: Cornell University Press, 1991).

15. Judith Shklar, *Ordinary Vices* (Cambridge, Mass.: Harvard University Press, 1984), 37ff. This liberal prejudice would probably need to be modified on the basis of the testimony of many people from more traditional cultures, where dishonoring others is an even greater abomination. See Mark Juergensmeyer, *Terror in the Mind of God* (Berkeley and Los Angeles: University of California Press, 2000), 187.

16. Václav Havel and Elie Wiesel, "A Tribute to Human Rights," in *The Universal Declaration of Human Rights: Fifty Years and Beyond*, ed. Yael Danieli, Elsa Stamatopoulou, and Clarence J. Dias (Amityville, N.Y.: Baywood, 1999), 3; Nadine Gordimer, "Reflections by Nobel Laureates," in *Universal Declaration of Human Rights*, viii.; Amartya Sen, "Human Rights and Economic Achievements," in *The East Asian Challenge for Human Rights*, ed. Joanne R. Bauer and Daniel A. Bell (New York: Cambridge University Press, 1999), 92–93.

17. Joseph Conrad, preface to *The Nigger of the Narcissus*, in *The Portable Conrad*, ed. Morton Dauwen Zabel (New York: Viking Press, 1947), 706.

18. Clifford Geertz, *The Interpretation of Cultures* (New York: Basic Books, 1973), 52.

19. Michael Ignatieff, *Blood and Belonging: Journeys into the New Nationalism* (New York: Noonday Press, 1995), 10.

20. Peter Gay, *The Cultivation of Hatred*, vol. 3 of *The Bourgeois Experience: Victoria to Freud* (New York: Norton, 1993), 536.

21. Orlando Patterson, *Rituals of Blood: Consequences of Slavery in Two American Centuries* (Washington, D.C.: Civitas/Counterpoint, 1998), 182–83.

22. Juergensmeyer, *Terror in the Mind of God*, 168–71.

23. René Girard, *The Scapegoat* (Baltimore: Johns Hopkins University Press, 1986).

24. Kenneth Burke, *A Grammar of Motives* (1945; Berkeley and Los Angeles: University of California Press, 1969), 406.

25. Burke, *Grammar of Motives*, 406.

26. Quoted in Patterson, *Rituals of Blood*, 184.

27. Giovanni Arrighi, *The Long Twentieth Century: Money, Power, and the Origins of Our Times* (London: Verso, 1994), 331.

28. See Stanley Jeyaraja Tambiah, "Ethnic Conflict in the World Today," *American Ethnologist* 16 (1989): 335–49; Arjun Appadurai, "Patriotism and Its Futures," *Public Culture* 5, no. 3 (1993): 411–430.

29. Appadurai, "Patriotism and Its Futures," 418.

30. Quoted in Stanley Edgar Hyman, *The Armed Vision*, rev. ed. (New York: Vintage Books, 1955), 380.

31. See Satya P. Mohanty, *Literary Theory and the Claims of History: Postmodernism, Objectivity, Multicultural Politics* (Ithaca, N.Y.: Cornell University Press, 1997).

32. William James, *Pragmatism and The Meaning of Truth* (Cambridge, Mass.: Harvard University Press, 1975), 31.

33. Nancy Fraser, "The Uses and Abuses of French Discourse Theories for Feminist Politics," *Boundary 2* 17, no. 2 (1990): 94.

34. Stephen Greenblatt, *Learning to Curse: Essays in Early Modern Culture* (New York: Routledge, 1990), 26.

35. Joseph Conrad, *Heart of Darkness* (New York: Penguin Books, 1995), 71.

36. The phrase is from Benedict Anderson's *Imagined Communities, Reflections on the Origin and Spread of Nationalism* (New York: Verso, 1983).

37. Benedict Anderson, *The Spectre of Comparisons* (London: Verso, 1998).

38. Anderson, *Spectre of Comparisons*, 48.

39. For a more extended discussion of these diasporan traditions, see James Clifford's chapter "Diasporas" in *Routes* (Cambridge, Mass.: Harvard University Press, 1997), 244–77.

40. Arjun Appadurai, *Modernity at Large: Cultural Dimensions of Globalization* (Minneapolis: University of Minnesota Press, 1996), 17.

41. Appadurai, *Modernity at Large*, 33.

42. Susanne Hoeber Rudolph, "Introduction: Religions, States, and Transnational Civil Society," in *Transnational Religion and Fading States*, ed. Susanne Hoeber Rudolph and James Piscatori (Boulder, Colo.: Westview Press, 1997), 1–24.

43. Saskia Sassen, *Globalization and Its Discontents* (New York: New Press, 1998), 100.

Chapter 3

1. All citations to William James's *Pragmatism* are taken from *Pragmatism and Other Writings*, ed. Giles Gunn (New York: Penguin Books, 2000); this quote is from page 112.

2. William James, *Pragmatism and Other Writings*, 112.

3. William James, *Pragmatism and Other Writings*, 194.

4. George Santayana, "A Brief History of My Opinions," in *The Philosophy of Santayana*, ed. Irwin Edman (New York: Charles Scribner's Sons, 1936), 16.

5. George Santayana, *Persons and Places* (London: Constable, 1944), 249; italics Santayana's.

6. Quoted in Richard J. Bernstein, introduction to *Essays in Radical Empiricism and A Pluralistic Universe* (New York: E. P. Dutton, 1971), xxv–xxvi.

7. For a further discussion of these assumptions, see Henry F. May, *The End of American Innocence* (1959; Chicago: Quadrangle Paperbacks, 1964), 3–51.

8. Wallace Stevens, *Opus Posthumous* (London: Faber and Faber, 1957), 237.

9. Wallace Stevens, *The Palm at the End of the Mind*, ed. Holly Stevens (New York: Vintage Books, 1972), 175.

10. William James, *The Correspondence of William James*, vol. 4. Edited by Ignas K. Skrupskelis and Elizabeth M. Berkeley (Charlottesville: University of Virginia Press, 1995), 241. Hereafter, all citations from James's early letters, unless otherwise noted, will be taken from this volume.

11. William James, *Correspondence of William James*, trans. from the French by Glenn Van Treese and Gilberte Van Treese, 393, 392.

12. William James, *Correspondence of William James*, 272.

13. William James, *Correspondence of William James*, 270.

14. William James, *Correspondence of William James*, trans. Glenn Van Treese and Gilberte Van Treese, 393.

15. William James, *Correspondence of William James*, 11.

16. William James, *Correspondence of William James*, 86.

17. Henry Samuel Levinson, *Santayana, Pragmatism, and the Spiritual Life* (Chapel Hill: University of North Carolina Press, 1992), 125–28.

18. Richard Poirier, *The Renewal of Literature* (New York: Random House, 1987), 10.

19. Henry James, Sr., "A Scientific Statement of the Christian Doctrine of the Lord, or Divine Man," *Moralism and Christianity* (New York: J. S. Redfield, 1850), 1–35; and "The Principle of Universality," in *Art, Lectures, and Miscellanies* (New York: J. S. Redfield, 1852), 101–34.

20. William James, *Correspondence of William James*, 98–99.

21. William James, *Correspondence of William James*, 103.

22. William James, *Correspondence of William James*, 111.

23. William James, *Correspondence of William James*, 122.

24. James's first two pieces of writing, placed in 1865, were reviews of *Lectures on the Elements of Comparative Anatomy* by Thomas Huxley (unsigned, in the *North American Review* 100 [January 1865]: 290–98) and *The Origin of Human Races* by Alfred R. Wallace (unsigned, in the *North American Review* 101 [July 1865]: 261–63). These reviews have been reprinted in *Essays, Comments, and Reviews* (Cambridge, Mass.: Harvard University Press, 1987).

25. William James, *Correspondence of William James*, 301, 302–03.

26. William James, *Correspondence of William James*, 194.

27. William James, *Correspondence of William James*, 182.

28. William James, *Correspondence of William James*, 300.

29. Quoted in F. O. Matthiessen, *The James Family* (New York: Knopf, 1947), 216.

30. Alice James, *The Diary of Alice James*, ed. Leon Edel (New York: Penguin Books, 1964), 96.

31. William James, *Correspondence of William James*, vol. 1, 159.

32. Henry, Senior's experience of vastation is recorded in his *Society: The Redeemed Form of Man:*

One day, however, towards the end of May, having eaten a comfortable dinner, I remained sitting at the table after the family had dispersed, idly gazing at the embers in the grate, thinking of nothing, and feeling only exhilaration incident to a good digestion, when suddenly—in a lightning-flash as it were—'fear came upon me, and trembling, which made all my bones to shake.' To all appearance it was a perfectly insane and abject terror, without ostensible cause, and only to be accounted for, to my perplexed imagination, by some damnèd shape squatting invisible to me within the precincts of the room, and raying out from his fetid personality influences fatal to life. The thing had not lasted ten second before I felt myself a wreck, that is, reduced from a state of firm, vigorous, joyful manhood to one of almost helpless infancy. The only self-control I was capable of exerting was to keep my seat. I felt the greatest desire to run incontinently to the foot of the stairs and shout for help to my wife,—to run to the roadside even, and appeal to the public to protect me; but by an immense effort I controlled these frenzied impulses, and determined not to budge from my chair till I had recovered my lost self-possession. This purpose I held for a good long hour, as I reckoned time, beat upon meanwhile by an ever-growing tempest of doubt, anxiety, and despair, with absolutely no relief from any truth I had ever encountered save a most pale and distant glimmer of the Divine existence,—when I resolved to abandon the vain struggle, and communicate without more ado what seemed my sudden burden of inmost, implacable unrest to my wife" (*Henry James, Senior: A Selection of His Writings*, ed. Giles Gunn (Chicago: American Library Association, 1974), 55–56.

33. William James, *The Varieties of Religious Experience* (Cambridge, Mass.: Harvard University Press, 1986), 134–35.

34. Quoted in Matthiessen, *James Family*, 204–5.

35. William James, *Correspondence of William James*, 195.

36. William James, *Correspondence of William James*, 203.

37. William James, *Correspondence of William James*, 195.

38. William James, *Correspondence of William James*, 248.

39. William James, *Correspondence of William James*, 302.

40. As H. S. Thayer has pointed out, the genealogical impulse can also be carried too far. When the pragmatic merely becomes another name for the practicable, its beginnings can be pushed back much further. Some have located its origins as far back as the era of primitive magic and early religion, from which, as Thayer proceeds to observe, it can then be said to have moved into ancient Greek literature, eventually became associated with certain Hellenistic schools of salvation, was subsequently discovered by early Christianity, later picked up and re-expressed during the Middle Ages by the Franciscans, eventually found its way into definitions of the "new knowledge" propounded by modern science, and was ultimately appropriated by the American colonists, who threaded it through Puritanism, the American Enlightenment, the opening of the West, and a host of other "American" moments since. But if the contexts differ, the effect is the same. Merely linking knowledge with results, thought with power, and ideas with action produces little that is new

and yields little that is distinctive: "The dictum holds for any interpretation of practical use, sacred or profane, whether it be taken as recommending the subservience of all things to a moral aim or to a material gain" (H. S. Thayer, *Meaning and Action: A Critical History of Pragmatism* [Indianapolis: Hackett Publishing, 1968], 6).

41. Charles Sanders Peirce, "How to Make Our Ideas Clear," in *Philosophical Writings of Peirce*, ed. Justus Buchler (New York: Dover Publications, 1955), 30, 31.

42. Charles Sanders Peirce, "The Essentials of Pragmatism," in *Philosophical Writings of Peirce*, 261.

43. Peirce, "How to Make Our Ideas Clear," 38.

44. William James, *A Pluralistic Universe* (New York: Longmans, Green, 1908), 97.

45. William James, *Pragmatism and Other Writings*, 27.

46. William James, "Philosophical Conceptions and Practical Results," in *William James: Writings, 1878–1899*, ed. Gerald Myers (New York: Library of America, 1992), 1080.

47. William James, *Pragmatism and Other Writings*, 25.

48. William James, *Some Problems of Philosophy*, in *William James: Writings, 1902–1910*, ed. Bruce Kuklick (New York: Library of America, 1987), 1013.

49. William James, *Pragmatism and Other Writings*, 28.

50. William James, *Pragmatism and Other Writings*, 28.

51. William James, *Pragmatism and Other Writings*, 29; italics James's.

52. William James, *Pragmatism and Other Writings*, 27.

53. William James, *Pragmatism and Other Writings*, 7.

54. William James, *Pragmatism and Other Writings*, 7.

55. William James, *Pragmatism and Other Writings*, 240.

56. William James, *Pragmatism and Other Writings*, 8.

57. William James, *Pragmatism and Other Writings*, 8–9.

58. William James, *Pragmatism and Other Writings*, 9.

59. William James, *Pluralistic Universe*, 131–32.

60. William James, *Pragmatism and Other Writings*, 91.

61. William James, *Pragmatism and Other Writings*, 31.

62. William James, *Pragmatism and Other Writings*, 75–76.

63. William James, *Pragmatism and Other Writings*, 76.

64. William James, *Pragmatism and Other Writings*, 112.

65. William James, *Pragmatism and Other Writings*, 38; italics James's.

66. William James, *Pragmatism and Other Writings*, 33, italics James's.

67. William James, *Pragmatism and Other Writings*, 93; italics James's.

68. William James, *Pragmatism and Other Writings*, 88; italics James's.

69. William James, *Pragmatism and Other Writings*, 96.

70. William James, *Pragmatism and Other Writings*, 94.

71. Hilary Putnam, "James's Theory of Truth," in *The Cambridge Companion to William James*, ed. Ruth Anna Putnam (New York: Cambridge University Press, 1997), 183.

72. William James, "Interview," *New York Times*, November 3, 1907.

73. William James, *Pragmatism and Other Writings*, 97–98; italics James's.

74. William James, *Pragmatism and Other Writings*, 159.

75. William James, *Pragmatism and Other Writings*, 140.

76. William James, *Pragmatism and Other Writings*, 113.

77. William James, *Pragmatism and Other Writings*, 113.

78. William James, *Pragmatism and Other Writings*, 114.

79. William James, "Does Consciousness Exist?" in *The Writings of William James*, ed. John J. McDermott (Chicago: University of Chicago Press, 1977), 178.

80. William James, *Pragmatism and Other Writings*, 138.

81. William James, *Pragmatism and Other Writings*, 199.

82. William James, *Varieties of Religious Experience*, 410.

83. William James, "The Continuity of Experience," in *Writings of William James*, ed. McDermott, 296.

84. William James, *Pragmatism and Other Writings*, 131.

85. Alice James, *The Diary of Alice James*, ed. Leon Edel (New York: Penguin Books, 1982), 96.

Chapter 4

1. The most important exception to this is Richard A. Hocks' *Henry James and Pragmatist Thought* (Chapel Hill: University of North Carolina Press, 1974); I also treat this relation at some length in my *Thinking Across the American Grain: Ideology, Intellect, and the New Pragmatism* (Chicago: University of Chicago Press, 1992), 143–44.

2. Quoted in F. O. Matthiessen, *The James Family* (New York: Knopf, 1947), 344.

3. Ross Posnock, *The Trial of Curiosity: Henry James, William James, and the Challenge of Modernity* (New York: Oxford University Press, 1991), 76; Henry James, *Letters*, vol. 3, ed. Leon Edel (Cambridge, Mass.: Belknap Press of Harvard University Press, 1980), 244.

4. Posnock, *The Trial of Curiosity*, 80.

5. This question is not meant to imply that Posnock is insensible of James's complex judgments on a variety of subjects; it merely suggests that he may be less interested in defining and analyzing the process by which James comes to those judgments than in characterizing the style of mind that enabled James to make them.

6. Henry James, *The American Scene*, ed. Leon Edel (Bloomington: Indiana University Press, 1968), 54.

7. W. H. Auden, *The Dyer's Hand and Other Essays* (New York: Random House, 1968), 314.

8. Wright Morris, *The Territory Ahead: Critical Interpretations in American Literature* (New York: Atheneum, 1963), 112.

9. Wallace Stevens, *The Collected Poems of Wallace Stevens* (New York: Knopf, 1964), 10.

10. Henry James, *The American Scene*, xxv.

11. Henry James, *The American Scene*, xxv–xxvi.

12. Henry James, *The American Scene*, 12–13.

13. Henry James, *The American Scene*, 12.

14. Henry James, *The American Scene*, 13.

15. Henry James, preface to *The Princess Casamassima* in *Henry James: Literary Criticism*, ed. Leon Edel (New York: Library of America, 1984), 1088.

16. James, preface to *Princess Casamassima*, 1088.

17. Henry James, "The Art of Fiction," in *The Future of the Novel*, ed. Leon Edel (New York: Random House, 1956), 13.

18. Henry James, *The American Scene*, 273.

19. Henry James, *The American Scene*, 273.

20. Henry James, *The American Scene*, 8.

21. Henry James, *The American Scene*, 9.

22. Henry James, *The American Scene*, 10.

23. Henry James, *The American Scene*, 159.

24. Henry James, *The American Scene*, 55.

25. Henry James, *The American Scene*, 162.

26. Henry James, *The American Scene*, 321.

27. Henry James, *The American Scene*, 320.

28. Henry James, *The American Scene*, 321.

29. Henry James, *The American Scene*, 372.

30. Henry James, *The American Scene*, 367–68.

31. Henry James, *The American Scene*, 406.

32. Henry James, *The American Scene*, 407.

33. Henry James, *The American Scene*, 408.

34. Gunn, *Thinking Across the American Grain*, 144.

35. Henry James, *The American Scene*, 35.

36. Henry James, *The American Scene*, 229.

37. Henry James, *The American Scene*, 228.

38. Henry James, *The American Scene*, 313.

39. Henry James, *The American Scene*, 337.

40. Henry James, *The American Scene*, 338.

41. Henry James, *The American Scene*, 369.

42. Henry James, *The American Scene*, 369–70.

43. Henry James, *The American Scene*, 370.

44. Henry James, *The American Scene*, 371.

45. Henry James, *The American Scene*, 377.

46. Henry James, *The American Scene*, 386.

47. Henry James, *The American Scene*, 385.

48. Henry James, *The American Scene*, 387.

49. Henry James, *The American Scene*, 394.

50. Henry James, *The American Scene*, 417.

51. Henry James, *The American Scene*, 418.

52. Henry James, *The American Scene*, 237.

53. Henry James, *The American Scene*, 425.

54. Henry James, *The American Scene*, 427.

55. Henry James, *The American Scene*, 428.

56. Kenneth W. Warren, *Black and White Strangers: Race and American Literary Realism* (Chicago: University of Chicago Press, 1993), 112.

57. Henry James, *The American Scene*, 388–89.

58. Henry James, *The American Scene*, 376.

59. Henry James, *The American Scene*, 132.

60. Henry James, *The American Scene*, 138.

61. Henry James, *The American Scene*, 136–37.

62. Henry James, *The American Scene*, 11.

63. Henry James, *The American Scene*, 401.

64. Henry James, *The American Scene*, 400.

66. Henry James, *The American Scene*, 401–2.

67. Henry James, *The American Scene*, 463.

68. Henry James, *The American Scene*, 465.

69. Henry James, *The American Scene*, 463.

70. Henry James, *The American Scene*, 463–64.

Chapter 5

1. Richard Rorty, *Consequences of Pragmatism* (Minneapolis: University of Minnesota Press, 1982), 143–55.

2. Richard Rorty, *Contingency, Irony, Solidarity* (Cambridge: Cambridge University Press, 1989), 22.

3. Isaiah Berlin, *Four Essays on Liberty* (London: Oxford University Press, 1969), 172.

4. Richard J. Bernstein, *Beyond Objectivism and Relativism: Science, Hermeneutics, and Praxis* (Philadelphia: University of Pennsylvania Press, 1982); Richard J. Bernstein, *The New Constellation: The Ethical-Political Horizons of Modernity/Postmodernity* (Cambridge: MIT Press, 1992).

5. John Edwin Smith, *Reason and God: Encounters of Philosophy and Religion* (New Haven, Conn.: Yale University Press, 1961); John Edwin Smith, *The Spirit of American Philosophy* (New York: Oxford University Press, 1963).

6. John J. McDermott, ed., *The Writings of William James: A Comprehensive Edition, Including an Annotated Bibliography Updated through 1977* (Chicago: University of Chicago Press, 1977); John J. McDermott, *The Philosophy of John Dewey* (New York: Putnam, 1973); John J. McDermott, *The Culture of Experience: Philosophical Essays in the American Grain* (New York: New York University Press, 1976); John J. McDermott, *Streams of Experience: Reflections on the History and Philosophy of American Culture* (Amherst: University of Massachusetts Press, 1986).

7. John Diggins, *The Promise of Pragmatism* (Chicago: University of Chicago Press, 1994), 8.

8. Indeed, near the end of his book, Diggins actually delineates the outlines of this worldview in what he describes as "the author's eleven theses on what we in American history always wanted to know until we came to realize that we already know it—thanks to [Reinhold] Niebuhr and the Calvinists." (*Promise of Pragmatism*, 435–36).

9. Diggins, *Promise of Pragmatism*, 235.

10. Bernard Meland, *Realities of Faith* (New York: Oxford University Press, 1962); Joseph Haroutunian, *God With Us: A Theology of Transpersonal Life* (Philadelphia: Westminster Press, 1965); Gordon D. Kaufman, *An Essay on Theological Method* (Missoula, Mont.: Scholars Press, 1975).

11. Kaufman, *Essay on Theological Method*, 76.

12. Cornel West, *The American Evasion of Philosophy: A Genealogy of Pragmatism* (Madison: University of Wisconsin Press, 1989).

13. Jeffrey Stout, *Ethics after Babel: The Languages of Morality and Their Discontents* (Boston: Beacon Press, 1988).

14. Henry Samuel Levinson, *Santayana: Pragmatism and the Spiritual Life* (Chapel Hill: University of North Carolina Press, 1994).

15. Joseph Brent, *Charles Sanders Peirce: A Life* (Bloomington: Indiana University Press, 1993); Alan Ryan, *John Dewey and the High Tide of American Liberalism* (New York: Norton, 1995); Bruce Kuklick, *Churchmen and Philosophers: From Jonathan Edwards to John Dewey* (New Haven, Conn.: Yale University Press, 1985).

16. William James, *Pragmatism* (Cambridge, Mass.: Harvard University Press, 1978), 28.

17. Quoted in Richard Rorty, "Pragmatism as Romantic Polytheism," in *The Revival of Pragmatism: New Essays on Social Thought, Law, and Culture*, ed. Morris Dickstein (Durham, N.C.: Duke University Press, 1998), 23.

18. Quoted in Rorty, "Pragmatism as Romantic Polytheism," 23.

19. Rorty, "Pragmatism as Romantic Polytheism," 23–24.

20. Rorty, "Pragmatism as Romantic Polytheism," 27–29.

21. Henry F. May, *The Enlightenment in America* (New York: Oxford University Press, 1976).

22. Sacvan Bercovitch, "The Biblical Basis of the American Myth," in *The Bible and American Arts and Letters*, ed. Giles Gunn (Philadelphia: Fortress Press, 1983), 219–29.

23. See Herbert N. Schneidau, *Sacred Discontent: The Bible and Western Tradition* (Berkeley and Los Angeles: University of California Press, 1976).

24. Rorty, "Pragmatism as Romantic Polytheism," 30.

25. John Dewey, *Art as Experience* (1934; New York: Perigee Books, 1980), 346.

26. This tradition originates in Emerson, the elder James, and his son William, and includes Whitman, Frost, Stein, and Stevens, while also conceding a place to a

host of other writers from Thoreau, Dickinson, Pound, and a part of T. S. Eliot (I would add Robinson and a bit later Cather) through Fenollosa, William Carlos Williams, and Kenneth Burke to contemporaries, or near contemporaries, like Frank O'Hara and John Ashbery.

27. Richard Poirier, *Poetry and Pragmatism* (Cambridge, Mass.: Harvard University Press, 1992) 42.

28. Richard Poirier, *Poetry and Pragmatism*, 4.

29. Henry David Thoreau, *Walden*, ed. J. Lyndon Shanley (Princeton, N.J.: Princeton University Press, 1971), 98.

30. Quoted in Dewey, *Art as Experience*, 349.

31. Ryan, *John Dewey and the High Tide of American Liberalism*, 367–69.

32. Rorty, "Pragmatism as Romantic Polytheism," 34.

Chapter 6

1. David A. Hollinger, *In the American Province: Studies in the History and Historiography of Ideas* (Baltimore: Johns Hopkins University Press, 1985), 3–43; James T. Kloppenberg, "Pragmatism: An Old Name for Some New Ways of Thinking?" in *The Revival of Pragmatism: New Essays on Social Thought, Law, and Culture*, ed. Morris Dickstein (Durham, N.C.: Duke University Press, 1998), 83–127; Thomas Bender, *Intellect and Public Life: Essays on the Social History of Academic Intellectuals in the United States* (Baltimore: Johns Hopkins University Press, 1993); Robert B. Westbrook, *John Dewey and American Democracy* (Ithaca: Cornell University Press, 1991); Joyce Appleby, Lynn Hunt, and Margaret Jacob, *Telling the Truth about History* (New York: Norton, 1994); James Livingston, *Pragmatism and the Political Economy of Cultural Revolution, 1850–1940* (Chapel Hill: University of North Carolina Press, 1994).

2. Hayden White, *Tropics of Discourse: Essays in Cultural Criticism* (Baltimore: Johns Hopkins University Press, 1978); Robert F. Berkhofer, *Beyond the Great Story: History as Text and Discourse* (Cambridge, Mass.: Belknap Press of Harvard University Press, 1995).

3. Several of the essays in which this marriage was originally proposed—"Rhetorical Hermeneutics in Theory," "Cultural Rhetorical Studies: Eating Books in Nineteenth-Century America," and "Rhetorical Hermeneutics as Reception Study: Huckleberry Finn and 'The Bad Boy Boom'"—were originally gathered in *Reconceptualizing American Literary/Cultural Studies: Rhetoric, History, and Politics in the Humanities*, ed. William E. Cain (New York: Garland, 1996), 3–56, but have now been published under slightly different titles, and with revisions, in Steven Mailloux, *Reception Histories: Rhetoric, Pragmatism, and American Cultural Studies* (Ithaca, N.Y.: Cornell University Press, 1998).

4. Mailloux, *Reception Histories*, 62.

5. Mailloux, *Reception Histories*, 71.

6. Paul Ricoeur, *Interpretation Theory: Discourse and the Surplus of Meaning* (Fort Worth: Texas Christian University Press, 1976), 81.

7. Ricoeur, *Interpretation Theory*, 92.

8. Ricoeur, *Interpretation Theory*, 93.

9. Mailloux, *Reception Histories*, 61.

10. Mailloux, *Reception Histories*, 61.

11. Mailloux, *Reception Histories*, 62.

12. Quoted in Mailloux, *Reception Histories*, 60.

13. Richard Rorty, *Consequences of Pragmatism* (Minneapolis: University of Minnesota Press, 1982), xxv.

14. Donald Davidson, *Inquiries into Truth and Interpretation* (Oxford: Clarendon Press, 1984), 192.

15. Davidson, *Inquiries into Truth and Interpretation*, 197.

16. Christopher Norris, *Deconstruction and the Interests of Theory* (Norman: University of Oklahoma Press, 1989), 60.

17. Mailloux, *Reception Histories*, 60.

18. Quoted in Mailloux, *Reception Histories*, 59.

19. Mailloux, *Reception Histories*, 129.

20. Alison Lurie, "She Had It All," *New York Review of Books*, March 2, 1995, 3.

21. Mailloux, *Reception Histories*, 137.

22. Wolfgang Iser, *The Implied Reader* (Baltimore: Johns Hopkins University Press, 1974), 24.

23. Mailloux, *Reception Histories*, 55.

24. Pierre Bourdieu, in *An Invitation to Reflexive Sociology*, by Pierre Bourdieu and Loïc J. D. Wacquant (Chicago: University of Chicago Press, 1992), 197.

Chapter 7

1. In this connection, see among others, John J. McDermott, *The Culture of Experience: Philosophical Essays in the American Grain* (New York: New York University Press, 1976); Richard Poirier, *The Renewal of Literature: Emersonian Reflections* (New York: Random House, 1987); Richard Poirier, *Poetry and Pragmatism* (Cambridge, Mass.: Harvard University Press, 1992); Hans Joas, *The Creativity of Action* (Chicago: University of Chicago Press, 1996); Richard A. Hocks, *Henry James and Pragmatist Thought: A Study in the Relationship between the Philosophy of William James and the Art of Henry James* (Chapel Hill: University of North Carolina Press, 1974); Joseph Brent, *Charles Sanders Peirce: A Life* (Bloomington: Indiana University Press, 1993); Ross Posnock, *The Trial of Curiosity: William James, Henry James, and the Challenge of Modernity* (New York: Oxford University Press, 1991); Ross Posnock, *Color and Culture: Black Writers and the Making of the Modern Intellectual* (Cambridge, Mass.: Harvard University Press, 1998); Ann Douglas, *Terrible Honesty: Mongrel Manhattan in the 1920s* (New York: Farrar, Straus & Giroux, 1995), 129–43; Henry Samuel Levinson, *Santayana, Pragmatism, and the Spiritual Life* (Chapel Hill: University of North Carolina Press, 1992); Richard Shusterman, *Pragmatist Aesthetics: Living Beauty, Rethinking Art* (Oxford: Blackwell, 1992); Thomas Alexander, *John*

Dewey's Theory of Art, Experience, and Nature: The Horizons of Feeling (Albany: State University of New York Press, 1987); Steven Mailloux, *Reception Histories: Rhetoric, Pragmatism, and American Cultural Politics* (Ithaca, N.Y.: Cornell University Press, 1998); Jonathan Levin, *The Poetics of Transition* (Durham, N.C.: Duke University Press, 1999).

2. Lewis Mumford, *The Golden Day* (New York: Viking Press, 1963), 93.

3. Mumford, *Golden Day*, 83.

4. Mumford, *Golden Day*, 83.

5. Brent, *Charles Sanders Peirce*, 203.

6. John Dewey, *The Quest for Certainty* (1929; New York: Capricorn Books, 1960), 311–12.

7. Richard Rorty, *Consequences of Pragmatism* (Minneapolis: University of Minnesota Press, 1982), 66.

8. Hayden White, "The Point of It All," *New Literary History* 2 (Autumn 1970): 179–80.

9. Barbara Herrnstein Smith, *On the Margins of Discourse: The Relation of Literature to Language* (Chicago: University of Chicago Press, 1978), 144–45.

10. Smith, *On the Margins of Discourse*, 145.

11. Smith, *On the Margins of Discourse*, 145.

12. Dorothy Van Ghent, *The English Novel: Form and Function* (New York: Harper Torchbooks, 1953), 3.

13. Pierre Macherey, *The Object of Literature*, trans. David Macey (New York: Cambridge University Press, 1995), 234.

14. J. V. Cunningham, *Tradition and Poetic Structure* (Denver: Alan Swallow, 1960), 141.

15. Arjun Appadurai, *Modernity at Large: Cultural Dimensions of Globalization* (Minneapolis: University of Minnesota Press, 1996), 4.

16. Benedict Anderson, *Imagined Communities: Reflections on the Origin and Spread of Nationalism* (London: Verso, 1983), 6–7.

17. Appadurai, *Modernity at Large*, 5.

18. Hannah Arendt, *Between Past and Future* (New York: Viking Press, 1968), 220.

19. Quoted in Hannah Arendt, *The Life of the Mind* (New York: Harcourt Brace Jovanovich, 1978), 257.

20. Arendt, *Life of the Mind*, 258.

21. Quoted in Arendt, *Life of the Mind*, 257.

22. Arendt, *Life of the Mind*, 257.

23. Arendt, *Life of the Mind*, 258.

24. Quoted in Arendt, *Life of the Mind*, 222.

25. Dewey, *Quest for Certainty*, 262.

26. Martha Nussbaum, *The Fragility of Goodness: Luck and Ethics in Greek Tragedy and Philosophy* (New York: Cambridge University Press, 1986), 14.

27. Martha Nussbaum, "Narrative Emotions: Beckett's Genealogy of Love," *Ethics* 98 (1988): 237.

28. Mark Johnson, *Moral Imagination: Implications of Cognitive Science for Ethics* (Chicago: University of Chicago Press, 1993), 10.

29. Ralph Waldo Emerson, "The Poet," in *Ralph Waldo Emerson: Selected Essays*, ed. Larzer Ziff (New York: Penguin Books, 1982), 271.

30. Peter Berger, *The Noise of Solemn Assemblies* (Garden City, N.Y.: Doubleday, 1961).

31. Kenneth Burke, quoted in William H. Rueckert, *Kenneth Burke and the Drama of Human Relations*, 2d ed. (Berkeley and Los Angeles: University of California Press, 1982), 162.

32. Poirier, *Renewal of Literature*, 202.

33. Poirier, *Renewal of Literature*, 181–223.

34. Poirier, *Revival of Pragmatism*, 347.

35. The phrase is Poirier's, though he uses it in a slightly different connection. Richard Poirier, *The Performing Self* (New York: Oxford University Press, 1971), xiii.

36. Poirier, *Performing Self*, xv.

37. Jonathan Levin correctly reminds us that such moments are often too unsettling of conventional understanding to be easily reducible to paraphrase or characterization even retrospectively. See *The Poetics of Transition* (Durham, N.C.: Duke University Press, 1999), xii.

38. Poirier, *Performing Self*, 186.

39. Poirier, *Performing Self*, 186.

40. Satya P. Mohanty, *Literary Theory and the Claims of History* (Ithaca, N.Y.: Cornell University Press, 1997), 231.

41. Amartya Sen, "Human Rights and Asian Values," *New Republic*, July 14 and 21, 1997, 33–40.

42. Mohanty, *Literary Theory and the Claims of History*, 248.

43. Mohanty, *Literary Theory and the Claims of History*, 248.

Chapter 8

1. Edward W. Said, *Culture and Imperialism* (New York: Knopf, 1993); Homi Bhabha, *The Location of Culture* (New York: Routledge, 1994); Gayatri Spivak, *The Post-Colonial Critic: Interviews, Strategies, Dialogues* (New York: Routledge, 1990); Benita Parry, *Conrad and Imperialism: Ideological Boundaries and Visionary Frontiers* (London: Macmillan Press, 1983); Aijaz Ahmad, *In Theory: Classes, Nations, Literatures* (London: Verso, 1992).

2. Albert Memmi, *The Colonizer and the Colonized* (New York: Orion Press, 1965).

3. Sara Suleri, *The Rhetoric of English India* (Chicago: University of Chicago Press, 1992), 3.

4. Frederick Buell, *National Culture and the New Global System* (Baltimore: Johns Hopkins University Press, 1994), 232.

5. Peter Hulme, cited by Said, *Culture and Imperialism*, 212.

6. Said, *Culture and Imperialism*, 214.

7. Said, *Culture and Imperialism*, 214.

8. Chinua Achebe, "An Image of Africa: Racism in Conrad's *Heart of Darkness*," in *Hopes and Impediments: Selected Essays 1965–1987* (London: Heinemann, 1988), 1–19.

9. Tayeb Salih, *Season of Migration to the North*, trans. Denys Johnson-Davies (Portsmouth, N.H.: Heinemann, 1969), 28.

10. Salih, *Season of Migration to the North*, 49–50.

11. Salih, *Season of Migration to the North*, 49.

12. Shoshana Felman, "Education and Crisis, or the Vicissitudes of Teaching," in *Testimony: Crisis of Witnessing in Literature, Psychoanalysis, and History*, ed. Shoshana Felman and Dori Laub (New York: Routledge, 1991), 28.

13. Cited in John Felstiner, "Translating Celan's Last Poem," *American Poetry Review*, July/August 1982, 23.

14. Cited in Felstiner, "Translating Celan's Last Poem," 23.

15. Felman, "Education and Crisis," 28–29.

16. Paul Celan, "Speech on the Occasion of Receiving the Literature Prize of the Free Hanseatic City of Bremen," in *Collected Prose*, trans. Rosmarie Waldrop (Manchester: Carcanet Press, 1986), 34.

17. Paul Celan, "The Meridian," in *Collected Prose*, 48.

18. Celan, "The Meridian," 49.

19. Paul Celan, "Todtnauberg," in *Poems of Paul Celan*, trans. Michael Hamburger (New York: Persea Books, 1988), 293.

20. *Poems of Paul Celan*, 271.

21. Primo Levi, *The Reawakening*, trans. Stuart Woolf (New York: Collier Books, 1987), 2.

22. Levi, *Reawakening*, 2.

23. Levi, *Reawakening*, 2–3.

24. Primo Levi, *Survival in Auschwitz* (New York: Touchstone Books, 1996), 26.

25. Levi, *Survival in Auschwitz*, 90.

26. Levi, *Survival in Auschwitz*, 91.

27. Levi, *Survival in Auschwitz*, 27.

28. Levi, *Survival in Auschwitz*, 121–22.

29. Levi, *Survival in Auschwitz*, 105–6.

30. See Paul Oppenheimer, *Evil and the Demonic: A New Theory of Monstrous Behavior* (New York: New York University Press, 1996), 9–11.

31. Levi, *Survival in Auschwitz*, 121.

32. Levi, *Survival in Auschwitz*, 171–72.

33. Levi, *Survival in Auschwitz*, 87.

34. Primo Levi, *The Drowned and the Saved*, trans. Raymond Rosenthal (New York: Vintage Books, 1989), 83.

35. Levi, *The Drowned and the Saved*, 82.

36. Lawrence W. Levine, *Black Culture and Black Consciousness: Afro-American Folk Thought from Slavery to Freedom* (New York: Oxford University Press, 1977), 80.

37. Gunnar Myrdal, *An American Dilemma: The Negro Problem and Modern Democracy* (New York: Harper and Brothers, 1944); E. Franklin Frazier, *The Negro in the United States*, rev. ed. (New York: Macmillan, 1949, 1957); Nathan Glazer and Daniel T. Moynihan, *Beyond the Melting Pot: The Negroes, Puerto Ricans, Jews, Italians, and Irish of New York City* (Cambridge, Mass: MIT Press, 1963); Frantz Fanon, *Toward the African Revolution: Political Essays* (1967; New York: Grove Press, 1988).

38. Alan Lomax, *Folk Song Style and Culture* (Washington, D.C.: American Association for the Advancement of Science, 1968); C. Eric Lincoln, *The Black Experience in Religion* (Garden City, N.Y.: Anchor Press, 1974); Herbert Gutman, *The Black Family in Slavery and Freedom, 1750–1925* (New York: Pantheon Books, 1976); Eugene D. Genovese, *Roll, Jordan, Roll: The World the Slaves Made* (New York: Pantheon Book, 1974); Albert J. Raboteau, *Slave Religion* (New York: Oxford University Press, 1978); to Thadious M. Davis, *Faulkner's "Negro": Art and the Southern Context* (Baton Rouge: Louisiana State University Press, 1983); Trudier Harris, *Exorcising Blackness: Historical and Literary Lynching and Burning Rituals* (Bloomington: Indiana University Press, 1984); Elizabeth Fox-Genovese, *Within the Plantation Household: Black and White Women of the Old South* (Chapel Hill: University of North Carolina Press, 1988); Henry Louis Gates, Jr., *The Signifying Monkey: A Theory of Afro-American Literary Criticism* (New York: Oxford University Press, 1988).

39. Ralph Ellison, *Shadow and Act* (New York: New American Library, 1964); W. E. B. Du Bois, *The Souls of Black Folk* (1902; New York: New American Library, 1969); Nathan Huggins, *Harlem Renaissance* (New York: Oxford University Press, 1971); Ann Douglas, *Terrible Honesty: Mongrel Manhattan in the 1920s* (New York: Farrar, Straus & Giroux, 1995).

40. Levine, *Black Culture and Black Consciousness*, xi.

41. Kenneth Burke, *The Philosophy of Literary Form*, 3d ed. (Berkeley and Los Angeles: University of California Press, 1973), 1–137.

42. Ellison, *Shadow and Act*, 301.

43. Quoted in Levine, *Black Culture and Black Consciousness*, 33.

44. Stuart Hall tells a similar story about the way the Rastafarians in Jamaica rewrote the Bible for themselves. Another people who were descendants of slaves, the Rastafarians initially associated their origins with the Ethiopia of the Bible and thus originally believed that they must necessarily be repatriated, like all African peoples, back to their homeland. But in order to make the Bible work for them in their new diaspora, they were eventually forced to take a text that did not belong to them, and that put them in the wrong place, and turn it "upside-down." In other words, to enable the Bible to legitimate their enforced existence in Jamaica, they were forced to reread the Bible—in song as well as speech—as authorizing the Africanization of Jamaica rather than the repatriation of Africans. Hence, Hall concludes, by "turning the text upside-down they remade themselves; they positioned

themselves differently as new political subjects; they reconstructed themselves as blacks in the new world: they became what they are." (Stuart Hall, "On Postmodernism and Articulation: An Interview with Stuart Hall, ed. by Lawrence Grossberg," in *Stuart Hall: Critical Dialogues in Cultural Studies*, ed. David Morley and Kuan-Hsing Chen [London: Routledge, 1996], 143.)

45. Donald G. Mathews, *Religion in the Old South* (Chicago: University of Chicago Press, 1977), 186.

46. Mathews, *Religion in the Old South*, 186.

47. Levine, *Black Culture and Black Consciousness*, 33.

48. Nelson Goodman, *Ways of Worldmaking* (Hassocks, England: Harvester Press, 1978).

49. Levine, *Black Culture and Black Consciousness*, 54.

50. Levine, *Black Culture and Black Consciousness*, xi.

51. Lionel Trilling, *The Liberal Imagination: Essays on Literature and Society* (1950; New York: Doubleday Anchor Books, 1957), 215.

52. For a thoughtful analysis of this discussion, see Richard Falk, *Predatory Globalization: A Critique* (Cambridge, England: Polity Press, 1999), 166–84.

53. Clifford Geertz, *Available Light: Anthropological Reflections on Philosophical Topics* (Princeton, N.J.: Princeton University Press, 2000), 218–60.

54. Geertz, *Available Light*, 260.

55. John Dewey, *Experience and Nature*, 2d ed. (La Salle, Ill.: Open Court Publishing, 1929), 332.

Acknowledgments

Earlier versions of several of these chapters have been published elsewhere, but all have been rewritten, some very substantially. A portion of chapter 1 was published as "Multiculturalism, Mourning, and the Americas: Towards a New Pragmatics of Cross- and Intercultural Criticism," in *John F. Kennedy Institut für Nordamerikastudien, Working Paper No. 75* (Berlin: Freie Universitat, 1995), 1–18. Segments of chapters 2 and 8 were published in "After Consensus: Multiculturalism, Alterity, and the Rethinking of Democratic Solidarity," in *After Consensus: Critical Challenge and Social Change in America*, ed. Hans Lofgren and Alan Shima (Göteborg: Acta Universitatis Gotheoburgensis, 1998), 11–26; and in "Consensus, Dissent, and Multi-culturalism: Conceptual Problems in Recreating a Common Democratic Purpose," *Negotiations of America's National Identity*, vol. 2, ed. Roland Hagenbuechle and Josef Raab, with Marietta Messmer (Munich: Stauffenburg Verlag, 2000), 427–44. Material from these two chapters will also appear in "Human Solidarity and the Problem of Otherness," in *Religion and Cultural Studies*, ed. Susan Mizruchi (Princeton: Princeton University Press, in press). Chapter 3 includes material from my introduction to *The Correspondence of William James*, vol. 4, ed. Ignas K. Skrupskelis and Elizabeth M. Berkeley (Charlottesville: University of Virginia Press, 1995), xix–lii; as well as my introduction to *Pragmatism and Other Writings*, by William James, ed. Giles Gunn (New York: Penguin Books, 2000), vii–xxxii. Chapter 4 appeared with some modifications as "Pragmatism, Rhetoric, and *The American Scene*," in *Rhetoric, Pragmatism, Sophistry*, ed. Steven Mailloux

(New York: Cambridge University Press, 1994), 155–79. Chapter 5 is a considerably revised and expanded version of "Religion and the Recent Revival of Pragmatism," which appeared in *The Revival of Pragmatism: New Essays on Social Thought, Law, and Culture*, ed. Morris Dickstein (Durham, N.C.: Duke University Press, 1998) 404–17; and includes several paragraphs from my introduction to *The Bible and American Arts and Letters* , copyright © 1983 Fortress Press (Philadelphia: Fortress Press, 1983), 1–9. A briefer version of chapter 6 was published as "Approaching the Historical," in *Reconceptualizing American Literary/Cultural Studies*, ed. William Cain (New York: Greenwood Press, 1996), 59–72. A much shortened version of chapter 7 was published as "The Pragmatics of the Aesthetic," *REAL* (*Yearbook of Research in English and American Literature*), vol. 15, ed. Winfried Fluck (Tübingen, Germany: Gunter Narr Verlag, 2000), 3–19. It will also appear under the same title in the same version in *Aesthetics and Difference*, ed. Emory Elliott (New York: Oxford University Press, 2001). Several passages from chapter 7 were also published in "Who Are You, Really, and What Were You Before?: Reflections on a Thinking Life" in *The Craft of Religious Studies*, ed. Jon R. Stone, copyright © Jon R. Stone (New York: St. Martin's Press, 1998), 277–99. A short portion of chapter 8 also appeared in "Forum: Neglected Resources in Scholarship," in *Religion and American Culture* 7, no.1 (Winter 1997): 8–14. I am grateful to all these publishers for permission to reprint this material here.

During the course of this project I have been the fortunate recipient of assistance from a number of individuals and institutions. My long absorption with pragmatist issues and problems has been supported, and often usefully critiqued, by Henry Samuel Levinson, John J. McDermott, Andrew Delbanco, John Carlos Rowe, Günter Lenz, Winfried Fluck, Mark Poster, Berndt Ostendorf, Heinz Ickstadt, Herwig Friedl, Klaus Milich, Renata Hoff, Forrest Robinson, Susan Mizruchi, Ross Posnock, Morris Dickstein, Richard Poirier, the late Alfred Kazin, Brook Thomas, Jonathan Levin, David B. Downing, and Emory Elliott. My concerns more generally with the criticism of an increasingly global intellectual culture in our late-modernist or postmodernist moment have been both broadened and sharpened by conversations with Alan Trachtenberg, John Seelye, Mitchell Breitwiesser, David Carrasco, Leo Marx, Charles Altieri, Paul Lauter, Wai Chee Dimock, Wendy Martin, Sacvan Bercovitch, Michael Cowan, Charles H. Long, Lawrence Buell, Eric J. Sundquist, William Spengemann, Philip Fisher, Peter Homans, Gerald Vizenor, Donald Pease, Mark Juergensmeyer, Sucheng Chan, Richard Hecht, Roger Friedland, Ninian

Smart, Shirley Lim, Everett Zimmerman, Elliott Butler-Evans, Carl Gutierrez-Jones, Enda Duffy, Christopher Craft, and the late Honorable Walter Capps (member of the U.S. House of Representatives).

My understanding of the hazards as well as rewards of cross-cultural education in the humanities was vastly expanded by the extraordinary colleagues from around the world who participated in two institutes I directed for the United States Information Agency on American literary cultures, and I also wish to thank in particular John Maxwell, Dean of Educational Extension at the University of California at Santa Barbara, for codirecting these institutes with me. I would also like to thank the members of various graduate seminars I have offered in English during the last several years who were willing to put aside conventional interpretations of their discipline and try out new ideas, particularly Parker Douglas, Rachel Borup, Elizabeth Olsen Byrne, Cheryl Weigand, Christopher Schedler, Laura Adams, Susanna Gilbert, and Robert Bennett.

Dick and Peggy Lamb, together with Dr. Jack Moxley and Doris Banchik, have been loyal friends extraordinaire during the long period of this book's development, providing wonderfully timely encouragement and support. Peter and Kathy Vasile have always been there when I needed them, as have my cousins Alexander Gunn and Peter Coveney, my brother and sister-in-law, Charles Gunn and Amy Patenaude, Rusty Kay, Berkeley and Karen Johnson, and "the boys," Nick, Sam, and Cooper.

In addition to this long list of acknowledgments, I owe a special debt of gratitude to Myra Jehlen and Steven Mailloux, both of whom read the manuscript in its entirety and made numerous, extensive, shrewd suggestions for its improvement. They have each given new dignity to the terms *colleague* and *critic*. My pages have been made considerably more readable because of the editorial intelligence of Clair James. Randolph Petilos has again resolved various problems and issues involved with the book's production with exceptional efficiency and consideration. And anyone who has been privileged to work with Alan Thomas shares my gratitude for the wisdom, candor, and understanding he brings to his work as editor. In this connection, I must also mention the strong support this project received from Lindsay Waters, who deserves my thanks for helping to bring it to conclusion. While none of the people mentioned above should be held accountable for any deficiencies this book may possess, all have helped to make it more honest and lucid.

I have been fortunate enough to be able to submit many of my ideas to criticism at various institutions both in the United States and abroad. In this connection, I wish to thank audiences at Keimung University, Pusan National University, and Kwangju University in Korea, as well as at the University of Colorado at Boulder, Vassar College, California Lutheran University, Dartmouth College, Mainz's Johannes Gutenberg University, Munich's Ludwig Maximilian University, the John F. Kennedy Institute for North American Studies at the Free University in Berlin, Humboldt University in Berlin, the University of Bratislava, Düsseldorf University, the University of Lisbon, the Interdisciplinary Humanities Center at the University of California at Santa Barbara, the University of California at Los Angeles, the University of California at Irvine, Westmont College, Göteborg University, the University of Eichstaett in Germany, the University of California at Berkeley, Boston University, the University of Texas at Dallas, the University of California at Santa Cruz, Barnard College, and the Society for the Advancement of American Philosophy, where I was invited to deliver the Coss Dialogues Lecture. To all these individuals and agencies, as well as to my colleagues in the Department of English and the Program in Global and International Studies at the University of California at Santa Barbara, who have provided a supportive and congenial atmosphere in which to do my work, I am deeply indebted.

Like many authors, I owe the largest debt of thanks to the members of my immediate family—to my children, Adam and Abby, for their affectionate support, forbearance, sense of humor, and abundance of goodwill; and to my wife, Deborah, for her always spirited, endlessly fascinating, and, in these years, extraordinarily courageous comradeship beyond solidarity. Without, in particular, Abby's great-heartedness, Adam's fidelity, and the inspiration of Deborah's example, the writing of this book would not have been possible.

Index

Abraham, Nicholas, 19

absolutism, xxv, 113, 148

Achebe, Chinua, 174–75

Adams, Henry, 90, 114

Addams, Jane, xix

Adorno, Theodor, xv, xvi, 58, 88, 180

Adventures of Huckleberry Finn, The (Twain), 132, 133, 138

aesthetic, the: as breaking free of high culture, xxvi; and ethics, 147, 150; as extending realm of the knowable, 152–53; heuristic value of, 153; Henry James, Sr., on the spiritual and, 63; as main solvent of culture as a whole, xxvi, 153–54; pragmatism and, xxiii, xxvi, 146–47; as realm apart, 148–50; in refiguring the global, 195; as sedimented into precincts of the ordinary, 155–65; as uttering the unutterable, 151–52. *See also* art

Africa, 174–76

African Americans: James's *The American Scene* on, 104–5; literature of as going beyond solidarity, 188–95; otherness of, 193–94; pragmatist tradition of, xvi–xvii; religion of, 189, 191–93; as studying African Americans, 10. *See also* Du Bois, W. E. B.; Ellison, Ralph; slavery

Agassiz, Louis, 64–65

aggression, 34

Ahmad, Aijaz, 171

Allende, Isabel, 13

Amado, Jorge, 13

Ambassadors, The (James), 99

America. *See* United States

American Dilemma, An (Myrdal), 188, 191

American Scene, The (James), 87–108; on African Americans, 104–5; on America's historical obligations, 128; on art enhancing life, 94; blind spots of, 104–6; on Boston house on Ashburton Place, 100; on Cape Cod's queerness, 99–100; on Charleston, 103; on culture of the hotel, 98; experience as portrayed in, 89; generosity of judgment of, 103–4; the "given case" in, 93; on immigrants, 27, 105; interpretive turn of, 92; James's mantle of genteel superiority at beginning of, 92–93; James's persona as restless analyst in, 88–89; James's trip to U.S. as basis of, 90; on Jews, 105; on the "Margin" in America, 106–8; on Mt. Vernon, 101; on New England, 103; on the "New Jersey condition," 96; on New York, 103; on Philadelphia, 103; on Rich-